RE

DA

ADVENT **2018** TO
EVE OF ADVENT **2019**

JUSTINE ALLAIN CHAPMAN
KATE BRUCE
STEVEN CROFT
PAULA GOODER
PETER GRAYSTONE
HELEN-ANN HARTLEY
DAVID HOYLE
GRAHAM JAMES
LIBBY LANE
JAN MCFARLANE
GORDON MURSELL
HELEN ORCHARD
JOHN PERUMBALATH
SARAH ROWLAND JONES
DAVID RUNCORN
JEANETTE SEARS
HARRY STEELE
RICHARD SUDWORTH
ANGELA TILBY
GRAHAM TOMLIN
MARGARET WHIPP

Church House Publishing
Church House
Great Smith Street
London SW1P 3AZ

ISBN 978 1 78140 007 4

Published 2018 by Church House Publishing
Copyright © The Archbishops' Council 2018

The opinions expressed in this book are those of the
authors and do not necessarily reflect the official policy of
the General Synod or The Archbishops' Council of the
Church of England.

Liturgical editor: Peter Moger
Series editor: Hugh Hillyard-Parker
Designed and typeset by Hugh Hillyard-Parker
Copy edited by Ros Connelly
Printed by CPI Group (UK) Ltd, Croydon CR0 4YY

What do you think of *Reflections for Daily Prayer*?

We'd love to hear from you – simply email us at

publishing@churchofengland.org

or write to us at

Church House Publishing, Church House,
Great Smith Street, London SW1P 3AZ.

Visit **www.dailyprayer.org.uk** for more
information on the *Reflections* series, ordering
and subscriptions.

Contents

Table of contributors

About the authors

Justine Allain Chapman has served as a parish priest and in theological education specializing in mission and pastoral care. She is currently Archdeacon of Boston in the Diocese of Lincoln committed to the wellbeing of clergy, congregations and churches. Her most recent book *The Resilient Disciple*, is for Lent.

Kate Bruce was Deputy Warden and Tutor in Preaching at Cranmer Hall, St John's College, until late 2017, and remains associated with Cranmer as Honorary Visiting Fellow. She now serves as an RAF Chaplain. She regularly offers day conferences in preaching around the country, and also preaches regularly. She enjoys running, and writes and performs stand-up comedy in her spare time.

Steven Croft is the Bishop of Oxford. He was previously Bishop of Sheffield and team leader of Fresh Expressions. He is the author of a number of books including *The Gift of Leadership* and *The Advent Calendar*, a novel for children and adults.

Paula Gooder is Director of Mission Learning and Development in the Birmingham Diocese. She is a writer and lecturer in biblical studies, author of a number of books including *Journey to the Empty Tomb, The Meaning is in the Waiting* and *Heaven*, and a co-author of the Pilgrim course. She is also a Reader in the Church of England.

Peter Graystone works for Church Army, developing projects that take Good News to people who have no real experience of Church. He edits the website Christianity.org.uk and reviews theatre for the *Church Times.*

Helen-Ann Hartley is the Bishop of Ripon in the Diocese of Leeds, a role she has held since early 2018. Prior to this appointment she was the Bishop of Waikato in New Zealand from 2014 until 2017, and before that she taught New Testament studies at Ripon College Cuddesdon and at the College of St John the Evangelist in Auckland, New Zealand.

David Hoyle is the Dean of Bristol. As a priest, he has worked in a Cambridge College, in a London parish and as Director of Ministry in the Diocese of Gloucester. His early academic work was as a church historian, but his latest book *The Pattern of Our Calling* is about ministry.

Graham James has been Bishop of Norwich since 1999. Previously, he was Bishop of St Germans in his native Cornwall and Chaplain to the Archbishop of Canterbury. He has served on the House of Lords Select Committee on Communications, and remains the Church of England's lead spokesperson on media issues. He has been a regular contributor to BBC Radio 4's 'Thought for the Day'.

Libby Lane is Bishop of Stockport in the Diocese of Chester. In 2015 she was consecrated as the Church of England's first woman bishop. She chairs the Diocesan Board of Education, and the Foxhill Diocesan Retreat House Committee. She is an elected Suffragan in the House of Bishops, Chair of Cranmer Hall Theological College Committee and nominated Vice Chair of The Children's Society.

Jan McFarlane is the Bishop of Repton in the Diocese of Derby. She has served as Archdeacon of Norwich, Director of Communications, Chaplain to the Bishop of Norwich, Chaplain of Ely Cathedral and Curate in the Stafford Team Ministry.

Gordon Mursell was Bishop of Stafford until his retirement in 2010. He now lives in south-west Scotland and is a writer on Christian spirituality and keen hillwalker.

Helen Orchard is Team Vicar of St Matthew's Church in the Wimbledon Team. She was previously Chaplain-Fellow at Exeter College, Oxford and before ordination worked for the National Health Service.

John Perumbalath is Archdeacon of Barking in Chelmsford Diocese. He has served as a theological educator and parish priest in the dioceses of Calcutta (Church of North India) and Rochester. He regularly guest lectures in the fields of faith and social engagement and in biblical studies.

Sarah Rowland Jones was a mathematician, then a British diplomat with postings in Jordan and Hungary, before ordination in the Church in Wales. After 11 years as researcher to successive Archbishops of Cape Town, she returned to Wales, and is now the Dean of St Davids. She serves on international Anglican think-tanks, broadcasts regularly, and writes on spirituality, public theology and ecumenism.

David Runcorn is a writer, speaker, spiritual director and theological teacher. He is currently Associate Director of Ordinands and Warden of Readers in the diocese of Gloucester.

Jeanette Sears formerly taught Christian Doctrine and Church History at Trinity College Bristol. She is now a freelance writer and carer. Her latest novel is *Murder and Mr Rochester* (www.jeanettesears.com).

Harry Steele is an Ordained Pioneer Minister in the Church of England currently serving as the Bishop's Interim Minister in Sheffield Diocese. He serves on the national Leading Your Church into Growth Team and is chaplain to the Sheffield Sharks Basketball team. Harry is passionate about helping parish churches grow.

Richard Sudworth is a Church of England parish priest in the Diocese of Birmingham and is the author of *Distinctly Welcoming: Christian Presence in a Multifaith Society* and *Encountering Islam: Christian-Muslim Relations in the Public Square*.

Angela Tilby is a Canon Emeritus of Christ Church Cathedral, Oxford. Prior to that she served in the Diocese of Oxford following a period in Cambridge, where she was at Westcott House and St Bene't's Church. Before ordination she was a producer for the BBC, and she still broadcasts regularly.

Graham Tomlin is Bishop of Kensington and President of St Mellitus College. He was formerly Vice Principal of Wycliffe Hall, Oxford and the first Principal of St Mellitus.

Rachel Treweek is the Bishop of Gloucester and the first female diocesan bishop in England. She served in two parishes in London and was Archdeacon of Northolt and later Hackney. Prior to ordination she was a speech and language therapist and is a trained practitioner in conflict transformation.

Margaret Whipp is the Lead Chaplain for the Oxford University Hospitals. Her first profession was in medicine. Since ordination she has served in parish ministry, university chaplaincy, and most recently as Senior Tutor at Ripon College Cuddesdon. She writes and researches in pastoral theology, enjoys singing and long-distance pilgrimage trails, and is an Honorary Canon of Christ Church Cathedral, Oxford.

About *Reflections for Daily Prayer*

Based on the *Common Worship Lectionary* readings for Morning Prayer, these daily reflections are designed to refresh and inspire times of personal prayer. The aim is to provide rich, contemporary and engaging insights into Scripture.

Each page lists the Lectionary readings for the day, with the main psalms for that day highlighted in **bold**. The Collect of the day – either the *Common Worship* Collect or the shorter additional Collect – is also included.

For those using this book in conjunction with a service of Morning Prayer, the following conventions apply: a psalm printed in parentheses is omitted if it has been used as the opening Canticle at that office; a psalm marked with an asterisk may be shortened if desired.

A short reflection is provided on either the Old or New Testament reading. Popular writers, experienced ministers, biblical scholars and theologians all contribute to this series, bringing with them their own emphases, enthusiasms and approaches to biblical interpretation.

Regular users of Morning Prayer and *Time to Pray* (from *Common Worship: Daily Prayer*) and anyone who follows the Lectionary for their regular Bible reading will benefit from the rich variety of traditions represented in these stimulating and accessible pieces.

This volume also includes both a simple form of *Common Worship:* Morning Prayer (see inside front and back covers) and a short form of Night Prayer – also known as Compline – (see pp. 326–7), particularly for the benefit of those readers who are new to the habit of the Daily Office or for any reader while travelling.

Building daily prayer into daily life

In our morning routines, there are many tasks we do without giving much thought to them, and others that we do with careful attention. Daily prayer and Bible reading is a strange mixture of these. These are disciplines (and gifts) that we as Christians should have in our daily pattern, but they are not tasks to be ticked off. Rather they are a key component of our developing relationship with God. In them is *life* – for the fruits of this time are to be lived out by us – and to be most fruitful, the task requires both purpose and letting go.

In saying a daily office of prayer, we make the deliberate decision to say 'yes' to spending time with God – the God who is always with us. In prayer and attentive reading of the Scriptures, there is both a conscious entering into God's presence and a 'letting go' of all we strive to control: both are our acknowledgement that it is God who is God.

> *… come into his presence with singing …*
>
> *Know that the Lord is God.*
> *It is he that has made us, and we are his;*
> *we are his people, and the sheep of his pasture.*
>
> *Enter his gates with thanksgiving…*
>
> *(Psalm 100, a traditional Canticle at Morning Prayer)*

If we want a relationship with someone to deepen and grow, we need to spend time with that person. It can be no surprise that the same is true between us and God.

In our daily routines, I suspect that most of us intentionally look in the mirror; occasionally we might see beyond the surface of our external reflection and catch a glimpse of who we truly are. For me, a regular pattern of daily prayer and Bible reading is like a hard look in a clean mirror: it gives a clear reflection of myself, my life and the world in which I live. But it is more than that, for in it I can also see the reflection of God who is most clearly revealed in Jesus Christ and present with us now in the Holy Spirit.

This commitment to daily prayer is about our relationship with the God who is love. St Paul, in his great passage about love, speaks of now seeing 'in a mirror, dimly' but one day seeing face to face: 'Now I know only in part; then I will know fully, even as I have been fully known' (1 Corinthians 13.12). Our daily prayer is part of that seeing in a mirror dimly, and it is also part of our deep yearning for an ever-clearer vision of our God. As we read Scripture, the past and the future converge in the present moment. We hear words from long ago – some of which can appear strange and confusing – and yet, the Holy Spirit is living and active in the present. In this place of relationship and revelation, we open ourselves to the possibility of being changed, of being reshaped in a way that is good for us and all creation.

It is important that the words of prayer and scripture should penetrate deep within rather than be a mere veneer. A quiet location is therefore a helpful starting point. For some, domestic circumstances or daily schedule make that difficult, but it is never impossible to become more fully present to God. The depths of our being can still be accessed no matter the world's clamour and activity. An awareness of this is all part of our journey from a false sense of control to a place of letting go, to a place where there is an opportunity for transformation.

Sometimes in our attention to Scripture, there will be connection with places of joy or pain; we might be encouraged or provoked or both. As we look and see and encounter God more deeply, there will be thanksgiving and repentance; the cries of our heart will surface as we acknowledge our needs and desires for ourselves and the world. The liturgy of Morning Prayer gives this voice and space.

I find it helpful to begin Morning Prayer by lighting a candle. This marks my sense of purpose and my acknowledgement of Christ's presence with me. It is also a silent prayer for illumination as I prepare to be attentive to what I see in the mirror, both of myself and of God. Amid the revelation of Scripture and the cries of my heart, the constancy of the tiny flame bears witness to the hope and light of Christ in all that is and will be.

When the candle is extinguished, I try to be still as I watch the smoke disappear. For me, it is symbolic of my prayers merging with the day. I know that my prayer and the reading of Scripture are not the smoke and mirrors of delusion. Rather, they are about encounter and discovery as I seek to venture into the day to love and serve the Lord as a disciple of Jesus Christ.

+ *Rachel Treweek*

Monday 3 December

Revelation 19

'Hallelujah! For the Lord our God the Almighty reigns' (v.6)

The book of Revelation is full of songs, and these words (or their King James equivalent) are from the most famous song of all, set by Handel in his oratorio *Messiah*. What is striking is that all the songs in the book come *before* the great battles with the beast (vv.19-20) and the dragon, or Satan (Revelation 20.2-3). Is this complacency – pious Christians trying to airbrush their problems away? No – and neither is it premature. It is praise, and in the Bible, especially in books such as Daniel and Revelation, praise is not the same as thanksgiving. Praise means lifting God's future into the present and celebrating it *as though it were happening now*.

Cleric and political activist Allan Boesak, writing about the songs of praise in the book of Revelation during the apartheid years in South Africa, understood this perfectly: 'Oppressed people in South Africa understand the need for singing ... And besides, it drives the dragon crazy when you sing about his downfall even though you are bleeding.'

Advent is supremely the time to shake off any apathetic feeling that we can do nothing to change the world. We can: we can sing a better one into being, and the praise songs of Revelation make an excellent place to start.

COLLECT

Almighty God,
give us grace to cast away the works of darkness
and to put on the armour of light,
now in the time of this mortal life,
in which your Son Jesus Christ came to us in great humility;
that on the last day,
when he shall come again in his glorious majesty
    to judge the living and the dead,
we may rise to the life immortal;
through him who is alive and reigns with you,
in the unity of the Holy Spirit,
one God, now and for ever.

| *Reflection by* **Gordon Mursell**

Psalms **80**, 82 *or* **5**, 6 (8)   **Tuesday 4 December**
Isaiah 43.1-13
Revelation 20

Revelation 20

'... they will be priests of God and of Christ, and they will reign with him for a thousand years' (v.6)

With these words, the writer of Revelation describes the Millennium, the thousand-year reign of Christ on earth before the final consummation of all things. Like everything in Revelation, it is a striking mix of this world and the next, a vision of all creation transfigured. But it begins here and now, with the transformation of the present world order into the realm of Christ the King. Furthermore, Christians will have a crucial role to play, as priests and kings. They will be priestly because they will share Christ's work of mediating between heaven and earth, reconciling each to the other, and because they will be there *for others*, not just for themselves. They will be royal because they will *matter* – and for all eternity – as sharers in the life and victory of Christ.

In this tremendous vision, no one will be unemployed, and no one will be preoccupied with self. At the heart of the vision stands a great throne, and on it will sit Someone greater than all the leaders of this world. But that Someone has the appearance and character of a lamb, whose self-offering opens the way to an upside-down creation in which the powerful will be brought low and the humble lifted high. Here, surely, is a vision of the future that is worth praying and striving for now.

Almighty God,
as your kingdom dawns,
turn us from the darkness of sin to the
light of holiness,
that we may be ready to meet you
in our Lord and Saviour, Jesus Christ.

COLLECT

Wednesday 5 December

Revelation 21.1-8

*'And the one who was seated on the throne said,
"See, I am making all things new"' (21.5)*

The Greek word for 'new' comes four times in these few verses: a new heaven, a new earth, the new Jerusalem, and finally 'I am making all things new'. The vision we are given here is nothing less than a new creation, with three distinctive features: first, there will be no more sea, because the old creation was made out of the watery chaos (Genesis 1.2) and was always liable to return to it, as it did in the days of Noah. No insularity in the new creation!

Second, there will be no more death, or mourning or crying, or pain – these tragic flaws in the old creation will be banished for ever from the new one.

Third, God will be with us; in fact, God's 'tent' or tabernacle will be pitched among us for ever. We will become in reality what we have always been in potential: God's children.

This, and nothing less than this, is what the Christian is to look forward to, and to begin to build here and now. The first citizens of this new creation will be precisely those who have grieved and wept and suffered the most in the old one; they will enjoy the front seats at a banquet at which the best wine is still to be served.

COLLECT

Almighty God,
give us grace to cast away the works of darkness
and to put on the armour of light,
now in the time of this mortal life,
in which your Son Jesus Christ came to us in great humility;
that on the last day,
when he shall come again in his glorious majesty
   to judge the living and the dead,
we may rise to the life immortal;
through him who is alive and reigns with you,
in the unity of the Holy Spirit,
one God, now and for ever.

Reflection by **Gordon Mursell**

Psalms **42**, 43 *or* 14, **15**, 16
Isaiah 44.1-8
Revelation 21.9-21

Thursday 6 December

Revelation 21.9-21

'... he showed me the holy city Jerusalem coming down out of heaven from God' (21.10)

There is a striking paradox at the heart of the Bible's closing vision of the new Jerusalem. It will have 'a great, high wall with twelve gates'. But (as we see in tomorrow's reading) the gates will never be shut. It will be a safe place, a refuge, which is why nothing unclean or evil will be found there. It will also be an inclusive place: we may be surprised at who turn out to be our fellow-citizens, and they may be surprised to see us!

More important still: it will be a *beautiful* place, transparent as glass; the precious stones and jewels that here are the privilege of the few will there be the delight of the many. In the New Testament, the Greek word for 'good' (*kalos*) also means 'beautiful', and that matters, because surely our greatest challenge in the twenty-first century is how to give birth to a vision of goodness that is not just about the absence of evil, but is truly attractive in its own right.

Well, here is that vision: a safe, inclusive and beautiful city where only those who freely choose a lifestyle and ideology hostile to its values will exclude themselves. Advent is the season to pray that vision into reality. Charles Wesley gave us the words:

Come, thou long-expected Jesus,
Born to set thy people free,
From our fears and sins release us,
Let us find our rest in thee.

Almighty God,
as your kingdom dawns,
turn us from the darkness of sin to the
light of holiness,
that we may be ready to meet you
in our Lord and Saviour, Jesus Christ.

COLLECT

Friday 7 December

Revelation 21.22 – 22.5

*'Then the angel showed me the river of the water of life,
bright as crystal' (22.1)*

The vision of the city with which the Bible ends is not the same as the Garden of Eden with which it begins, but they do have much in common. Eden is a paradise garden, and the first man and woman are commanded 'to till it and keep it' (Genesis 2.15) – nature and human culture belonged together in the presence of God, before everything went wrong. In the new Jerusalem, nature and human culture will be perfectly integrated: the tree of life, with its fruit and leaves 'for the healing of the nations', and the river that flows through the city, will be complemented by 'the glory and the honour of the nations'. No temple will be needed: everyone will enjoy direct access to the presence of God.

This tremendous vision of a creation made new comes *from exile* (Revelation 1.9). In our world today, borders and barriers are increasingly closed against refugees, asylum seekers and others forced into exile. Yet the Bible suggests that those excluded may be precisely the ones capable of envisioning, and helping us build, a new and better world.

Advent is the time to ask: what can we do to develop a vision of that new world, and who are the people who can help us to build it?

COLLECT

Almighty God,
give us grace to cast away the works of darkness
and to put on the armour of light,
now in the time of this mortal life,
in which your Son Jesus Christ came to us in great humility;
that on the last day,
when he shall come again in his glorious majesty
    to judge the living and the dead,
we may rise to the life immortal;
through him who is alive and reigns with you,
in the unity of the Holy Spirit,
one God, now and for ever.

Reflection by **Gordon Mursell**

Saturday 8 December

Revelation 22.6-end

'Amen. Come, Lord Jesus!' (v.20)

The Greek verb 'to come' appears seven times in these closing verses of Revelation, just as it appears three times in the opening verses. In his wonderful Advent hymn, based directly on texts from Revelation, Charles Wesley captures this emphasis on a God who comes: 'Lo! He comes with clouds descending' echoes Revelation 1.7 ('Behold, he cometh with clouds' in the KJV), and his closing line, 'Alleluia! Come, Lord, come!' echoes verse 20 of this chapter. The whole hymn, like the book, is focused on the need for expectant, even defiant, waiting for the God who comes among us – at Christmas, in the word made flesh; at the end of time, as our Judge; and every day, wherever and whenever people have hearts and minds ready to make that God welcome.

Like any good preacher, Wesley follows John of Patmos in verse 20 by moving from testimony (talking *about* God, in the first three verses of his hymn) to prayer (talking *to* God) in the closing verse. It is sad that, in his equally famous Christmas hymn ('Hark! The herald angels sing'), the closing verse, where he again moves from talking about God to talking to God, is invariably omitted today, for it is precisely in these closing words that we are invited to make the message of Scripture our own, and open our hearts to the God who comes:

> *Come, Desire of nations, come,*
> *Fix in us thy humble home…*

Almighty God,
as your kingdom dawns,
turn us from the darkness of sin to the
light of holiness,
that we may be ready to meet you
in our Lord and Saviour, Jesus Christ.

COLLECT

Monday 10 December

1 Thessalonians 1

'For the people of those regions report ... how you turned to God from idols, to serve a living and true God, and to wait for his Son from heaven' (vv.9-10)

These words give us a fascinating insight into how members of one of the very earliest churches became Christians, and the three stages involved in doing this. First, they 'turned to God from idols' – the verb 'turn' occurs rarely in Paul's letters and always involves some kind of change of life and direction. There were plenty of idols for those first Christians to turn from (including the growing cult of emperor worship), and there are plenty today.

Second, they turned in order 'to serve a living and true God'. At the heart of Christian life is this costly willingness to put self second, and service of God and neighbour first.

Third, they committed themselves 'to wait for his Son from heaven'. The Greek word for 'wait' occurs nowhere else in the New Testament, and has about it a sense of hanging on in there (it comes from a root meaning 'abide').

Here is the spirituality of Advent: what idols do we need to turn from? What service of God and neighbour do we need to commit to? And are we waiting expectantly for what God longs to do in our lives today?

COLLECT

O Lord, raise up, we pray, your power
and come among us,
and with great might succour us;
that whereas, through our sins and wickedness
we are grievously hindered
in running the race that is set before us,
your bountiful grace and mercy
may speedily help and deliver us;
through Jesus Christ your Son our Lord,
to whom with you and the Holy Spirit,
be honour and glory, now and for ever.

| *Reflection by* **Gordon Mursell**

Tuesday 11 December

1 Thessalonians 2.1-12

'But we were gentle among you, like a nurse tenderly caring for her own children' (v.7)

The image of the apostle as a nurse caring for her own children is striking, and not only because it complements the more traditional image of the apostle 'like a father with his children' that follows it. The image carries overtones of feeding and nurturing, just as the Greek word for 'tenderly caring' carries overtones of keeping warm.

Two implications of the apostle as nurse are worth noting. First, Paul sees the vocation of an apostle as far more than dispensing professional skills – it involves ministering with one's own self, making oneself vulnerable to rejection. This makes Christian pastoral care costly; it also makes it potentially life changing. Second, the nurse does not care for her dependent children indefinitely; there will come a time to let them go, even though the nurse will never cease to care about them.

What this nurse offers her children is nothing less than unconditional love, which is why Paul goes on to speak of sharing his own self with the Thessalonian Christians, 'because you have become very dear to us'. Above all, Paul wants those Christians to know that they are loved, and his ministry as a nurse embodies the love that God shows to all of us at Christmas by becoming human among us.

Almighty God,
purify our hearts and minds,
that when your Son Jesus Christ comes again as
judge and saviour
we may be ready to receive him,
who is our Lord and our God.

COLLECT

Wednesday 12 December

Psalms **62**, 63 *or* **34**
Isaiah 47
1 Thessalonians 2.13-end

1 Thessalonians 2.13-end

'...but Satan blocked our way' (v.18)

Suddenly, Paul's letter to the Thessalonians is overshadowed by evil. The best-laid plans of even the greatest Christian apostle are unexpectedly thwarted – and by Satan. We need to be careful here: there is no suggestion that Paul attributes all or most of human sin and suffering to the work of a personal devil, turning us into helpless pawns in an epic cosmic battle. But the Bible does suggest that evil is a real and active force in the world, which, like cancer, can take over entire people and organizations if not confronted and challenged.

Advent is supremely the season to remember that. The beauty of the Christmas story is stained by Herod's terrible massacre of the Innocents. And we are told in the Gospel of John that Satan entered into Judas Iscariot, not when he was conspiring with others to betray Jesus but right in the middle of the Last Supper (John 13.27).

It's easy, and tempting, to view Herod or Judas as embodiments of pure evil; it would be wiser to admit that in any situation, no matter how spiritual, human frailty is exposed to the reality of evil. Rigorous and vigilant self-examination are essential here. In an Advent sermon, John Henry Newman wrote: 'we are destined to come before Him; nay, and to come before Him in judgment; and that on our first meeting; and that suddenly.'

COLLECT

O Lord, raise up, we pray, your power
and come among us,
and with great might succour us;
that whereas, through our sins and wickedness
we are grievously hindered
in running the race that is set before us,
your bountiful grace and mercy
may speedily help and deliver us;
through Jesus Christ your Son our Lord,
to whom with you and the Holy Spirit,
be honour and glory, now and for ever.

| *Reflection by* **Gordon Mursell**

Psalms 53, **54**, 60 *or* 37*
Isaiah 48.1-11
1 Thessalonians 3

Thursday 13 December

1 Thessalonians 3

'And may the Lord make you ... abound in love for one another and for all, just as we abound in love for you' (v.12)

If (as many scholars argue) St Paul's first letter to the Thessalonians is the earliest piece of writing in the New Testament, then verses 11 to 13 of chapter 3 form the earliest Christian prayer in written form. Notice that it comes in the middle of the letter: Paul has no difficulty moving from pastoral encouragement to prayer and back again, rather than (as can sometimes happen today) cordoning prayer off from the rest of Church life by restricting it to the beginning and end of a meeting or other activity.

Paul's prayer for God to strengthen their hearts in holiness so that they may be blameless 'at the coming of our Lord Jesus' captures exactly what we might call the spirituality of Advent. What is even more striking is his prayer for them to abound in love for one another and for all. From the very beginning, Christians were to be concerned with all humanity, not just a chosen few; hence the writer of 1 Timothy urges the recipient to pray 'for everyone ... in the sight of God our Saviour, who desires everyone to be saved' (1 Timothy 2.1-4).

Advent is a time to enlarge the focus of our prayer and witness to embrace nothing less than the whole of creation.

Almighty God,
purify our hearts and minds,
that when your Son Jesus Christ comes again as
judge and saviour
we may be ready to receive him,
who is our Lord and our God.

COLLECT

Friday 14 December

1 Thessalonians 4.1-12

'... you yourselves have been taught by God to love one another'
(v.9)

The first letter to the Thessalonians gives us a fascinating picture of a young and fragile Christian community struggling to survive and grow against a background of what seems to have been a mix of indifference and active hostility. Paul speaks in this chapter about the 'lustful passion' of the gentiles, and earlier he writes about adherents of Judaism who 'drove us out' (1 Thessalonians 2.15; Bishop Tom Wright helpfully suggests that they should be described as 'Judeans' rather than 'Jews', since all the earliest Christians were Jews, including Paul himself).

Paul wants those first Christians to stand out by their love for one another. But many good Judeans and pagans will also have loved one another. What surely made the followers of Jesus distinctive was their assurance that they were themselves unconditionally loved (Paul calls them 'beloved by God', 1 Thessalonians 1.4), irrespective of whether they were Jews or gentiles in origin. This is the unique gift and the living heart of Christian faith: that all people, whatever our upbringing, orientation or ethnicity, can come to know that we are loved with the love that is made flesh in the incarnation and crucifixion of God's only Son, and which should find living and outgoing expression in the life of the Church.

COLLECT

O Lord, raise up, we pray, your power
and come among us,
and with great might succour us;
that whereas, through our sins and wickedness
we are grievously hindered
in running the race that is set before us,
your bountiful grace and mercy
may speedily help and deliver us;
through Jesus Christ your Son our Lord,
to whom with you and the Holy Spirit,
be honour and glory, now and for ever.

Reflection by **Gordon Mursell**

Psalms **145** *or* 41, **42**, 43
Isaiah 49.1-13
1 Thessalonians 4.13-end

Saturday 15 December

1 Thessalonians 4.13-end

'For the Lord himself, with a cry of command ... will descend from heaven' (v.16)

With these dramatic words, Paul seeks to reassure the Thessalonian Christians, who were evidently anxious that those of their number who had already died would miss out on the resurrection, by contrast with those who were still alive at Christ's second coming. This may not be a major concern for us today, but what Paul writes remains of enduring importance. Those who have died 'in Christ' will be the first to experience the fullness of resurrection life.

Paul doesn't specify what it means to be 'in Christ', or whether this includes righteous non-believers. What he does say is that we will be reunited with those we love but see no longer, and that, like the father of the Prodigal Son, the risen Christ will already be on the road, so to speak, to meet us and bring us home.

What's more, we will *hear* his coming ('with a cry of command, with the archangel's call and with the sound of God's trumpet'). In Scripture, hearing is always the primary sense, and Advent is the season for attuning our ears so we can hear, as Mary and Zechariah both did, the call of God into a new and life-changing future. If we can hear God's call to us now, then God's final call at the end of time will be nothing less than a welcome home.

Almighty God,
purify our hearts and minds,
that when your Son Jesus Christ comes again as
judge and saviour
we may be ready to receive him,
who is our Lord and our God.

COLLECT

Monday 17 December

Psalm **40** *or* **44**
Isaiah 49.14-25
1 Thessalonians 5.1-11

1 Thessalonians 5.1-11

'For God has destined us not for wrath …' (v.9)

In the 1970s, when there were serious troubles in Northern Ireland, Dr Ian Paisley became the most prominent – and belligerent – of the Protestant leaders. The Prime Minister, James Callaghan, once said to him, 'We are all children of God, are we not?' 'No,' Paisley thundered, 'we are children of wrath.'

In Ephesians 2.3 Paul says of himself and his fellow Christians, 'we were by nature children of wrath, like everyone else'. But writing to the Thessalonians, Paul tells them that their faith means they are destined 'not for wrath' but for 'salvation through our Lord Jesus Christ'.

There is an innate tendency in human beings to do the wrong thing even when we desire to do what is right. Paul could wax eloquently about it. We call it original sin, and it is now a very unfashionable concept in the western world. It is what has led many people to believe they are under condemnation and subject to God's wrath. But the most grievous judges of human beings are frequently human beings themselves. Even in an age that scarcely believes in sin, wrath and hell, many people remain deeply dissatisfied with their lives and with themselves. A saviour is still needed. Jesus Christ looks upon us not as captive to the evil one but as liberated by his saving love. That's why we can claim truly to be children of God.

COLLECT

O Lord Jesus Christ,
who at your first coming sent your messenger
to prepare your way before you:
grant that the ministers and stewards of your mysteries
may likewise so prepare and make ready your way
by turning the hearts of the disobedient to the wisdom of the just,
that at your second coming to judge the world
we may be found an acceptable people in your sight;
for you are alive and reign with the Father
in the unity of the Holy Spirit,
one God, now and for ever.

Reflection by **Graham James**

Psalms **70**, 74 *or* **48**, 52
Isaiah 50
1 Thessalonians 5.12-end

Tuesday 18 December

1 Thessalonians 5.12-end

'... encourage the faint-hearted, help the weak' (v.14)

The Greek word translated here as 'faint-hearted' makes its only appearance in the whole of the New Testament in this letter from Paul to the Thessalonians. A literal translation would be 'little-souled'. 'Faint-hearted', if used at all in English now, would be likely to refer to people who are nervous, anxious and afraid, passing through life in a permanent state of underconfidence. But Paul seems to be thinking of the diffident people in the Thessalonian congregation, the ones who don't place much value on themselves or think they have little to offer. That's why they're described as 'little-souled'.

In Greek culture, someone with lots of self-confidence and self-assurance was thought to be a 'great-souled' person. Such people were endowed, it was believed, with qualities of leadership. Yet it may well be the diffident and modest who have much more of the meekness and humility that Jesus said in the Sermon on the Mount would cause them to inherit the earth. The contemporary world is as liable to admire the 'great-souled' self-confident leader as ancient Greece. As Christmas approaches and we celebrate God coming to earth in the defenceless humility of a newborn baby, perhaps we should spare a thought for the faint-hearted, diffident and humble people in congregations everywhere. They are often the ones most ready to serve. They should be encouraged to believe they have greater souls than they think.

God for whom we watch and wait,
you sent John the Baptist to prepare the way of your Son:
give us courage to speak the truth,
to hunger for justice,
and to suffer for the cause of right,
with Jesus Christ our Lord.

COLLECT

Wednesday 19 December

2 Thessalonians 1

'... we ... boast of you among the churches of God' (v.4)

One of Aesop's fables is about a boastful traveller. He claims that when staying in Rhodes many people witnessed him leaping further than any other human being. A bystander asks him to pretend it is Rhodes and repeat his feat. It put an end to his boasting.

In the contemporary world, boasting seems almost compulsory. Some job applications or curriculum vitae I read make me feel rather inferior to the possessors of such great talents. Yet when I meet such people in the flesh they are frequently far from boastful. In their applications for jobs they are simply doing what the culture requires.

Sometimes in his letters, Paul boasts ironically of his sufferings, imprisonments and persecutions, the signs that he's an authentic apostle of Jesus Christ (2 Corinthians 10.12). In this letter he isn't boasting about himself or his achievements but the faith and perseverance of the Thessalonians, a young church facing persecution. We don't know the precise circumstances, but what impresses Paul is their love for each other and refusal to abandon Christ despite the pressure put upon them. He tells the Thessalonians he boasts of their story to other churches to encourage them.

Many churches across the world are experiencing persecution in our own age, notably in Egypt and Pakistan, Syria and elsewhere in the Middle East. Do we even know the extent of their sufferings? Do we boast of them enough?

COLLECT

O Lord Jesus Christ,
who at your first coming sent your messenger
to prepare your way before you:
grant that the ministers and stewards of your mysteries
may likewise so prepare and make ready your way
by turning the hearts of the disobedient to the wisdom of the just,
that at your second coming to judge the world
we may be found an acceptable people in your sight;
for you are alive and reign with the Father
in the unity of the Holy Spirit,
one God, now and for ever.

Reflection by **Graham James**

Psalms **46**, 95
Isaiah 51.9-16
2 Thessalonians 2

Thursday 20 December

2 Thessalonians 2

'Let no one deceive you in any way…' (v.3)

One of the members of the nonconformist church I attended in my childhood believed strongly that the end times were imminent. He distributed tracts and preached at street corners. Sadly, he had a very unsmiling countenance and carried with him a deep gloom.

The Thessalonians to whom Paul writes believed the end times were imminent too. They were much more cheerful about it, though. For them, the world had been so recently turned upside down by the resurrection of Christ and the coming of the Holy Spirit that they thought God would surely bring things to completion very soon. Some of them even believed the day of the Lord had already come. The gifts of the Spirit were such that miraculous things were happening. Lives were being changed. Surely that was what was promised when Christ would return?

Paul is concerned that they should not be deceived. But it's hard not to have some sympathy with the Thessalonians. When lives are so transformed in Christ that people have become a new creation, doesn't it seem like an anticipation of the 'day of the Lord'?

Two thousand years of Christian history have dulled such expectation. The Christian Church has long been an established institution. Yet we still live in an interim time between Pentecost and the second coming of Christ, however we may understand it. A touch of Thessalonian excitement might do us all some good.

God for whom we watch and wait,
you sent John the Baptist to prepare the way of your Son:
give us courage to speak the truth,
to hunger for justice,
and to suffer for the cause of right,
with Jesus Christ our Lord.

COLLECT

Reflection by **Graham James**   25

Friday 21 December

2 Thessalonians 3

'I, Paul, write this greeting with my own hand' (v.17)

Paul sometimes finishes his letters with a greeting in his own handwriting to authenticate them. It was common in the ancient world for letter writers (Cicero comes to mind) to dictate them to a scribe and then add a personal greeting of their own at the end. Here Paul seems almost to overdo it, saying 'this is the mark in every letter of mine; it is the way I write'.

A handwritten letter has now become something of a rarity in the western world. Yet it is often the more precious as a result. A bereaved person will read letters of condolence again and again. Phone calls don't have the same permanence. 'Thank you for writing in your own hand,' I've been told at such times. Electronic communication cannot be cherished in quite the same way.

In 2016 the Bishop's Art Prize in Norwich (a competition I sponsor each year at the Norwich University of the Arts) was won by a bronze simply called *Epistle*. It was cast from a pile of handwritten letters, given weight and permanence, a sign of how much they meant to the people who received them.

The weight the Church has given to Paul's letters as scripture may cause us to forget just how personal they were for those who first read them. Do we write enough letters in our own hand? When and to whom should we write them?

COLLECT

O Lord Jesus Christ,
who at your first coming sent your messenger
to prepare your way before you:
grant that the ministers and stewards of your mysteries
may likewise so prepare and make ready your way
by turning the hearts of the disobedient to the wisdom of the just,
that at your second coming to judge the world
we may be found an acceptable people in your sight;
for you are alive and reign with the Father
in the unity of the Holy Spirit,
one God, now and for ever.

Reflection by **Graham James**

Psalms **124**, 125, 126, 127
Isaiah 52.1-12
Jude

Saturday 22 December

Isaiah 52.1-12
'How beautiful ... are the feet ...' (v.7)

It's estimated that in an average life span most people will walk 20,000 miles, and frequently a great deal more than that. It's the rough equivalent of walking round the world. Our feet have a lot of work to do, though we tend to take them for granted. That's why this verse in Isaiah is such an arresting and intriguing one.

Our feet can be a mirror to our general health. Problems with the circulation of our blood as well as signs of arthritis or diabetes may be detected first in our feet. But we don't generally regard our feet as the most attractive part of the human body.

The word in Hebrew, *na'ha*, which we translate as 'beautiful' does not mean pretty or alluring. It's more to do with being appropriate and fitting, entirely aligned with God's purpose. So feet are beautiful when they do the right work, God's work. Here it's the feet of heralds that are beautiful because they are proclaiming a message of freedom for the people of Israel, announcing their homecoming.

In Romans 10.15, Paul takes this verse and applies it to those who are sent into the world to preach the gospel. The good news of Jesus Christ has been carried on foot to every part of the globe in Christian mission. Where will our feet take us today and for what purpose?

COLLECT

God for whom we watch and wait,
you sent John the Baptist to prepare the way of your Son:
give us courage to speak the truth,
to hunger for justice,
and to suffer for the cause of right,
with Jesus Christ our Lord.

Reflection by **Graham James**   27

Monday 24 December
Christmas Eve

Psalms **45**, 113
Isaiah 52.13 – end of 53
2 Peter 1.1-15

Isaiah 52.13 – end of 53

'... we held him of no account' (53.3)

Isaiah's vision of the suffering servant 'wounded for our transgressions, crushed for our iniquities' seems a natural reading for Good Friday. So it's something of a surprise when it appears on Christmas Eve, read in churches already festooned with Christmas trees, their cribs set up awaiting only the addition of the child in the manger.

Among the things that unite Christmas Eve and Good Friday is the indifference of the local population, whether to the birth of Jesus in Bethlehem or to his crucifixion in Jerusalem. A few shepherds apart, Bethlehem 'held him of no account'. Only later, after the visit of Eastern sages, did Herod fear for his kingdom and try to trace this special child. On the eve of Christ's birth, his parents were homeless travellers, also of no account. On Good Friday in Jerusalem, his mother Mary and a few others were at the foot of the cross, but the life of the city was barely interrupted by yet another felon going to his execution. The central events of Christianity took place largely unnoticed by the world.

More people go to church in England nowadays on Christmas Eve than on any other day of the year. Perhaps it's especially at Christmas, when suddenly what the Church offers becomes popular, we need to recall not just the harsh circumstances of Christ's birth but remember the world at the time 'held him of no account', both at his birth and death.

COLLECT

Almighty God,
you make us glad with the yearly remembrance
    of the birth of your Son Jesus Christ:
grant that, as we joyfully receive him as our redeemer,
so we may with sure confidence behold him
when he shall come to be our judge;
who is alive and reigns with you,
in the unity of the Holy Spirit,
one God, now and for ever.

Reflection by **Graham James**

Tuesday 25 December
Christmas Day

Matthew 1.18-end
'God is with us' (v.23)

John Tavener's anthem *A Christmas Proclamation* begins quietly with the words 'God is with us', sung unaccompanied. A haunting melody then unfolds with a solo tenor voice complemented by crescendos from a choir until 'God is with us' is repeated. The organ is then introduced, and eventually an emphatic 'Christ is born' is sung loudly and triumphantly with the organ at full blast. This composition seems unmistakably to have been written by a man of faith.

The brilliance of Tavener's work is that it captures the way Jesus slips almost unannounced into the world, born under the cover of darkness in the outhouse of a pub. Yet this obscure birth marks the most emphatic turning point in world history, demanding the loudest proclamation.

It's not that God had not been with his people before Christ was born. But his birth reveals something entirely new. There is scarcely any creature more helpless than a newborn human baby. None of us would have survived at all if no one had cared for us in the first days and weeks of our lives. That was as true for Jesus as for the rest of us. We think of God caring for us but in the birth of the infant Christ, God places himself into our care. That's how we know that God is truly with us.

Almighty God,
you have given us your only-begotten Son
to take our nature upon him
and as at this time to be born of a pure virgin:
grant that we, who have been born again
and made your children by adoption and grace,
may daily be renewed by your Holy Spirit;
through Jesus Christ your Son our Lord,
who is alive and reigns with you,
in the unity of the Holy Spirit,
one God, now and for ever.

COLLECT

Wednesday 26 December

Stephen, deacon, first martyr

Psalms **13**, 31.1-8, 150
Jeremiah 26.12-15
Acts 6

Acts 6

'They chose Stephen, a man full of faith ...' (v.5)

St Stephen's Day does not get much prominence in our liturgical observances. Even the most devout Christians are ready for a day off church on December 26th. The placing of the remembrance of the first martyr for the Christian faith so near the celebration of the birth of Christ is no accident. No greater love can be shown to Christ than to lay down one's life for him.

Stephen's rise to prominence came as the result of being given a menial task. The Greek-speaking widows in the church in Jerusalem were being treated unfairly in the daily distribution of food. The apostles seemed to think that serving tables would lead them to neglect 'prayer' and 'serving the word'. They were wise enough, however, to choose men 'of good standing' to distribute the food. The unity of this early Christian community depended on treating everyone in the same way. As it turned out, Stephen was a powerful preacher too, as his sermon in Act 7 demonstrates. Caring for the poor and preaching the word of God should not be divided.

In Greek, *Stephanos* means 'crown'. The birth of the infant King is followed immediately in our calendar by the commemoration of the first of countless Christians to wear a martyr's crown. Well before the wise men arrive at the stable with their myrrh, there's a reminder here that whenever and wherever we encounter Jesus, his cross and all that it means stands in the shadows.

COLLECT

Gracious Father,
who gave the first martyr Stephen
grace to pray for those who took up stones against him:
grant that in all our sufferings for the truth
we may learn to love even our enemies
and to seek forgiveness for those who desire our hurt,
looking up to heaven to him who was crucified for us,
Jesus Christ, our mediator and advocate,
who is alive and reigns with you,
in the unity of the Holy Spirit,
one God, now and for ever.

| *Reflection by* **Graham James**

Psalms **21**, 147.13-end
Exodus 33.12-end
1 John 2.1-11

Thursday 27 December
John, Apostle and Evangelist

1 John 2.1-11
'I abide in him...' (v.6)

The word 'abide' is not much used nowadays. If it is, it's frequently given a negative twist. 'I can't abide him' or 'I can't abide TV quiz shows' emphasizes an inability to tolerate someone or something.

The theologian Ben Quash in his book simply called *Abiding* explores how this unfashionable word conveys more about the quality of Christian life than almost any other. It's a word found frequently in John's Gospel and the Johannine letters. Abiding is about perseverance and constancy. It includes relinquishing anything that prevents us living with Christ and those he has called to follow him.

The glory of following Christ is that he also abides in us. It's reciprocal. Perhaps our biggest challenge is to love the others Christ has called to follow him. They include those we would never choose to count as our friends. Yet we are called not merely to tolerate them but to be fully at home with them and open our hearts to them.

Ben Quash points to the example of Ruth in the Old Testament as a fine illustration of what abiding meant. When her widowed mother-in-law Naomi decides to return to Bethlehem from Moab, Ruth, herself widowed, insists on going with her to this foreign land. 'Where you go, I will go; where you lodge, I will lodge; your people shall be my people, and your God my God' (Ruth 1.16).

With whom will we abide today?

Merciful Lord,
cast your bright beams of light upon the Church:
that, being enlightened by the teaching
of your blessed apostle and evangelist Saint John,
we may so walk in the light of your truth
that we may at last attain to the light of everlasting life;
through Jesus Christ your incarnate Son our Lord,
who is alive and reigns with you,
in the unity of the Holy Spirit,
one God, now and for ever.

COLLECT

Reflection by **Graham James**   31

Friday 28 December

The Holy Innocents

Psalms **36**, 146
Baruch 4.21-27
or Genesis 37.13-20
Matthew 18.1-10

Matthew 18.1-10

'... unless you ... become like children, you will never enter the kingdom of heaven' (v.3)

Holy Innocents' Day reminds us of the helplessness of infants in an adult world. But Herod was not uniquely wicked. In our own age the callous disregard for children's lives in the world's worst conflicts makes today's remembrance chillingly contemporary. Infants are entirely dependent on parents, guardians or other carers even to live.

Jesus says we are to become like children when answering the question 'Who is the greatest in the kingdom of heaven?' The disciples (who asked the question) should have understood the need for such dependence. Earlier (in Matthew 10) the Twelve were sent out to proclaim the good news. They were allowed no money, no change of clothes and no bag. They were to go barefoot, a sign of extreme poverty. They were to know what it was to be entirely dependent on the generosity of others in their mission. They were to learn how to receive.

The art of receiving is well practised by children, but we seem to lose it gradually as we grow. Perhaps instead of so many references to 'the servant Church', we should hear more frequently of 'the receiving Church'. We have nothing that we have not first received from God. We call our acts of worship 'services', whereas they may more appropriately be termed 'receptions'. For we are always on the receiving end of God's grace, as dependent upon him as the youngest infants on those around them.

COLLECT

Heavenly Father,
whose children suffered at the hands of Herod,
though they had done no wrong:
by the suffering of your Son
and by the innocence of our lives
frustrate all evil designs
and establish your reign of justice and peace;
through Jesus Christ your Son our Lord,
who is alive and reigns with you,
in the unity of the Holy Spirit,
one God, now and for ever.

| *Reflection by* **Graham James**

Psalms **19**, 20
Isaiah 57.15-end
John 1.1-18

Saturday 29 December

John 1.1-18

'... yet the world did not know him' (v.10)

At the end of the Christmas midnight eucharist in Norwich Cathedral, the great west doors are flung open and John's prologue is read. The gospeller faces the city beyond. There are usually a few Christmas revellers taken by surprise, but since it is around 1 o'clock in the morning, the city is dark and fairly quiet. John's poetic and glorious words about God speaking to the world in Christ ring out – and meet no response. It's a potent symbol. 'He was in the world ... yet the world did not know him.'

The prologue is about the Word. In Jesus, God spoke in all his fullness, holding nothing back. As the distinguished American professor Thomas Gardner says in his remarkable book *John in the Company of Poets*: 'When God spoke Jesus to the world, Jesus was everything he intended to say.'

Behind the gospeller at the midnight eucharist, a huge congregation suggests that even in secular Britain there are those drawn to the 'Word made flesh'. In the prologue, John quickly modifies his assertion that the whole world does not recognize Christ, reminding us that 'to all who received him ... he gave power to become children of God'. At the end of that Christmas eucharist, John's words hang in the air, helping us realize how frequently we live between recognizing Christ and not knowing him, poised between darkness and light. We know, too, we are being addressed directly by the God who speaks in Jesus everything he intended to say.

COLLECT

Almighty God,
you have given us your only-begotten Son
to take our nature upon him
and as at this time to be born of a pure virgin:
grant that we, who have been born again
and made your children by adoption and grace,
may daily be renewed by your Holy Spirit;
through Jesus Christ your Son our Lord,
who is alive and reigns with you,
in the unity of the Holy Spirit,
one God, now and for ever.

Reflection by **Graham James**   33

Monday 31 December

Isaiah 59.15*b*-end

'And he will come to Zion as Redeemer' (v.20)

I gave my mother a mobile phone for Christmas. She was overjoyed. I rang on Boxing Day to see how she was getting on. There was no reply from the mobile so I resorted to the landline. My father answered: 'To tell the truth, the telephoning and the texting and the directory and the voicemail are all proving a bit complicated.'

'Bring Mum to the phone,' I replied. 'I'll give her some more instructions.' I could sense him hesitating. 'Just give her the message.'

He came back a minute later: 'She says that, to be honest, she doesn't need more messages or instructions. The only way she's going to understand the wretched thing is if her son comes in person.'

This chapter of Isaiah is set five centuries before Jesus. The Jews had been released from decades of exile in Babylon and had returned to the lands surrounding Jerusalem (Zion, v.20). But God is dismayed at the injustice that fills the land. No messenger has arisen to instruct the people.

God gathers his armour, but it's not a warrior's armour. Instead he plans to fight for the people he loves with judgement, righteousness and salvation. And the people God loves are not a privileged few, but anyone from east to west who honours him. Who will come? God himself will come.

That is why Jesus walked and talked on our planet. The Son came in person.

COLLECT

Almighty God,
who wonderfully created us in your own image
and yet more wonderfully restored us
through your Son Jesus Christ:
grant that, as he came to share in our humanity,
so we may share the life of his divinity;
who is alive and reigns with you,
in the unity of the Holy Spirit,
one God, now and for ever.

Reflection by **Peter Graystone**

Psalms **103**, 150
Genesis 17.1-13
Romans 2.17-end

Tuesday 1 January
Naming and Circumcision of Jesus

Genesis 17.1-13
'... an everlasting covenant' (v.7)

The story of the Hebrew people (later the Jews) begins with Abram. He lived in the region we would now call Iraq. He must have been regarded as eccentric or mad by his neighbours because he believed two things that had been revealed to him. First, there is only one God, not hundreds of gods who control the harvest, the weather and so on. And second, God is invisible, so idols are useless.

That belief was so strong that it compelled Abram and his family to leave the town in which they were born and travel hundreds of miles to make a new home in the lands in which Jesus would live centuries later.

On the journey God gave him three new things. The first was a name: Abraham. It means 'father of many'.

The second was a covenant: a vow that put God and Abraham's descendants into an eternal relationship. God's promise was that the childless Abraham would have sons and be the ancestor of millions. And no matter what happened, he would never cease to be their God.

The third was a sign: the circumcision of males. Most unmistakeable during the intimate moments at which children are conceived, this was a mark to remind Jews that the God of miracles sustains life from generation to generation. At every point in history, from the days of Abraham to the present, they have been precious to him.

Almighty God,
whose blessed Son was circumcised
in obedience to the law for our sake
and given the Name that is above every name:
give us grace faithfully to bear his Name,
to worship him in the freedom of the Spirit,
and to proclaim him as the Saviour of the world;
who is alive and reigns with you,
in the unity of the Holy Spirit,
one God, now and for ever.

COLLECT

*Reflection by **Peter Graystone***

Wednesday 2 January

Psalm **18.1-30**
Isaiah 60.1-12
John 1.35-42

Isaiah 60.1-12

'Arise, shine; for your light has come' (v.1)

Here is a picture of a world overwhelmed with gloom except for one brilliant patch of light. The light is shining from the Jews, newly re-established in and around Jerusalem. Gentiles in the darkness find the light of God's people so attractive that they flood towards it bearing gifts.

This passage sets echoes reverberating. Five centuries later in the Jerusalem temple, an old man realized that he was witnessing the fulfilment of God's promise. 'My eyes have seen your salvation, which you have prepared in the presence of all peoples, a light for revelation to the gentiles' (Luke 2.30-32). The old man's name was Simeon. And what had his eyes seen? They had seen Jesus.

God's plan for humankind has always embraced more than just the Jews. Jesus' family became aware of that during his earliest days. Intellectuals from gentile lands came to worship him, following a star and also bearing gifts. What were those gifts? Verse 6 sets off another echo.

However, the most telling echo is of Jesus commissioning his followers, 'You are the light of the world. A city built on a hill cannot be hidden ... Let your light shine before others' (Matthew 5.14,16). The responsibility to be the light that attracts people struggling in darkness towards God began centuries ago with the Jews. Then it passed to Jesus. He in turn has passed it to you and me. Our moment has come. Arise! Shine!

COLLECT

Almighty God,
who wonderfully created us in your own image
and yet more wonderfully restored us
through your Son Jesus Christ:
grant that, as he came to share in our humanity,
so we may share the life of his divinity;
who is alive and reigns with you,
in the unity of the Holy Spirit,
one God, now and for ever.

| *Reflection by* **Peter Graystone**

Psalms **127**, 128, 131
Isaiah 60.13-end
John 1.43-end

Thursday 3 January

Isaiah 60.13-end

'... your days of mourning shall be ended' (v.20)

Chapter 60 of Isaiah is flooded with light. Considering how dark had been the years of exile that the Jews had suffered, the contrast is remarkable. Their return to the lands around Jerusalem would bring years of hope. Salvation was imminent for God's people. However, God's plan for their salvation this time included all the other nations of the known world.

Something else about this vision was startling and new. The nations of the world would be drawn to the God of the Jews not because they were violently conquered, but because of the beauty and appeal of his kingdom. God's light would shine and the nations of the world would come towards it willingly. They would see the peace with which God's people lived and long to share it. They would observe righteousness in the way the most vulnerable were treated and want to copy it.

What could at first glance seem to be a prejudiced vision of Israelite (or even Christian) supremacy becomes instead a missionary challenge. When the light of God transforms people's lives, those who encounter it find it deeply attractive and want to experience it for themselves.

There is still darkness in the world. However, the light has dawned. God's people, then and now, are called to be witnesses to how compelling that light truly is.

God in Trinity,
eternal unity of perfect love:
gather the nations to be one family,
and draw us into your holy life
through the birth of Emmanuel,
our Lord Jesus Christ.

COLLECT

Reflection by **Peter Graystone** | 37

Friday 4 January

Psalm **89.1-37**
Isaiah 61
John 2.1-12

Isaiah 61

'... good news to the oppressed' (v.1)

Who is the 'me' that speaks here in verse 1? This is the last of several appearances in Isaiah of the character often called 'the Servant'.

There is a sense in which the Servant is Isaiah himself. His message of good news for the oppressed Jews has threaded its way through these chapters. To a people in exile he has spoken with hope of release.

At another level, the Servant is the whole people of God in the years following their captivity. They were literally repairing the ruined cities. The Jews were to receive huge blessings as they were recompensed for all their years of suffering. In response, they were to be people who embraced justice.

In addition, Christians have always viewed Jesus as fulfilling the role of the Servant. He identified himself with these words when preaching at Nazareth (Luke 4.16-19). He omitted the phrase about God's vengeance as if he knew that the world's salvation would be worked out with love and not with violence.

However, each of us needs to recognize that the 'me' might refer to each of us individually. Christians are called to be servants of a needy world in our own times and places. Wherever people are broken-hearted or oppressed or poor, that is where the Spirit of God sends the followers of Jesus. Who do these words remind you of, and what would it mean for you to serve them?

COLLECT

Almighty God,
who wonderfully created us in your own image
and yet more wonderfully restored us
through your Son Jesus Christ:
grant that, as he came to share in our humanity,
so we may share the life of his divinity;
who is alive and reigns with you,
in the unity of the Holy Spirit,
one God, now and for ever.

Reflection by **Peter Graystone**

Psalms 8, **48**
Isaiah 62
John 2.13-end

Saturday 5 January

Isaiah 62

'See, your salvation comes' (v.11)

There is a restlessness about these verses. Watchmen are appointed on the walls of Jerusalem and they are people of prayer. They act as 'remembrancers' (ERV) – a slightly archaic political term. In England in the 12th century, the role of King's Remembrancer was created by Henry II to ensure that the king remembered who owed him tax. It still exists as a senior judicial post, and in 2014 Barbara Fontaine was the first woman appointed to the role.

Ancient customs often have modern equivalents. The God who knows every prayer before it is uttered still longs for his people to be remembrancers. The coming of Jesus, born in circumstances of great humility, has inaugurated a kingdom that God is building. It is a kingdom in which salvation comes and forsaken people are redeemed. Everyone who prays, 'Your kingdom come,' today acts as a remembrancer for God.

Creating that kingdom does not come quickly. Working so that the poor and desolate can be renamed with delightful names is laborious but it comes steadily, like the rebuilding of ruined Jerusalem all those centuries ago. Idling away time is not an option. Get building!

The twentieth-century Japanese reformer Toyohiko Kagawa lived and worked in the slums of Japan. This was his restless reflection: 'I read in a book that a man called Christ went about doing good. It is very disconcerting that I am so easily satisfied with just going about.'

COLLECT

God in Trinity,
eternal unity of perfect love:
gather the nations to be one family,
and draw us into your holy life
through the birth of Emmanuel,
our Lord Jesus Christ.

Reflection by **Peter Graystone**   39

Monday 7 January

Isaiah 63.7-end

'For you are our father' (v.16)

Yesterday I celebrated my father's ninetieth birthday. The year has also featured his sixtieth wedding anniversary and the birth of a great granddaughter. My father made a short speech in which he embarrassed his children by saying how proud he was of what they had achieved.

Today I read of God describing himself as father to his people. Is he proud of their achievements? Well, he had high expectations. He anticipated that they would respond to his love with gratitude. He imagined that they would not 'deal falsely' or wish they had a different father. As a distressed people who were saved, he expected faithfulness. This image of a father with estranged children has reappeared in Isaiah since the very beginning (Isaiah 1.2,4).

Later in this reading, we see the relationship from the perspective of God's people. They acknowledge him as their father. They know he is both mighty and compassionate, and that the relationship between child and parent is not as it should be. But with an extraordinary arrogance, they blame God for it. It is *his* fault because he made them harden their hearts, and that is why they have stopped revering him. In the place where you expect a sob of repentance comes a plea to God to 'turn back'. Surprised? Well, to me there is something very familiar about choosing to blame God first and examining my own failings second.

COLLECT

O God,
who by the leading of a star
manifested your only Son to the peoples of the earth:
mercifully grant that we,
who know you now by faith,
may at last behold your glory face to face;
through Jesus Christ your Son our Lord,
who is alive and reigns with you,
in the unity of the Holy Spirit,
one God, now and for ever.

| *Reflection by* **Peter Graystone**

Psalms **46**, 147.13 – end of **73**
Isaiah 64
1 John 4.7-end

Tuesday 8 January

Isaiah 64

'... we are the clay, and you are our potter' (v.8)

Today's Bible reading continues yesterday's poem. This is where a sob of repentance finally comes. It starts by remembering how thrilling the relationship between the people and their God used to be. It was so hot you could boil a kettle on it. It's not unusual, even today, to look back at how vivid one's experience of God was at an earlier stage of life and long for old excitements to return.

It continues with a realization that God is almighty. Only those who 'wait for' and 'remember' him are able to put themselves and God in proper perspective. Those who take time to do so realize that their failings make them truly unworthy. Our sins diminish us so much that we become like an autumn leaf, in danger of being blown away from God.

That's the point at which true repentance comes. It involves a plea to God for forgiveness. And it involves submitting to God for him to reshape our lives as if we were clay in the hands of a potter.

The poem ends with uncertainty. Even after all this, might God still appear silent? How wonderful to live as a Christian in the knowledge that the Saviour for whom Isaiah longed has come. Because of all that Jesus has done, those who come to God asking for forgiveness can do so with absolute assurance that it is freely, lovingly given.

COLLECT

Creator of the heavens,
who led the Magi by a star
to worship the Christ-child:
guide and sustain us,
that we may find our journey's end
in Jesus Christ our Lord.

Reflection by **Peter Graystone** | 41

Wednesday 9 January

Isaiah 65.1-16

'Here I am, here I am' (v.1)

This poem begins with a depressing list of all the reasons why God could justifiably have rejected his people. And then comes a most surprising moment of hope.

Our God is one who has opened his arms and made himself obvious to everyone. Not even just those who are searching for him, but anyone. And how did the Jews who lived all those centuries before Jesus respond? They provocatively worshipped in ways that were forbidden. They toyed with necromancy and defiantly ate prohibited foods. And they claimed that this made them holier than anyone else.

Does all that wrongdoing grind you down? Then take heart because God's graciousness is greater than you could imagine. You would expect a bunch of grapes that's withered and dry to be thrown away. But instead God intends to use even the most unpromising resources. He will not reject those grapes but will use every last one to make wine. That is his extraordinary blessing.

Like a bruised reed that is not chopped down, but tended back to life; like a flickering candle that isn't extinguished, but coaxed into flame (Isaiah 42.3, Matthew 12.20), God will keep working on our lives with loving determination. No one is ever regarded as too useless for his purposes. He even sees the potential in a dried-up grape like me. How can I resist when he calls out, 'Here I am'?

COLLECT

O God,
who by the leading of a star
manifested your only Son to the peoples of the earth:
mercifully grant that we,
who know you now by faith,
may at last behold your glory face to face;
through Jesus Christ your Son our Lord,
who is alive and reigns with you,
in the unity of the Holy Spirit,
one God, now and for ever.

| *Reflection by* **Peter Graystone**

Psalms 97, **149** *or* 78.1-39*
Isaiah 65.17-end
1 John 5.13-end

Thursday 10 January

Isaiah 65.17-end

'But be glad and rejoice for ever in what I am creating' (v.18)

God is building a kingdom. The coming of Jesus announced that it was near. His resurrection from the dead made it inevitable. One day, when heaven and earth are renewed, it will become a reality so perfect that the suffering of this uncertain life will be completely forgotten.

Isaiah spells out what a vision of that kingdom can and should mean in the present as well as in the future. It means children surviving childbirth and thriving in infancy. It means people living healthily to a good age. It means stable societies free from war, famine and the other catastrophes that force people to leave their homes.

It is marked by an end to a mother's nagging fear about what the future holds for her child. It is marked by such a closeness to God that every whisper will be heard. It is marked by a world in which humans are at one with the created order – neither threatened by nor a threat to the environment.

Christians are called to be beacons, shining in today's world by working to make the values of the kingdom a reality and illuminating the path that leads to our future in heaven where it will be perfected eternally. In our world of shocking inequalities, this vision is not just a comforting hope; it is an urgent challenge.

Creator of the heavens,
who led the Magi by a star
to worship the Christ-child:
guide and sustain us,
that we may find our journey's end
in Jesus Christ our Lord.

COLLECT

Friday 11 January

Psalms 98, **150** *or* 55
Isaiah 66.1-11
2 John

Isaiah 66.1-11

'... when I called, no one answered' (v.4)

The Jews learnt much about God during their years of exile in Babylon. When they were brutally defeated and dragged into captivity, they had assumed that their God was dead as well, crushed under the ruins of the temple in Jerusalem where they had made their sacrifices. But slowly they came to realize that God was not dead. In fact, he had come to Babylon with them and wanted them to thrive even in that loathsome place. Furthermore, God was everywhere in the world and longing for people to respond to his call. Thanks to the Jews' discoveries, Christians now hold these things central to their beliefs.

With that learning came a new attitude to temple worship. After the Jews returned to the lands surrounding Jerusalem, the temple was rebuilt. The Western Wall ('Wailing Wall'), which still stands in the city, survives from that rebuild. But there was a new attitude to it that rejected the idea that humans could build walls around God. What God was and is looking for is honesty and humility in his presence. If you go through the motions of sacrificing an animal without listening to and responding to God's call on your heart, the action is useless. Or worse, it could turn you into an intolerant, religious bigot. Still today, immaculate religious practices mean nothing without a heart open to and changed by the gracious love of Jesus.

COLLECT

O God,
who by the leading of a star
manifested your only Son to the peoples of the earth:
mercifully grant that we,
who know you now by faith,
may at last behold your glory face to face;
through Jesus Christ your Son our Lord,
who is alive and reigns with you,
in the unity of the Holy Spirit,
one God, now and for ever.

Reflection by **Peter Graystone**

Psalms **96**, 145 *or* **76**, 79
Isaiah 66.12-23
3 John

Saturday 12 January

Isaiah 66.12-23

'I will comfort you' (v.13)

Endings are not always pleasing. The Old Testament ends with the threat of a curse if ancient laws are forgotten (Malachi 4.4-6). The book of Isaiah ends just after today's reading with a vision of the death of those who reject the Lord (v.24). In fact, when it is read in synagogues, it is customary to read verses 22 and 23 again at the end to soften the blow. In contrast, the New Testament ends with Jesus' grace resting on all believers (Revelation 22.21). It is a vision of a peaceful future that Isaiah prepares us for in verses 12-14 of today's reading.

Here is one of the precious Bible passages that encourage us to think about the actions of God in female terms. God has made Jerusalem a source of security and wellbeing. The city has become a mother with tender care for her children. She is the source of comfort, the kind that a baby can only find in a mother's arms. Body and soul flourish because the context is peace.

The prophetic poem continues with a list of what must have seemed earth's remotest places, Tarshish (Spain) to Javan (Greece). Jews and gentiles alike will be drawn to worship the glory of God. This peaceful vision is a precursor to the promise of the new Jerusalem, the very image with which the Bible comes to a climax – the glorious destiny of all who long for God's kingdom to come (Revelation 21.2).

Creator of the heavens,
who led the Magi by a star
to worship the Christ-child:
guide and sustain us,
that we may find our journey's end
in Jesus Christ our Lord.

COLLECT

Reflection by **Peter Graystone**   45

Monday 14 January

Psalms **2**, 110 *or* **80**, 82
Amos 1
1 Corinthians 1.1-17

1 Corinthians 1.1-17

'... called into the fellowship of ... Jesus Christ' (v.9)

Deep party divisions are the background to one of Paul's most passionate letters. The Corinthian church had been founded by Paul around AD 50, and now, only a few years later, he is writing to beg these fledgling Christians not to tear their fellowship apart through social and spiritual exclusivism. His letter is full of feeling and concern for this young church and its witness to the gospel.

The work of healing divisions must be active and practical. Paul urges a spirit of unity using language reminiscent of the mending of nets, or the healing of a broken bone. In older translations, his phrase for being 'united' in verse 10 is translated as 'knit together'.

There is a rich theological basis to this plea for unity. The Corinthians are 'called' to be God's holy people, to be saints, just as Paul knows himself to be 'called' to be an apostle of Christ Jesus. Central to this shared vocation is a 'calling' into fellowship one with another. The beautiful Greek word *koinonia* emphasizes the solidarity and strength of the common life to which Christ calls every one of us, despite our disagreements and difficulties.

Whenever this organic fellowship is broken, it is as if Christ himself is torn in pieces. I wonder how we may be called to heal the body of Christ in our own day?

COLLECT

Eternal Father,
who at the baptism of Jesus
revealed him to be your Son,
anointing him with the Holy Spirit:
grant to us, who are born again by water and the Spirit,
that we may be faithful to our calling as your adopted children;
through Jesus Christ your Son our Lord,
who is alive and reigns with you,
in the unity of the Holy Spirit,
one God, now and for ever.

| *Reflection by* **Margaret Whipp**

Tuesday 15 January

1 Corinthians 1.18-end

'For Jews demand signs and Greeks desire wisdom' (v.22)

Partisan pretensions are usually a symptom of much deeper problems within the Christian community. Paul probes beneath the surface of the Corinthians' quarrelling to expose the root causes of their competitiveness and spiritual pride. While they are so easily impressed by worldly showmanship, how can they face up to the profoundly radical challenge of the cross?

Corinth was a cosmopolitan city where travelling sophists and popular wonder-workers could readily command a hearing. Cultured Greeks flocked to hear these eloquent debaters who flattered their intellect, whilst the fervent hopes of pious Jews could be inflamed by firework displays of supernatural power. Though their cultural appetites were different, the two communities felt the same underlying cravings for influence, excitement and power.

All this is folly, according to Paul and his gospel. The great paradox of the cross is to contradict all human pretensions of wisdom and strength, revealing the grace of God in the shocking humility of Christ crucified.

Human beings have always gathered around leaders who promise easy assurances to heart and mind. In our own generation, whole nations have been seduced by the clever manipulation of popular agendas or the showy rhetoric of loud-mouthed leaders, some of them self-proclaimed Christians, whose boastfulness is profoundly and seriously at odds with the gospel of Christ. Then, as now, the message of the cross invites a far deeper conversion of life.

Heavenly Father,
at the Jordan you revealed Jesus as your Son:
may we recognize him as our Lord
and know ourselves to be your beloved children;
through Jesus Christ our Saviour.

COLLECT

Reflection by **Margaret Whipp** | 47

Wednesday 16 January

Psalms 19, **20** *or* 119.105-128
Amos 3
1 Corinthians 2

1 Corinthians 2

'... not with plausible words of wisdom' (v.4)

It seems that the Corinthians could be easily impressed. A little fancy oratory, or a few verbal flourishes, were enough to bend their ears away from the stark simplicity of the Christian message. The apostle eschews the shallowness and spin of mere 'lofty words', determined that his medium should match the message of a crucified Christ, whose obedience subverts every form of worldly cleverness or self-seeking pretension.

The abuse of language is one of the pervasive temptations of a media age, where plausible words and catchy straplines easily capture the attention of gullible mass audiences. In contrast, the poet T. S. Eliot wrote of his longing to 'purify the dialect of the tribe' (*Little Gidding*), harnessing human speech and language to holier purposes of goodness, beauty and truth.

Paul himself knew the temptations of a keen mind and forceful personality. Even in translation, we sense in his strongly worded letters the persuasive power of a formidable rhetorical training. But the true force of his gospel was something far more challenging – the uncompromising message of 'Jesus Christ, and him crucified'.

In another letter, Paul wrote that Christian language and everyday conversation should be something pungent and purposeful. 'Let your speech always be gracious, seasoned with salt' (Colossians 4.6). What might be our own contribution to 'purifying the dialect' of our communities?

COLLECT

Eternal Father,
who at the baptism of Jesus
revealed him to be your Son,
anointing him with the Holy Spirit:
grant to us, who are born again by water and the Spirit,
that we may be faithful to our calling as your adopted children;
through Jesus Christ your Son our Lord,
who is alive and reigns with you,
in the unity of the Holy Spirit,
one God, now and for ever.

| *Reflection by* **Margaret Whipp**

Psalms **21**, 24 *or* 90, **92**   **Thursday 17 January**
Amos 4
1 Corinthians 3

1 Corinthians 3

'... you are God's field, God's building' (v.9)

Paul holds a strong affection for the young Christian community in Corinth. He could be forgiven for indulging in possessiveness or pride towards this vibrant church that he had founded. But in the face of their damaging factionalism, he chooses to take a step back, to remind them that their primary relationship is with God.

Here is a good model for anyone facing conflict or division. It is foolish to put human leaders on a pedestal, or to squabble and compete, pitting one against the other. After all, what is Apollos? Or what is Paul? It is absurd to undermine the fellowship of God's people on the basis of merely human allegiances.

Instead, Paul offers a larger view, painting a vivid picture of the Church as God's own active enterprise. Human labourers will come and go, like so many contractors on a farm or a building site. But the work of God presses forward, according to his great plan and purpose of redemption. No individual worker, however gifted or influential, may steal the glory that belongs to God alone.

I find this a deeply encouraging perspective when struggling with the perennial problems of immaturity and strife within the family of God. All of us, leaders and led, are part of God's work in progress; and it is God alone who is the source of our life in Christ Jesus (1 Corinthians 1.30).

> Heavenly Father,
> at the Jordan you revealed Jesus as your Son:
> may we recognize him as our Lord
> and know ourselves to be your beloved children;
> through Jesus Christ our Saviour.

COLLECT

Friday 18 January

Psalms **67**, 72 *or* **88** (95)
Amos 5.1-17
1 Corinthians 4

1 Corinthians 4

'... why do you boast?' (v.7)

The theme of boasting is very prominent in Paul's letters. Perhaps it reflects something in his own psychological make-up, and the intense struggles through which he came to embrace the gospel of Christ crucified.

Honour and shame were potent dynamics in Greco-Roman society, and in Paul's passionate encounters with the Corinthian church we glimpse how the importance of social esteem sometimes ran counter to essential gospel values. The Corinthians became 'puffed up' with inflated self-importance, congratulating themselves on their spiritual sophistication, as they bragged about one teacher while disparaging another. No wonder Paul was indignant!

His reaction to these invidious comparisons is more than a matter of personal pique, however. Underneath their boastfulness and infighting lay a deeper problem of misplaced pride. Paul puts his finger on this arrogance and entitlement. What's so special about you? What do you have that you did not receive as a pure gift? What is at stake here is the entire gospel of grace.

Self-congratulation takes many forms in different cultures and societies, churches and individuals. Whenever we pride ourselves that we are a cut above the rest, then we forget the ultimate source of all our blessings. 'Let the one who boasts, boast in the Lord' (1 Corinthians 1.31).

COLLECT

Eternal Father,
who at the baptism of Jesus
revealed him to be your Son,
anointing him with the Holy Spirit:
grant to us, who are born again by water and the Spirit,
that we may be faithful to our calling as your adopted children;
through Jesus Christ your Son our Lord,
who is alive and reigns with you,
in the unity of the Holy Spirit,
one God, now and for ever.

| *Reflection by* **Margaret Whipp**

Saturday 19 January

1 Corinthians 5

'Clean out the old yeast' (v.7)

Paul's anxious indignation reaches a new peak in today's chapter, where he confronts the challenge of blatant sexual immorality in a prominent member of the Corinthian church.

What was the problem? We know that the moral boundaries of sexual behaviour can be 'hot-button' issues in any generation, even if the norms of what is deemed acceptable may vary according to current social and scientific perspectives. But it seems that there is more to Paul's outrage than a particular horror of incest.

Cosy collusion with bad behaviour was having a corrupting influence, like stale yeast, on the whole community. Jesus often drew on the imagery of yeast to remind his disciples of the pervasive effect – for good or ill – of our moral and spiritual attitudes (cf. Mark 8.15). Here Paul extends the metaphor to evoke the Passover custom of cleaning out every trace of old leavened dough from the household in preparation for a new year of redemption (Exodus 12.15).

The real target here is complacency. There is nothing pretty about the arrogance of this socially comfortable, but morally compromised, Corinthian church. They have scarcely begun to recognize the utter newness and radical challenge of Christ's sacrificial life and death.

In questions of moral behaviour, there is always a fine line to be drawn between judgementalism and collusion. Where do you think our churches are at risk of complacency today?

Heavenly Father,
at the Jordan you revealed Jesus as your Son:
may we recognize him as our Lord
and know ourselves to be your beloved children;
through Jesus Christ our Saviour.

COLLECT

Reflection by **Margaret Whipp** | 51

Monday 21 January

Psalms 145, **146** *or* **98**, 99, 101
Amos 6
1 Corinthians 6.1-11

1 Corinthians 6.1-11

'When any of you has a grievance ...' (v.1)

Wouldn't it be nice if Christians always got along with each other? But, like the Corinthians of Paul's day, we know what it is to encounter conflict and hurt, even within the fellowship of the Church.

We cannot know the precise issue that was serious enough for Christians to be going to court against one another. Most likely, they were falling out over the usual problem areas of money, sex and power. Feelings were running high, and Paul writes to offer guidance and perspective at several levels.

Between Christian brothers and sisters, litigious behaviour is grossly unedifying. Like many well-educated Greek citizens, the Corinthians may have enjoyed nothing better than a good argument, but Paul begs them not to air their grievances in public. Surely, they have enough good sense to sort things out among themselves without taking their squabbles to a court of scoffing unbelievers.

At a deeper level, we must ask what drives Christians to argue with each another. Where is the gentle and eirenic spirit of Jesus' teaching (cf. Matthew 5.21-26)? When we feel aggrieved, for whatever reason, we must search our own hearts for a less vexatious attitude. Perhaps we feel that we always have to be right?

Fundamentally, Paul urges Christians to be true to their baptism. Faithfulness is not about winning or losing, being right or wrong, but seeking a common spirit in the Lord Jesus Christ.

COLLECT

Almighty God,
whose Son revealed in signs and miracles
the wonder of your saving presence:
renew your people with your heavenly grace,
and in all our weakness
sustain us by your mighty power;
through Jesus Christ your Son our Lord,
who is alive and reigns with you,
in the unity of the Holy Spirit,
one God, now and for ever.

| *Reflection by* **Margaret Whipp**

Psalms **132**, 147.1-12 *or* **106*** (*or* 103)   **Tuesday 22 January**
Amos 7
1 Corinthians 6.12-end

1 Corinthians 6.12-end

'... glorify God in your body' (v.20)

The perennial genius of Paul, amid searing conflict and moral outrage, is to hold firmly to the deeper spiritual and theological issues for his fellow-believers. We can sense, in this chapter, the enormity of his indignation, as he confronts flagrant immorality with a determination to expose the underlying challenge to the good news of Christ.

'Shun fornication!' The idea that Christian people could demean their own bodies through sexual immorality was appalling to the apostle. Is nothing sacred? So licentious was the prevailing culture in Corinth that the human body had become cheapened and disrespected, as something of little or no worth.

Paul does not meet this permissiveness with mere prudery. Instead, he elevates his argument against sexual immorality with a plea for proper Christian reverence for the human body. Just as he has earlier argued for the integrity of the Church as the Body of Christ and the temple of God (1 Corinthians 3.16), he now urges respect for the individual body as a temple of the Holy Spirit to be honoured for the glory of God.

Our own culture is awash with incitements to abuse and dishonour the body, often masquerading as voices of liberation. Seeing the true worth of our body as the gift of God, gloriously redeemed by Christ, and indwelt by his Spirit, lifts our eyes to a far greater beauty and authentic freedom.

God of all mercy,
your Son proclaimed good news to the poor,
release to the captives,
and freedom to the oppressed:
anoint us with your Holy Spirit
and set all your people free
to praise you in Christ our Lord.

COLLECT

Wednesday 23 January

Psalms **81**, 147.13-end
or 110, **111**, 112
Amos 8
1 Corinthians 7.1-24

1 Corinthians 7.1-24

'... each has a particular gift from God' (v.7)

Further tricky moral questions now unfold, as the apostle ventures into the tangled web of marital ethics. Anyone who has had to deal with awkward questions or angry emails will sympathize with Paul, turning his pastoral attention toward 'the matters about which you wrote'. There is some comfort in the recognition that Christians have always had to reckon with controversy and changing social expectations.

Paul's answers and arguments may differ from our own, in some respects, but it is hard not to admire the care and honesty with which he engages the burning issues of real people in real relationships. There is an engaging humility in the way he offers his own example, as well as his theological and pastoral wisdom, without trying to over-assert his personal authority.

At the heart of tendentious ethical debate, it is important to maintain a gracious respect for real people – including ourselves. Paul clearly values the social status and story of the individual Corinthians under question, each one of whom 'has a particular gift from God'. This is a very different mindset from the dismissive and objectifying way in which Christians sometimes portray others as problems to be resolved, rather than sisters and brothers to be embraced.

Within the complex story of your own life and relationships, could there be 'a particular gift from God' that surprises you?

COLLECT

Almighty God,
whose Son revealed in signs and miracles
the wonder of your saving presence:
renew your people with your heavenly grace,
and in all our weakness
sustain us by your mighty power;
through Jesus Christ your Son our Lord,
who is alive and reigns with you,
in the unity of the Holy Spirit,
one God, now and for ever.

| *Reflection by* **Margaret Whipp**

Thursday 24 January

1 Corinthians 7.25-end

'... to promote good order and unhindered devotion to the Lord' (v.35)

There is great pastoral warmth in Paul's advice relating to virgins. He is writing, of course, for Christians in a very different social context from our own, where girls and women would be given in marriage by their male guardians as part of a costly contractual arrangement between families.

The religious context, also, is strikingly different, as the apostle contemplates the imminent return of Christ (cf. 1 Corinthians 1.8), which, to his mind, renders all long-term social institutions finally irrelevant (v.31).

For all that we must weigh his words, there is nonetheless a wealth of pastoral wisdom underlying Paul's carefully balanced advice. Far from a simplistic rejection of marriage, we find a nuanced pragmatism and humanity that aims at liberty, for the sake of untrammelled devotion to the Lord.

It is remarkable how often religious groups distort their moral and spiritual priorities when it comes to questions of marriage, as if these transitory social arrangements were of supreme and ultimate importance. When Jesus argued with the Sadducees, he brought a similarly radical and heavenly corrective to their narrow-minded idealization of the earthly institutions of marriage (Mark 12.25).

In a more individualistic age, Christians grapple with a bewildering diversity of moral and social alternatives, with all the attendant anxieties for their own commitments and the witness of the church. How might we, in our context, best pursue 'good order and unhindered devotion to the Lord'?

God of all mercy,
your Son proclaimed good news to the poor,
release to the captives,
and freedom to the oppressed:
anoint us with your Holy Spirit
and set all your people free
to praise you in Christ our Lord.

COLLECT

Reflection by **Margaret Whipp** | 55

Friday 25 January
Conversion of Paul

Psalms 66, 147.13-end
Ezekiel 3.22-end
Philippians 3.1-14

Philippians 3.1-14
'... straining forward to what lies ahead' (v.13)

The *chiaroscuro* technique of Renaissance artists portrays deep contrasts between darkness and light with subtlety and force. Something of similar intensity comes across in the repeated New Testament accounts of Saul's encounter with the risen Christ.

Caravaggio captures the drama of the Damascus Road experience in a famous painting in Santa Maria del Popolo in Rome. Such is the force of blinding light that we see Saul flung from his horse onto the ground, overwhelmed by the epiphany that called him from the shadows of false confidence into the luminous experience of faith in the risen Lord.

One moment of conversion can take a lifetime to fully embrace. Paul, as he now became, had to abandon the tunnel vision of his religious exclusivity to learn and practise the transformational gospel of Christ's death and resurrection.

We see some of the implications worked out in his message to the Philippians. Knocked off his Pharisaic high-horse, he had to relinquish all ideas of religious superiority and narrow-mindedness. The kind of piety he had once prized had to be overturned and radically challenged by this devastating encounter with grace. Never again could Paul feel smug in his own credentials. From now on, he would be straining forward in the faith of Christ alone.

What does ongoing conversion mean for you?

COLLECT

Almighty God,
who caused the light of the gospel
to shine throughout the world
through the preaching of your servant Saint Paul:
grant that we who celebrate his wonderful conversion
may follow him in bearing witness to your truth;
through Jesus Christ your Son our Lord,
who is alive and reigns with you,
in the unity of the Holy Spirit,
one God, now and for ever.

| *Reflection by* **Margaret Whipp**

Saturday 26 January

1 Corinthians 9.1-14

'Are you not my work in the Lord?' (v.1)

The epistle takes a fresh turn in chapter 9, as Paul passionately debates the glorious liberties of the Christian life (cf. Romans 8.21). In the previous chapter he had tackled the scandalous arguments arising from different opinions about food sacrificed to idols. Should believers flaunt their new-found freedom in Christ, by sitting loose to age-old questions of purity and contamination? Or is it more important, for the sake of unity, to have regard to the tender conscience of those for whom these may be deeply divisive issues? We may recognize similar dynamics in some of the unresolved issues over which contemporary Christians agonize.

The apostle cuts through this debate by courageously offering his own example. Rightly or wrongly, Paul had decided to show restraint in the very personal area of his own lifestyle. He could have flaunted his apostolic right to insist on financial remuneration for his gospel ministry and also, interestingly, for the upkeep of a wife. Instead, he chose the controversial path of self-supporting ministry, which would commend the gospel through relationships unburdened by expectation of economic reward.

For Christians, there are some questions that can only be settled in the context of open, loving and generous relationships. Perhaps this is what Paul felt so keenly, as he insisted that *you* are my work in the Lord.

Almighty God,
whose Son revealed in signs and miracles
the wonder of your saving presence:
renew your people with your heavenly grace,
and in all our weakness
sustain us by your mighty power;
through Jesus Christ your Son our Lord,
who is alive and reigns with you,
in the unity of the Holy Spirit,
one God, now and for ever.

COLLECT

Reflection by **Margaret Whipp** | 57

Monday 28 January

Psalms 40, **108** *or* 123, 124, 125, **126**
Hosea 2.18 – end of 3
1 Corinthians 9.15-end

1 Corinthians 9.15-end

'I do it all for the sake of the gospel ...' (v.23)

As Paul writes to the Church in Corinth, offering them advice, encouragement and direction in light of the problems they face, we can perhaps imagine the complaint some of those members may have had. Maybe Paul himself imagined the same complaint as he wrote his letter; did he imagine them asking him, 'Who put you in charge? What authority do you have?'

Paul informs the Church that he isn't a paid professional (although he points out he could have been), nor has he made use of any of the entitlements he earned as an apostle. Had he done, he might have appeared like the sophists – paid teachers and philosophers who often plied their trade in Corinth. Paul is not like them: he shares the gospel, not for money or reward, but because it is the light of Christ for a world in darkness. The gospel is its own reward.

Paul is willing to give up entitlements and to become weak (the very thing his opponents accused him of) in order to share the good news; he is willing to change and make sacrifices. He is able to do this because his status and sense of worth are not based on human standards, but on God's call on his life. Paul is a child of God, and so are you. Paul is a minister of the gospel, and you can be too.

COLLECT

God our creator,
who in the beginning
commanded the light to shine out of darkness:
we pray that the light of the glorious gospel of Christ
may dispel the darkness of ignorance and unbelief,
shine into the hearts of all your people,
and reveal the knowledge of your glory
in the face of Jesus Christ your Son our Lord,
who is alive and reigns with you,
in the unity of the Holy Spirit,
one God, now and for ever.

Reflection by **Harry Steele**

Psalms 34, **36** *or* **132**, 133
Hosea 4.1-16
1 Corinthians 10.1-13

Tuesday 29 January

1 Corinthians 10.1-13

'Now these things occurred as examples for us ...' (v.6)

A long time before the philosopher George Santayana wrote, 'Those who cannot remember the past are destined to repeat it', Paul sought to convince the Corinthians to learn from the past mistakes of the Israelites and do all they could to avoid idolatry.

The issue was one that may not become a key question for us: is it permissible for the Corinthians to eat meat purchased from the public market in Corinth, even if it may have come from an animal that had been sacrificed to an idol (1 Corinthians 8)? Evidently, some of the Corinthians were confident in the knowledge and freedom they had. They had been baptized; they had met with Christ through gathering around the table of the Lord, so they were sure there was no spiritual danger in eating this meat.

The ancient Israelites also had reasons to feel confident. They had been led out of Egypt; 'baptized' as they crossed the Red Sea; and God had been ever-present as the Rock in their wilderness journey, but they weren't immune to idolatry.

Epiphany can be a time to recall and be thankful for key spiritual moments in our own lives. As we recall times we felt close to Christ, listen to Paul's concern not to let anything become more important to us than Jesus. For the Corinthians, this was both the things they had learnt, and their sense of entitlement to do as they wished – perhaps showing us that we can make idols out of things that are not inherently bad.

God of heaven,
you send the gospel to the ends of the earth
and your messengers to every nation:
send your Holy Spirit to transform us
by the good news of everlasting life
in Jesus Christ our Lord.

COLLECT

Wednesday 30 January

1 Corinthians 10.14 – 11.1

'Be imitators of me, as I am of Christ' (11.1)

Paul is concluding his argument with the Corinthians about food. The Corinthian Christians lived in a society where there would be frequent invitations to eat meals at pagan temples. To us that may sound like something a Christian ought not do, but in that society they were the restaurants of the day. There were also questions around food that was purchased in the market. It was not clear if this meat had been used as a pagan sacrifice, and if it had, would it be okay for a Christian to eat it?

The heart of the argument is that of freedom for a Christian. Some behaviour is always wrong for someone who professes to be a follower of Jesus, and some things don't really matter (but one still might avoid them, just so as to help fellow believers, or even non-believers, in their understanding of faith). The problem is where to draw that line: what is clearly wrong, and what is inconsequential? It is a question the Church is still asking, and there are nearly as many different answers as there are people asking the question.

Whereas the Corinthian's argument is based on knowledge and wisdom, Paul's argument implores them to imitate him imitating Christ. 'What would Jesus do?' is a question that is notoriously difficult to answer, and some think it oversimplifies the challenge of how to respond in different circumstances, but it is a good place to start.

COLLECT

God our creator,
who in the beginning
commanded the light to shine out of darkness:
we pray that the light of the glorious gospel of Christ
may dispel the darkness of ignorance and unbelief,
shine into the hearts of all your people,
and reveal the knowledge of your glory
 in the face of Jesus Christ your Son our Lord,
who is alive and reigns with you,
in the unity of the Holy Spirit,
one God, now and for ever.

| *Reflection by* **Harry Steele**

Psalms **47**, 48 *or* **143**, 146
Hosea 5.8 – 6.6
1 Corinthians 11.2-16

Thursday 31 January

1 Corinthians 11.2-16

'… any woman who prays or prophesies' (v.5)

In these verses it is notoriously difficult to grasp exactly what practices were going on in Corinth and what Paul is advising. It seems one of the mistakes that the Church in Corinth made is the blurring of differences between genders; thinking that doing so makes them less 'physical' and more holy.

In the midst of many questions raised, verse 3 is one that can't be ignored, as it has been used to discuss differences between male and female and define roles in the Church. Does the word 'head' to explore the relationship between man/Christ, woman/man, and Christ/God imply 'authority', or does Paul mean 'source'? Does Christ have authority over man, man authority over woman, and God authority over Christ? Or does the passage mean that Christ is the source and creator of man, that woman was made out of man in the creation accounts, and that God is the source of Christ incarnate? (I believe vv.11-12 suggest the latter understanding.)

In the midst of this, and other difficult questions, one thing we can know is that in verse 4 men are expected to pray and prophesy, and in verse 5 women are expected to do the same. The passage is not speaking here of professional clergy, but Paul's expectation that both men and women play an active role in worship. So a good question to ask is: how does Paul's expectation that *all* pray and prophesy challenge our current practices in our worshipping communities?

God of heaven,
you send the gospel to the ends of the earth
and your messengers to every nation:
send your Holy Spirit to transform us
by the good news of everlasting life
in Jesus Christ our Lord.

COLLECT

Reflection by **Harry Steele** | 61

Friday 1 February
Psalms 61, **65** or 142, **144**
Hosea 6.7 – 7.2
1 Corinthians 11.17-end

1 Corinthians 11.17-end

'This is my body that is for you. Do this in remembrance of me'
(v.24)

Paul is remembering and recounting the words that Jesus used when he shared a last supper – the Last Supper – with his friends. Even though that meal happened not many years before Paul wrote his letter to the Church in the city of Corinth, the times were very different.

The Church Paul writes to is divided. The tradition at the time was to celebrate the Lord's Supper in the context of a meal, but, whereas nowadays we observe the sacrament and forget the meal, it seems that members of that early Christian community were enjoying the meal and forgetting the sacrament. The meal would have taken place in someone's home. We know, through archaeological studies, that homes then didn't have a dining room large enough for much more than ten, so if there were more people, they would have to eat in the atrium – a kind of large hallway with space, in large houses, for perhaps 50 people. It seems members of the Church were offering the use of their home, but trying to make sure their friends were in the 'dining room', whilst everyone else slummed it in the atrium. The church was divided at the very place it ought to be expressing unity.

On Maundy Thursday, and every resurrection day, we remember that in the broken bread we encounter Jesus' body. As we, the Church, share that, we also become the body of Christ. So the Church can be broken, but it ought never be divided.

COLLECT

God our creator,
who in the beginning
commanded the light to shine out of darkness:
we pray that the light of the glorious gospel of Christ
may dispel the darkness of ignorance and unbelief,
shine into the hearts of all your people,
and reveal the knowledge of your glory
    in the face of Jesus Christ your Son our Lord,
who is alive and reigns with you,
in the unity of the Holy Spirit,
one God, now and for ever.

Reflection by **Harry Steele**

Psalms **48**, 146
Exodus 13.1-16
Romans 12.1-5

Saturday 2 February
Presentation of Christ
in the Temple

Romans 12.1-5

'... present your bodies as a living sacrifice' (v.1)

Forty days after his birth, Jesus was taken to the temple in Jerusalem and presented to God in fulfilment of Jewish Law. After giving birth the mother was to make herself ritually clean by sacrificing a lamb and a pigeon (Leviticus 12.1-8). At the same time, Jesus, as the firstborn male, was presented to God as described in Exodus 13.2 and 12-16. This is what Mary did. It gave her the opportunity to thank God for the safe birth of her child and to offer Jesus in service to God. She let go of the gift that had just been given.

Just after Christmas, especially among those school-aged, there is a question often asked: 'What did you get for Christmas?' The presentation of Christ in the temple prompts a very different question: not 'What did you get?' but 'What did you give?'

For Mary there was no going back, but if there had been, it might have been tempting, as she is told Jesus will cause the rise and the fall of many in Israel, and that a sword will pierce Mary's own soul too (Luke 2.35).

According to Paul, there ought to be no going back either for the believers who are willing, as a response to all God has done, to offer their lives to God. As has been noted before, sacrifices that have been offered aren't in a position to change their mind and un-offer themselves. May your sacrifice this day be wholehearted.

Almighty and ever-living God,
clothed in majesty,
whose beloved Son was this day presented in the Temple,
in substance of our flesh:
grant that we may be presented to you
with pure and clean hearts,
by your Son Jesus Christ our Lord,
who is alive and reigns with you,
in the unity of the Holy Spirit,
one God, now and for ever.

COLLECT

Reflection by **Harry Steele** | 63

Monday 4 February

Psalms 1, 2, 3
1 Chronicles 10.1 – 11.9
John 13.1-11

John 13.1-11

*'... he poured water into a basin and began to wash
the disciples' feet' (v.5)*

Jesus knows he will soon die, so gathers with those he loves for a final meal. In John's Gospel, instead of rituals we perform at parties – cutting a cake, giving gifts, or perhaps making a speech – Jesus performs a different ritual, so unusual that the other Gospel writers decide not to use it in their accounts of the life of Jesus.

Jesus, to show his love for his friends and to mark this poignant moment, elects to play the role of a servant, and wash the dust of the road off the feet of his disciples. Jesus kneels on the floor in front of each disciple, one after another. No one is left out: all are washed, all are loved.

Did this act of Jesus washing Judas' feet make Judas' plan to betray Jesus easier – would he have been angry that Jesus would humble himself with this menial task? Or did it make it harder – did Jesus' action cause him to pause and be moved by the love that Jesus showed him?

In this reading, Jesus shows his love to his disciples in a new way, at the heart of which is humility and service. May you experience the love of Jesus in new ways today; then show it to others, being sure no one misses out.

COLLECT
Almighty God,
by whose grace alone we are accepted and called to your service:
strengthen us by your Holy Spirit
and make us worthy of our calling;
through Jesus Christ your Son our Lord,
who is alive and reigns with you,
in the unity of the Holy Spirit,
one God, now and for ever.

| *Reflection by* **Harry Steele**

Psalms **5**, 6 (8)
1 Chronicles 13
John 13.12-20

Tuesday 5 February

John 13.12-20
'Do you know what I have done to you?' (v.12)

The disciples were probably still perplexed. It was the role of a servant to wash the feet of travellers – in fact it was a role for the lowliest servant in the household. What Jesus had just done was a powerful and provocative example of willed powerlessness. I wonder if it helped them understand the cross and Jesus' imminent death?

At times we make excuses for why we are not doing the humbling and difficult jobs. The Church in general has always struggled with getting a correct balance between doing a good thing and doing the right thing. Some of these same disciples, in Acts 6, would explain that they were too busy with important ministry to serve sandwiches to the poor widows (Acts 6.2). I can't help but wonder about how valid their excuses were. Jesus reminds his disciples, and us, that none of them are greater than he; no one is above assuming the role of a servant.

Reflect on that question of Jesus: do you know what I have done for you? While you are considering it, think about your own attitudes and actions: how can you love the world? How can you serve the world?

God of our salvation,
help us to turn away from those habits which harm our bodies
and poison our minds
and to choose again your gift of life,
revealed to us in Jesus Christ our Lord.

COLLECT

Wednesday 6 February

John 13.21-30

'Jesus was troubled in spirit ...' (v.21)

This part of the passion story is full of human emotion. Jesus Christ, the divine *Logos*, is troubled. If we pause to reflect, we might wonder whether, at this moment, it is the forthcoming outcome of the action or the act of betrayal itself that troubles Jesus.

The beloved disciple is close to Jesus, close enough to ask the painful question of who the betrayer is. And yet, when he finds out that it is Judas Iscariot, what good does this information do him, Simon Peter, or any of the disciples? No one present understands Jesus' command to Judas to do what he will do quickly. None can stop the betrayal.

Judas is frustrated and disappointed, failing to know Jesus. He exercises the free will available to all, but is a pawn of Satan, and even in the act of betrayal is fulfilling God's plan of salvation.

In all these emotions – which we may be able to relate to: feeling troubled; feeling loved yet afraid to act; betraying a close friend or being betrayed; struggling to know Jesus – it is easy to lose sight of the cosmic scope of these events. Satan casts a net of darkness to bring fear, failure, death and defeat. But God wills and acts: to save and redeem, to bring light and life.

COLLECT

Almighty God,
by whose grace alone we are accepted and called to your service:
strengthen us by your Holy Spirit
and make us worthy of our calling;
through Jesus Christ your Son our Lord,
who is alive and reigns with you,
in the unity of the Holy Spirit,
one God, now and for ever.

Reflection by **Harry Steele**

Thursday 7 February

John 13.31-end

'Lord, where are you going?' (v.36)

Judas has stepped into the night: the act of betrayal has begun. The remaining disciples are faithful, but are perhaps unsettled by Jesus' recent washing of their feet, his prediction of betrayal and Judas' rushing off for reasons they can't fathom.

Peter is certainly unsettled. The author of John's Gospel uses his full name in verse 36, and so sounds a little like a frustrated parent calling for scattered children. Jesus has just given a 'new commandment' to the disciples: that they should love one another just as Jesus has loved them. Simon Peter, in the confusion misses the significance of the newness of this command, and how the love that is commanded is linked to the humble act of foot washing. Instead of dwelling on the command to love, Peter asks Jesus where he is going.

Ultimately, Peter wants to lay down his life for Jesus, without understanding it is Jesus who must die for him (and you and me). Peter is not aware of his own shortcomings: he is not ready to stand for Jesus when all else is crumbling.

We often think of, and pray about, the things we want to do for Jesus. Less frequently do we take time, real time, to meditate on what Jesus has done for us. There is no better day than today to meditate on the sacrificial and humble love that Jesus has for you.

God of our salvation,
help us to turn away from those habits which harm our bodies
and poison our minds
and to choose again your gift of life,
revealed to us in Jesus Christ our Lord.

COLLECT

Friday 8 February

Psalms 17, **19**
I Chronicles 21.1 – 22.1
John 14.1-14

John 14.1-14

'Do not let your hearts be troubled' (v.1)

The disciples have clean feet *and* have learned a lesson about the extent to which Jesus will humble himself in order to serve those he loves (John 13.5), but they have heavy hearts. The reason for this is that Jesus has just told them that he is leaving them, and the place he is going to is somewhere they can't yet follow. So the disciples will soon be in the position we find ourselves in today: we can't see Jesus, or reach out and touch him – not physically. In light of this, the instruction 'Do not let your hearts be troubled' is simple enough, but when times are tough, it is seemingly impossible to do.

When we are in situations that trouble us, the answer is to have a trust-relationship with Jesus – or to put it another way, to have faith. When we have a relationship with Jesus, we know the one who died to defeat death and rose again to give us life eternal. However, we are – each one of us – at one time or another just like Thomas: 'We don't know the way', we cry. The very fact that we share how we feel with Jesus means we do know the way: Jesus is the way.

In the near future, the disciples will find it hard to not be troubled, but in the midst of those troubles, they know Jesus. Followers of Christ have light, even in the dark valleys.

COLLECT

Almighty God,
by whose grace alone we are accepted and called to your service:
strengthen us by your Holy Spirit
and make us worthy of our calling;
through Jesus Christ your Son our Lord,
who is alive and reigns with you,
in the unity of the Holy Spirit,
one God, now and for ever.

Reflection by **Harry Steele**

Psalms 20, 21, **23**
1 Chronicles 22.2-end
John 14.15-end

Saturday 9 February

John 14.15-end

'... those who love me will be loved by my Father' (v.21)

Towards the end of the time of his final meal with his disciples, Jesus tells them again that he will leave them soon, but they ought not worry, as they will soon experience Jesus in a new way. In response, Judas (not that one) asks a question that most of us will have wondered about: why doesn't Jesus just reveal himself to all the world?

Today's reading emphasizes love, and in that is the answer. John is clear that Jesus loves all the world (John 3.16), but love cannot be revealed in power. Throughout this Gospel, the miracles of Jesus are described as signs: they point those who pay attention to the true nature of Jesus, but they don't force anyone to have faith in Jesus, nor even create a situation where faith is an inevitable response.

Jesus will not make himself plain to the whole world, only to those who have, in love, turned to Jesus because of his loving actions. When we discover Jesus, we can't help but love, and when we love, we obey; those who love and obey are loved in a special way by the Father. It is special because God dwells in them.

This is the essence of faith – a loving response to God who loved us first. The Holy Spirit is key to this. That is not surprising given that the Holy Spirit continues the work of Jesus who loves us first.

God of our salvation,
help us to turn away from those habits which harm our bodies
and poison our minds
and to choose again your gift of life,
revealed to us in Jesus Christ our Lord.

COLLECT

Monday 11 February

Psalms 27, **30**
I Chronicles 28.1-10
John 15.1-11

John 15.1-11

'I am the true vine, and my Father is the vine-grower' (v.1)

From the promise of the Holy Spirit, the 'Advocate' who 'will teach you everything' (John 14.25), Jesus introduces the idea of the vine. This picture of connectedness and growth provides the foundation for the gift of the Holy Spirit. The Holy Spirit is the comforter who will be sent by the Father to continue the ministry of Jesus to and through the disciples, even in the physical absence of Jesus. The disciples themselves are the branches, all connected, all imbued with the life and love of God and tasked with bearing fruit: the works of God.

The disciples would have been very familiar with the picture of the vine for Israel in the Hebrew Bible: 'Israel is a luxuriant vine' (Hosea 10.1). It is tempting to make the mistake of thinking that Jesus is therefore *replacing* the Jews in God's purposes, especially as non-Jews responding to this text. Rather, Jesus is expanding the originating promise of God to the whole world and offering His living presence to all peoples. This is the presence that accompanied the Jewish people through their desert wanderings and was there in the temple. Amazingly, this glory of God is now promised to us.

For each of us who have been 'grafted in' and who are therefore indebted to Jewish roots, there is the wonder and humility that we can participate in the re-creative and loving energy of God even through the discipline of the vine-grower.

COLLECT

O God,
you know us to be set
in the midst of so many and great dangers,
that by reason of the frailty of our nature
we cannot always stand upright:
grant to us such strength and protection
as may support us in all dangers
and carry us through all temptations;
through Jesus Christ your Son our Lord,
who is alive and reigns with you,
in the unity of the Holy Spirit,
one God, now and for ever.

70 *Reflection by* **Richard Sudworth**

Psalms 32, **36**
1 Chronicles 28.11-end
John 15.12-17

Tuesday 12 February

John 15.12-17

*'This is my commandment, that you love one another
as I have loved you' (v.12)*

Dwelling in the life of the Father God, in Jesus, by the Holy Spirit will mean that we love the things of God: the teachings of Jesus (John 15.10). Not only that, but we will love all other disciples. There is no qualification here; no exemption. Just like in a family, we are bound to each other regardless of our likes and our choices. Today, that Christian family stretches across bounds of culture, race, language, class, sexuality and denomination. There is an exchange of love because ultimately we have first of all been loved by God in Christ.

Whilst we are bound to one another and to the works of God, in one sense to the 'family business', Jesus goes even further. We are not servants but friends of Jesus, and therefore by extension, friends of God. The thread running through John 14 to 17 is of intimacy: first, of Jesus' intimacy with God, and then, in turn, the intimacy of followers of Jesus with him, with God, and with each other.

Jesus is making an astonishing promise here. The Christian destiny is not simply to follow the example of Jesus as a role model; Jesus is more than just a good man, and the implications are therefore so much greater. We are called to be drawn up into the very life of God in Jesus. To quote St Athanasius, 'God became man, that man [and woman], might become God.'

Lord of the hosts of heaven,
our salvation and our strength,
without you we are lost:
guard us from all that harms or hurts
and raise us when we fall;
through Jesus Christ our Lord.

COLLECT

Reflection by **Richard Sudworth** | 71

Wednesday 13 February

Psalm **34**
I Chronicles 29.1-9
John 15.18-end

John 15.18-end

'If the world hates you, be aware that it hated me before it hated you' (v.18)

As Jesus addresses the disciples, it seems that it's good news/bad news time. The bad news is, he is going away; the good news, the Holy Spirit is being sent upon them. The good news is, the disciples are friends of God; the bad news, they will therefore get some of the same treatment that Jesus has had.

When Jesus talks of the 'world' as hating the things of God, it is helpful to understand the world as signalling a contrast to the reign of God. Being disciples of Jesus does not mean that the physical realities of daily living in the world are somehow sub-Christian. The teachings of Jesus are not about escaping the world for some super-spiritual heavenly realm. Rather, they are about living in the light of God's reign: making decisions that are shaped by the kind of relationships, work, politics, earth, that God intended for us.

It means that we should expect struggle and opposition, even persecution, because we live in a world that is too often shaped by different values: the worship of money, sex and power. In the midst of struggles, the Holy Spirit witnesses to the way of Christ and we too are called to witness to an alternative way of living. Looking at both the beauty and the fractures in our world, our hearts often ache with the pain and we would pray 'Your kingdom come ...'

COLLECT

O God,
you know us to be set
in the midst of so many and great dangers,
that by reason of the frailty of our nature
we cannot always stand upright:
grant to us such strength and protection
as may support us in all dangers
and carry us through all temptations;
through Jesus Christ your Son our Lord,
who is alive and reigns with you,
in the unity of the Holy Spirit,
one God, now and for ever.

| *Reflection by* **Richard Sudworth**

Psalm 37*
1 Chronicles 29.10-20
John 16.1-15

Thursday 14 February

John 16.1-15

*'When the Spirit of truth comes, he will guide you into all
the truth' (v.13)*

Throughout the Gospel of John, truth is linked inextricably to the person of Jesus. He is 'full of grace and truth' (1.14) and 'the way, and the truth, and the life' (14.6). The disciples are being warned about the trials that are to come, trials that will be faced without Jesus. How will they know what to do? Where will they find truth if so much around them will be opposed to the things of God? Once again, the promise of the Holy Spirit provides the comfort they need because the Advocate will point them towards Jesus and confirm to the disciples all that Jesus taught.

When John talks about truth, you get the sense of several layers of meaning. There is the simple meaning of truthfulness: what is right, correct, or in order. This is truth as objective fact. What Jesus says is true, in this sense, and can be relied upon as a better way even throughout opposition and struggle. There is the truthfulness of character: Jesus is truth*ful*. His words and actions command respect because of his integrity and they ultimately carry the authority of God. But the final sense of 'truth' is that Jesus himself *is* truth.

When we meet Jesus, we encounter humanity rightly ordered, as humans should be, bearing the divine life. The gift of the Holy Spirit brings us, mysteriously, into the presence of God in Christ.

> Lord of the hosts of heaven,
> our salvation and our strength,
> without you we are lost:
> guard us from all that harms or hurts
> and raise us when we fall;
> through Jesus Christ our Lord.

COLLECT

Reflection by **Richard Sudworth**   73

Friday 15 February

Psalm 31
1 Chronicles 29.21-end
John 16.16-22

John 16.16-22

'... you will have pain, but your pain will turn into joy' (v.20)

The US rock star Bruce Springsteen has identified his songs with the black Gospel-music tradition. He has said that in his songs, 'the verses are the blues, the chorus is the gospel'. Whether it is blues, gospel, rock, in folk or classical music traditions, humans seek to express the darkness of suffering, and the yearning of hope. In preparing the disciples for his death and absence, Jesus is giving space to the realities of grief and loss, of confusion and persecution that will be a part of their experience, as it is ours.

But that grief and loss does not have the last word. The blues that is the suffering of the human condition and of the struggle of building lives on the values of the kingdom of God will be followed by the chorus – the gospel – literally, the good news of redemption. As a mother waits patiently for the birth of her child, actively involved, seeing the visible signs of growth, she knows there is pain ahead that will be superseded by the joy of new life.

As men and women following Jesus now, we are in an in-between time frame of struggles and suffering intermingled with present joys and anticipations of the kingdom of God. Like that picture of the new creation in C. S. Lewis' *The Great Divorce*, the world of real permanence and substance is found whenever we encounter the truth, beauty and goodness of Jesus.

COLLECT

O God,
you know us to be set
in the midst of so many and great dangers,
that by reason of the frailty of our nature
we cannot always stand upright:
grant to us such strength and protection
as may support us in all dangers
and carry us through all temptations;
through Jesus Christ your Son our Lord,
who is alive and reigns with you,
in the unity of the Holy Spirit,
one God, now and for ever.

74 | *Reflection by* **Richard Sudworth**

Psalms 41, 42, 43
2 Chronicles 1.1-13
John 16.23-end

Saturday 16 February

John 16.23-end

'I have said this to you, so that in me you may have peace' (v.33)

This text completes John's account of Jesus' words of comfort prior to his crucifixion. A shadow looms over this final exchange as Jesus responds to the confusion of the disciples by promising that picture language will soon no longer be needed: things will become clear. The disciples jump ahead now believing that time has arrived, and they don't need to ask any more questions of Jesus. We know where the story leads, and Jesus tells them that the 'the hour is coming ... when you will be scattered'. The disciples think they understand, have grasped the totality of who Jesus is, but they have little idea that shortly they will be deserting Jesus in his hour of need.

It is easy to see the disciples as a hapless band forever misunderstanding Jesus and blundering about like cartoon characters. The Gospel accounts come alive to us when we see ourselves in their tentative explorations and very human confusions. There is a paradox at the heart of our understanding of God as present to us in Christ: God has come close to us in the life of Jesus, but that human life is at the same time strange and cannot be boxed in by our limited understanding.

The strangeness of Jesus is what the disciples are struggling with, and what we sometimes struggle with too. While we are encouraged to ask for *anything*, what we are promised are not 'things' but complete joy.

COLLECT

Lord of the hosts of heaven,
our salvation and our strength,
without you we are lost:
guard us from all that harms or hurts
and raise us when we fall;
through Jesus Christ our Lord.

Monday 18 February

John 17.1-5

'... glorify your Son' (v.1)

Before we enter into the painful drama of the Passion narrative, Jesus shifts from preparing his disciples to praying to his Father in heaven. We are privileged to listen in to this pivotal prayer, which must have been charged with the emotion of the loss that Jesus knew lay ahead.

Again, Jesus returns to the theme of glory, of the presence of God in and with him at this decisive hour, boldly looking up to heaven. There is a remarkable claim in verse 5, echoing the Prologue of John 1, where Jesus prays for 'the glory that I had in your presence before the world existed'. Somehow, in this carpenter's son, people will encounter the reality of the Eternal One of Israel.

What is even more startling is that, more specifically, the glory of YAHWEH could be made manifest in the horrific death that we know is looming. In John's Gospel, a shocking link is made between the lifting up of Jesus on the cross, and the glory of God. In so many ways, this does not make sense and is even contradictory: the power and presence of the one, creator God being realized in the shameful, public execution at the hands of the Roman Empire of this innocent man.

As we meditate on the Passion story, we begin to enter into the mystery of God's love taking on flesh, and dwelling among us.

COLLECT

Almighty God,
who alone can bring order
to the unruly wills and passions of sinful humanity:
give your people grace
so to love what you command
and to desire what you promise,
that, among the many changes of this world,
our hearts may surely there be fixed
where true joys are to be found;
through Jesus Christ your Son our Lord,
who is alive and reigns with you,
in the unity of the Holy Spirit,
one God, now and for ever.

Reflection by **Richard Sudworth**

Tuesday 19 February

John 17.6-19

'As you have sent me into the world, so I have sent them into the world' (v.18)

As Jesus prays for his disciples, he continues to identify his words and ministry with God's: 'everything you have given me is from you'. If Jesus was saying something scandalous in identifying his own coming trials with the glory of God then he goes further here by saying that the disciples, too, will embody God's glory.

Again, we know how the drama unfolds, how the disciples end up betraying, denying and fleeing from the pressure-cooker of Jesus' trial and crucifixion. And yet Jesus prays, 'All mine are yours, and yours are mine; and I have been glorified in them'. God's love and mercy cascade out in the life and death of Jesus and draw his friends and followers into a similar pattern of giving and blessing.

The celebrated missionary-scholar Lesslie Newbigin pointed out that Jesus never wrote a book for posterity; he didn't leave behind an ideal or a programme. Jesus left behind a community – the Church. This ramshackle community, full of weakness and flaws, is also mysteriously a place of encounter with the divine life: sent by God, made holy by God, guarded by God.

A constant challenge for the Church is how we are to be in the world but not of it. If we are sent by God after the pattern of Jesus, how might we seek to respond to suffering, struggles and rejection? And where might God be calling us to go?

COLLECT

Eternal God,
whose Son went among the crowds
and brought healing with his touch:
help us to show his love,
in your Church as we gather together,
and by our lives as they are transformed
into the image of Christ our Lord.

Reflection by **Richard Sudworth** | 77

Wednesday 20 February

John 17.20-end

'... so that they may be one' (v.22)

Wonderfully, Jesus prays for us: those that believe Jesus through the testimony of those disciples. Again, we too are included in this identification with Jesus and therefore God. We are called to be fruitful and to witness to this good news 'that the world may believe that you have sent me'.

There is a long Anglican tradition stretching back to the sixteenth-century theologian Richard Hooker of understanding the Church as a 'participation' in the godhead, which goes to the heart of this prayer. It is a way of thinking about the nature of the Church that has a twofold effect: it undermines the temptation to build hard and fast barriers to the work of God in the world, and it highlights the fact that our particular local church or even denomination is not the limit of God's community on earth.

When Jesus prays that God's glory, which has been given to him, is also given to us, it is both a reminder of the seriousness of our charge and our humbling dependence upon God. The mission of the Church is 'joining in with what God is doing in the world': no human concern should be closed off from the concerns of the Church. It is fitting, then, that Jesus completes his prayer as this section began back in Chapter 13.1 with a reaffirmation of God's love in him and us, making unity a vital part of our calling.

COLLECT

Almighty God,
who alone can bring order
to the unruly wills and passions of sinful humanity:
give your people grace
so to love what you command
and to desire what you promise,
that, among the many changes of this world,
our hearts may surely there be fixed
where true joys are to be found;
through Jesus Christ your Son our Lord,
who is alive and reigns with you,
in the unity of the Holy Spirit,
one God, now and for ever.

Reflection by **Richard Sudworth**

Psalms 56, **57** (63*)
2 Chronicles 6.1-21
John 18.1-11

Thursday 21 February

John 18.1-11

'For whom are you looking?' (v.4)

John's Passion narrative opens in a garden, just as the creation narrative began in Genesis 2.8 and how the gospel itself begins. A garden will be the place of Jesus' burial (19.41) and the scene of resurrection in the encounter with the 'gardener' of 20.15. All these resonances situate the story of Jesus in cosmic terms: the death and resurrection of Jesus are part and parcel of the big story of God's redemption of the world. It is a story that will culminate in a garden city in the vision of Revelation 21–22.

In the sordid betrayal of Jesus by Judas and his arrest by the soldiers, we glimpse the mismatched clash of earthly and heavenly powers. Jesus only has to identify himself speaking the simple words literally translated in the Greek, 'I am', for Judas and the soldiers all to fall to the ground. Peter's pitiful effort to rescue Jesus by cutting off the ear of the high priest's slave is comical in its uselessness.

The reality is that they are all in the presence of another type of power. Any control that the soldiers exert over Jesus is because it has been freely given over to them. One lens with which to view the whole passion narrative is as a clash of kingdoms, where the kingdom of Christ is ultimately victorious in the embrace of self-giving love. A question for us to ponder may well be 'For whom are you looking?'

Reflection by **Richard Sudworth** 79

Friday 22 February

Psalms **51**, 54
2 Chronicles 6.22-end
John 18.12-27

John 18.12-27

'Again Peter denied it, and at that moment the cock crowed' (v.27)

Peter's denial of Jesus is just one of the features of the Passion narrative that make such a compelling human drama. That Peter, the friend of Jesus who was so determined to stick by him through thick and thin, should falter at the last, echoes through the ages in our comparable failures. Even and most agonizingly, especially with those closest to us, we can cause the deepest pain. This is nothing if not a very human story shot through with divine mercy.

The shabby denials are given greater poignancy by the ordinariness of the people that Peter is talking to: the gatekeeper of the high priest's courtyard, and the slaves and the officers warming their hands by the fire. Peter is not on formal trial but tangled up in his own test and a drama off-stage from the heart of the story.

These denials by Peter frame the assured authority of Jesus under his interrogation by the high priest. The insecure questioning from the high priest and the random and petty violence of his officer are in stark contrast to the authority of Jesus. While the religious authorities may hold human power and force in this instance, we are left under no illusion that the real power rests in the bound figure before them. The concluding words following Peter's denials – 'at that moment the cock crowed' – are given to us without any comment. Nothing more need be said.

COLLECT

Almighty God,
who alone can bring order
to the unruly wills and passions of sinful humanity:
give your people grace
so to love what you command
and to desire what you promise,
that, among the many changes of this world,
our hearts may surely there be fixed
where true joys are to be found;
through Jesus Christ your Son our Lord,
who is alive and reigns with you,
in the unity of the Holy Spirit,
one God, now and for ever.

| *Reflection by* **Richard Sudworth**

Psalm **68**
2 Chronicles 7
John 18.28-end

Saturday 23 February

John 18.28-end

'For this I was born, and for this I came into the world, to testify to the truth' (v.37)

As we enter the climax to the trial of Jesus before Pilate, the clash of earthly and heavenly kingdoms becomes most apparent. It is worth noticing the repeated stage directions throughout this chapter. Jesus, Peter, and then Pilate are either 'entering' or 'outside' or 'going into' various settings. It is as if the story alternates between two stages: the 'inner' and the 'outer'. The outside is a world of mob rule, of noise and violence; the inside is the calm authority of Jesus.

Underpinning the scene of Jesus' trial is a question about who is king. Pilate refers to Jesus as 'King of the Jews' three times. Jesus speaks truthfully, is truthful and dependable, and embodies truth. The inner world of Jesus is formed by the clarity of his calling and identity in God. This is an identity that bumps up against the political jostlings and manoeuvrings of Pilate and Caiaphas. It is no less political, no less full of implication for public life. The kingship of Jesus is of a different order, though.

When Pilate says 'What is truth?', he is denying his responsibility and disqualifying his own authority. Only Jesus comes out of this exchange looking like he has any real authority. At the crucifixion, the sin of the world is brought to a head and shown for what it is. As God in Christ willingly suffers at the hands of humanity, so that sin can finally be forgiven.

COLLECT

Eternal God,
whose Son went among the crowds
and brought healing with his touch:
help us to show his love,
in your Church as we gather together,
and by our lives as they are transformed
into the image of Christ our Lord.

Reflection by **Richard Sudworth** | 81

Monday 25 February

Psalm **71**
2 Chronicles 9.1-12
John 19.1-16

John 19.1-16

'You would have no power over me unless it had been given you from above' (v.11)

Where does true power lie in this passage? With Pontius Pilate, official representative of the most powerful person on the earth at that time, Emperor Tiberius Caesar? Or with Jesus, dressed mockingly in a purple robe, a crown of cruel thorns pushed onto his head, seemingly completely powerless at the hands of Pilate, who boasts that he has power of life and death over him?

John clearly sees the meaning beneath the meaning. On the surface Pilate is obviously the powerful one. But ultimately Pilate's power is thwarted. He doesn't want to put Jesus to death. He is awkward in his presence, sensing that in this bedraggled so-called criminal who is so clearly hated by the crowds, there is more than meets the eye. But after claiming that he holds the power to put Jesus to death or let him live, in the end he is dictated to by the crowd. Ultimately, Pilate has no power at all.

And the 'king who is not a king', dressed up and mocked, is in the end the one who holds the power. Not the temporal power of an earthly kingdom but the eternal truth of an everlasting kingdom. Jesus refuses the title of king, but lives out what it means to live under God's reign. Real power in God's kingdom is found not in cruel bullying, nor in displays of aggressive strength, but in humility, truth and love.

COLLECT

Almighty God,
you have created the heavens and the earth
and made us in your own image:
teach us to discern your hand in all your works
and your likeness in all your children;
through Jesus Christ your Son our Lord,
who with you and the Holy Spirit reigns supreme over all things,
now and for ever.

| *Reflection by* **Jan McFarlane**

John 19.17-30

'What I have written I have written' (v.22)

In the light of yesterday's reflection, we can't help but be drawn to the sign Pilate has nailed above Jesus' head as he hangs on the cross. For citizens of an occupied country, the words 'King of the Jews' above the head of someone executed as a common criminal – and what's more, in three languages so that it can be read by everyone – is more than uncomfortable. Pilate is asked to change the wording, but this time he won't be pushed around by the crowd. He has written what he has written, and it will remain as it is, recorded for all time. Pilate at last understands where the true power and authority lie. The title that Jesus never claimed is now truly his, in the moment of his greatest vulnerability and weakness. No earthly kingdom this.

Jesus carries his cross by himself. There is no Simon of Cyrene to help him in John's account. He is surrounded by those who shout and jeer and want him dead. His disciples, whom he has called friends, have fled. Only John is left, together with Jesus' mother, his aunt, Mary Magdalene and Mary the wife of Clopas. A crucified God is not a crowd-puller for those seeking a mighty secular king. But here we see God's kingdom inaugurated – with blood, sweat and tears, and through the power of love.

Almighty God,
give us reverence for all creation
and respect for every person,
that we may mirror your likeness
in Jesus Christ our Lord.

COLLECT

Reflection by **Jan McFarlane**

Wednesday 27 February

Psalm **77**
2 Chronicles 12
John 19.31-end

John 19.31-end

'Nicodemus, who had at first come to Jesus by night, also came' (v.39)

Jesus is dead. Undeniably dead, not just unconscious – and pierced in the side to prove it. It would seem that the story is over. The crowds disperse.

And then, stage left, appear two characters, once hidden and shadowy, now boldly out in the open. Or to use John's constant refrain, two who have moved from darkness to light.

First Nicodemus. We met him earlier in John's Gospel. He first came to Jesus 'by night' and we assume he has stayed in the shadows ever since. Nicodemus represents perhaps those who long to believe, but who are held back by some secret fear, remaining peripheral, on the edge, watching from a distance, too scared to commit.

And then Joseph of Arimathea, a prominent member of the Sanhedrin, a 'secret disciple' held back because of fear of what might happen to his reputation if he were seen to be following Jesus. Plenty of people today would identify with Joseph.

What causes them to suddenly step out of the shadows? What causes them to commit themselves to Jesus? Perhaps through his death the truth of his teachings and all that he had lived out suddenly took on new meaning. Millions of those across the globe who have stood at the foot of the cross ever since have experienced that same transforming power. Quite simply, the power of love.

As the hymn writer, Isaac Watts, wrote some 1700 years later: 'Love so amazing, so divine, demands my life, my soul, my all.'

COLLECT

Almighty God,
you have created the heavens and the earth
and made us in your own image:
teach us to discern your hand in all your works
and your likeness in all your children;
through Jesus Christ your Son our Lord,
who with you and the Holy Spirit reigns supreme over all things,
now and for ever.

| *Reflection by* **Jan McFarlane**

Psalm **78.1-39***
2 Chronicles 13.1 – 14.1
John 20.1-10

Thursday 28 February

John 20.1-10
'... for as yet they did not understand' (v.9)

We're told that it's somewhere between 3am and 6am when Mary goes to the tomb. Whatever the actual time, it's still dark. John's great themes of light and dark are used to great effect once more as the physical darkness mirrors the disciples' inability to see what Jesus has been trying to tell them.

First Mary, and then Peter and John, witness the empty tomb. The grave clothes, which John had been careful to tell us yesterday were wrapped tightly around Jesus' body, are discarded. Confusion reigns. What the three encounter is an *absence*, an *emptiness*. They don't know where Jesus is. Jesus is simply not there.

Mary, Peter and John would have spent the Saturday Sabbath numb with grief. They would still have been in shock, the events of that first Good Friday moving as quickly as they did. They would have been exhausted, physically, mentally and emotionally.

When we find ourselves in a dark place, emotionally and physically shattered, sometimes all we encounter is an absence. It seems as if God is no longer with us. It takes determination to hang on in there, to live with the questions, to dwell in the emptiness of Easter Eve, trusting that like that first Easter morning eventually the darkness will recede and a new dawn will break. And then we will encounter God once more. And then we will understand.

> Almighty God,
> give us reverence for all creation
> and respect for every person,
> that we may mirror your likeness
> in Jesus Christ our Lord.

COLLECT

Friday 1 March

John 20.11-18

'Jesus said to her, "Mary!"' (v.16)

The truth of the resurrection is revealed to us in one word. As the Good Shepherd speaks to one of his flock by name, the scales fall from our eyes. We understand. Jesus is not dead. He is alive. And he calls us by name.

Jesus meets his disciples personally and intimately, often at unexpected times and in unexpected places. Our faith must be based not on the hearsay of others, not by simply knowing the story of Jesus, but through a personal encounter with him. And then, like Mary, we must turn. We remember this Easter morning encounter when in the baptism service, the candidate (or godparent on behalf of the candidate) is asked, 'Do you turn to Christ?' If we turn to Christ, our encounter with him has the potential to be as life changing as it was for Mary and the first disciples.

Jesus tells Mary not to cling to him. Instead she is to go and tell the others what she has witnessed. Mary, the first apostle, obeys and goes. It's all too easy to sit in church, clinging to Jesus' feet. But we're commanded by Jesus to go. To go and tell those who don't yet know him of his life-changing, life-affirming presence in our lives. And then to bring them to the empty tomb so they can encounter the risen Christ for themselves – the risen Christ who calls them by name.

COLLECT

Almighty God,
you have created the heavens and the earth
and made us in your own image:
teach us to discern your hand in all your works
and your likeness in all your children;
through Jesus Christ your Son our Lord,
who with you and the Holy Spirit reigns supreme over all things,
now and for ever.

| *Reflection by* **Jan McFarlane**

Saturday 2 March

John 20.19-end
'Unless I see the mark of the nails in his hands' (v.25)

Thank God, quite literally, for Thomas. Thomas the belligerent. Thomas the obstinate. Thomas the realist. Thomas the doubter. Thomas who is not going to believe what the others tell him. He wants proof. He won't believe until he sees for himself physical evidence for what the others claim. Thomas represents all those who struggle to believe. And when he is granted his proof, his doubts fall away and he utters the greatest confession of all: 'My Lord and my God!'. It is Thomas the Doubter who recognizes that the risen Christ is God.

There is something both moving and reassuring about the fact that Jesus is recognized by his scars. If ever we are struggling with our faith, it is by sitting at the foot of the cross and contemplating the nail marks in Christ's hands and the spear wound in his side that we can find evidence, physical proof, that we are known, called by name, and loved unconditionally.

Few of us travel through life without acquiring scars, be they physical, mental or emotional. The temptation is to think that we are only healed when the scars fade. But our wounds are what make us who we are. Our scars show that we have fought and won. The fourteenth-century mystic, Julian of Norwich said in her *Revelations of Divine Love* that 'though a soul be healed, its wounds are seen before God, no longer as wounds but as trophies'. We stagger on, rejoicing.

Almighty God,
give us reverence for all creation
and respect for every person,
that we may mirror your likeness
in Jesus Christ our Lord.

COLLECT

Monday 4 March

Jeremiah 1

'... they have ... worshipped the works of their own hands' (v.16)

Hold on to your hats! We're heading towards Lent with the roller-coaster prophet, Jeremiah. It won't make for easy reading, but Jeremiah is a prophet for our times and we need to heed his wisdom.

Jeremiah lived through one of the most difficult and challenging times in Hebrew history: the time leading up to the fall of Jerusalem and the exile of God's people in Babylon. The prophet could see what was happening. God's people had gone soft. They had abandoned God for an easy life. They had adopted the culture of those around them. They felt they could live easily without God's help.

Jeremiah could see that there was nothing but disaster on the horizon – and his prophecies came true. But he was able to promise too that ultimately, as a result of all that would happen, the relationship between God and his people would be stronger than ever before.

In the Western world today, the Church is in crisis. Numbers are falling; more and more people profess to follow no religion at all; it's hard to see a hopeful future. Jeremiah challenges us to consider how we will respond. By abandoning God? By clinging desperately to the old traditions and the old ways? By devising endless human strategies?

Or by watching and waiting, quietly listening for what God wants us to do; and being prepared to step out of our comfort zone, with courage and with faith?

COLLECT

Almighty Father,
whose Son was revealed in majesty
before he suffered death upon the cross:
give us grace to perceive his glory,
that we may be strengthened to suffer with him
and be changed into his likeness, from glory to glory;
who is alive and reigns with you,
in the unity of the Holy Spirit,
one God, now and for ever.

Reflection by **Jan McFarlane**

Psalms 87, **89.1-18**
Jeremiah 2.1-13
John 3.22-end

Tuesday 5 March

Jeremiah 2.1-13

'... cracked cisterns that can hold no water' (v.13)

There is an old saying, 'you are what you eat'. Eat good food and you'll be lean, fit and healthy. Eat food full of fat and sugar and your body will reveal on the outside what has been stored on the inside. Jeremiah here says something similar. That God's people have become what they have worshipped. God's people have turned away from him. They have failed to be distinctive. They have become like the false idols they revere. The lesson is clear: we will become whatever it is that takes up our time, our money and our attention. Our priorities in life will shape us and mould us.

For those who live in a semi-desert, water – and a good source of water – is a matter of life and death. Jeremiah accuses the people of Judah of turning away from the sparking, flowing, underground spring, which is God, the source of all life, and looking instead to cisterns carved by human hands from solid rock, with no water source, and leaking what little water it may already hold.

If we're struggling, tired and weary, might it be that we're trying to survive on the muddy dregs from an edifice made in our own strength? We're told by doctors that if we're tired, we should drink more water. What might it mean for us to return to that source of living water, Jesus himself?

Holy God,
you know the disorder of our sinful lives:
set straight our crooked hearts,
and bend our wills to love your goodness
and your glory
in Jesus Christ our Lord.

COLLECT

Reflection by **Jan McFarlane** | 89

Wednesday 6 March
Ash Wednesday

1 Timothy 6.6-19

'For the love of money is a root of all kinds of evil' (v.10)

Money, money, money. All too often the bane of Church life and the cause of our most fractious disagreements. Many clergy and lay preachers shy away from preaching about money, yet the reality is that we need hard cash to finance the mission and ministry of the Church, and both Jesus and Paul are bold in their teaching that the desire to hoard rather than give away our money is evidence of spiritual dis-ease.

As both an archdeacon and a bishop, I have been on the receiving end of anger and all manner of accusations when asking parishes to give more to our common fund – the fund that allows those who have more to help those who have less. It's all very biblical, but somehow talk of money (and note the problem is the love of money, not money itself) causes many people to feel defensive and threatened. I imagine it's something to do with a natural desire for security, but the Bible teaches us that ultimately money is not where true security is found. In fact, the opposite can be true. The more money you have, the more you have to lose and so it becomes a cause of great anxiety. Maybe that's why the poorest parishes are the best at giving their money away.

Perhaps this Ash Wednesday we might consider once again how much we give to the mission and ministry Church. It will reveal to us where our true priorities lie.

COLLECT

Almighty and everlasting God,
you hate nothing that you have made
and forgive the sins of all those who are penitent:
create and make in us new and contrite hearts
that we, worthily lamenting our sins
and acknowledging our wretchedness,
may receive from you, the God of all mercy,
perfect remission and forgiveness;
through Jesus Christ your Son our Lord,
who is alive and reigns with you,
in the unity of the Holy Spirit,
one God, now and for ever.

Reflection by **Jan McFarlane**

Thursday 7 March

Jeremiah 2.14-32

'Yet my people have forgotten me, days without number' (v.32)

The tirade against God's wayward people continues. See, there is that water imagery again. Desert-living people need a good source of water for survival, and yet God's people have turned their back on the spring of living waters, preferring dirty river water instead. Jeremiah doesn't hold back. He vents his spleen. They are like a prostitute; a vine that has turned unruly; a people so unclean that no soap will be strong enough; a camel with no driver, running round in circles and going nowhere; an animal wild with desire and refusing to see sense; a thief left with nothing when caught and found guilty.

Jeremiah despairs. What will it take for them to see sense?

This passage is much more than an interesting story from the history books. Jeremiah is speaking to us today. What is the modern equivalent of turning away from God? Perhaps it's that thing known as 'institutional atheism'. We, the Church, say that we believe in God; that God is in charge. And then we ignore him and carry on in our own strength as if God didn't exist; as if we didn't really believe that he's in charge at all. We plough on with our human strategies, applying management techniques from the secular world, as if it's up to us to save the world.

God must despair. What will it take for us to see sense?

Holy God,
our lives are laid open before you:
rescue us from the chaos of sin
and through the death of your Son
bring us healing and make us whole
in Jesus Christ our Lord.

COLLECT

Friday 8 March

Jeremiah 3.6-22

'I will give you shepherds after my own heart' (v.15)

Suddenly the tone changes. God has vented his spleen through his prophet. And now his anger subsides and God's pastoral heart is revealed once again. God cannot help himself. He loves his people and he cannot, will not, let them go. The divorce laws of Jeremiah's time were clear. There was to be no second chance. But God is willing to go against the law. If only they will see the error of their ways and turn back to him, God will welcome his wayward children home with open arms. There are echoes here of Jesus' parable of the prodigal son. Echoes too of the relationship God will have with his children as revealed in Jesus' prayer, 'Our Father...'

And another echo: God will in time send not only shepherds after his own heart, but his very self to be the Good Shepherd who knows each sheep by name and who will gently tend his flock.

How successfully do we share this good news today? The good news that no matter what we have done, God does not remain angry forever. We only have to say sorry and turn back to him, and he will run towards us with loving arms, gather us back into the fold, and never let us go.

Is that how the gospel message is perceived by those around us? Or is 'church' still seen as a place where people will be judged and condemned, if not by God, then by God's people?

COLLECT

Almighty and everlasting God,
you hate nothing that you have made
and forgive the sins of all those who are penitent:
create and make in us new and contrite hearts
that we, worthily lamenting our sins
and acknowledging our wretchedness,
may receive from you, the God of all mercy,
perfect remission and forgiveness;
through Jesus Christ your Son our Lord,
who is alive and reigns with you,
in the unity of the Holy Spirit,
one God, now and for ever.

Reflection by **Jan McFarlane**

Saturday 9 March

Jeremiah 4.1-18

'Your ways and your doings have brought this upon you' (v.18)

Yesterday's glimpse of a future of sincere repentance and genuine reconciliation fades once more as we return to the present. There is much more to go through first; the enemy is on the horizon. It's going to get worse before it gets better. And God's people have no one to blame but themselves.

How easy it is to look for someone to blame when things go wrong. And, if all else fails, we blame God. Yet nearly always we have to learn to take full responsibility for our deeds. We make our beds and we must lie in them. Taking responsibility, owning up and saying sorry are mature actions that can take a lifetime to master.

And there is no room for judging others. Father Brown, the clerical sleuth created by author G. K. Chesterton, has a well-worn technique for solving his crimes. He looks within his own heart to find the criminals' motives. 'You see it was I who killed all these people', he explains ruefully. There is no room for judgement here. We are all capable of the actions described by Jeremiah. And the only salvation is God and God's grace.

Those of us who preach and pastor have a delicate balancing act on our hands. We must help God's people to take responsibility for their own actions, and then, as fellow sinners, be agents of God's reconciling forgiveness, grace and peace.

COLLECT

Holy God,
our lives are laid open before you:
rescue us from the chaos of sin
and through the death of your Son
bring us healing and make us whole
in Jesus Christ our Lord.

Reflection by **Jan McFarlane**

Monday 11 March

Psalms 10, 11 *or* 98, 99, 101
Jeremiah 4.19-end
John 5.1-18

Jeremiah 4.19-end

'... the whole land shall be a desolation' (v.27)

Lent beckons us into penitential reflection. Our readings set the tone. We break into a speech by Jeremiah against a backdrop of political ferment and spiritual desolation. Jeremiah had warned repeatedly that faithlessness has consequences. It did. In 598 Jerusalem was defeated and 10 years later its leading citizens deported to Babylon. Jeremiah links the people's 'stupidity', 'foolishness' and 'evil' to war, disaster and destruction. The sin of the people has consequences.

The scale of the damage Jeremiah recounts is breathtaking: barren lands, earthquake, ruination of country and city. It's hard to read these ancient words without juxtaposing them with contemporary pictures of bombed-out towns, buildings haemorrhaging their contents into rubble-strewn streets; a seabird garlanded in plastic netting; a family perched on a rooftop as the flood water rises. Sin has global consequences.

Sin: the human propensity to bend everything to selfish ends eclipses worship and inverts the divine order. When humanity repudiates right relationship to God, it creates idols to fulfil the need to worship. Whether it's a carved wooden pole (Jeremiah 10.3-4), or a contemporary status symbol, unmask the idol and see salutation of the self at the altar of greed, lust and selfishness; there is nothing new under the sun.

The gift of Lent bends our hearts to penitential reflection; at whose altar do I worship, and at what cost?

COLLECT

Almighty God,
whose Son Jesus Christ fasted forty days in the wilderness,
and was tempted as we are, yet without sin:
give us grace to discipline ourselves in obedience to your Spirit;
and, as you know our weakness,
so may we know your power to save;
through Jesus Christ your Son our Lord,
who is alive and reigns with you,
in the unity of the Holy Spirit,
one God, now and for ever.

| *Reflection by* **Kate Bruce**

Psalm **44** *or* **106*** (*or* 103)   **Tuesday 12 March**
Jeremiah 5.1-19
John 5.19-29

Jeremiah 5.1-19
'But I will not make a full end of you' (v.18)

'Jeremiah' has become a byword for one who is pessimistic and doom laden. At first glance, today's reading suggests the prophet has earned this moniker; all seems so bleak. There is no justice or truth in Jerusalem; rich and poor alike are unrepentant, and Jeremiah prophesies God's punishment on an 'utterly faithless' people. Babylon becomes a weapon of discipline in God's hand, a nation that will wreak devastation on them.

However, a closer reading indicates that far from being an agent of doom, Jeremiah is a man of integrity and hope. He speaks truth where other prophets 'are nothing but wind'. He is not peddling cheap grace. Jeremiah utters divine judgement with courage, aiming to convince the people to turn back to the God who is utterly faithful. In spite of the rebellion and the judgement they have brought down upon their own heads, we read that a remnant of the people will survive the experience of punishment. God will not make a 'full end' of them, in the hope that new life will come from the remnant that is left.

As we journey through Lent, confronting the sin that lurks and corrupts, we must hold on to hope – hope in the grace that stirs repentance, the gift of forgiveness and renewal.

Heavenly Father,
your Son battled with the powers of darkness,
and grew closer to you in the desert:
help us to use these days to grow in wisdom and prayer
that we may witness to your saving love
in Jesus Christ our Lord.

COLLECT

Reflection by **Kate Bruce**   95

Wednesday 13 March

Psalms **6**, 17 *or* 110, **111**, 112
Jeremiah 5.20-end
John 5.30-end

Jeremiah 5.20-end

'They do not say in their hearts, "Let us fear the Lord our God ..."'
(v.24)

Boundaries create safe spaces, setting limitation and creating order. Just as God creates boundaries in the natural world, he sets them in the social and political world. But this order has been breached by 'scoundrels' who 'know no limits in deeds of wickedness'. Jeremiah paints a picture: those without power are abused, their rights disregarded, their boundaries ignored. At the heart of this appalling corruption is a monumental failing of imagination, the unwillingness to 'see' God aright and therefore a wrong perception of the self and the other. The strong set snares; the powerless become prey. The situation becomes even more horrifying since the voices of those who should speak truth are corrupted: 'the prophets prophesy falsely, and the priests rule as the prophets direct.'

Jeremiah's voice reverberates uncomfortably in our own context: abuse in the Church and wider society, followed by years of collusion and cover-up; the increasing poverty of the poorest, and the indifference of some in highest office.

The Lenten questions are sharp: where is my heart's focus – on God, or on myself? Do I stand up for the rights of the powerless? Do I respect the boundaries God has ordered? Jeremiah's voice is a summons to prayer and penitence. Have I ears to hear?

COLLECT

Almighty God,
whose Son Jesus Christ fasted forty days in the wilderness,
and was tempted as we are, yet without sin:
give us grace to discipline ourselves in obedience to your Spirit;
and, as you know our weakness,
so may we know your power to save;
through Jesus Christ your Son our Lord,
who is alive and reigns with you,
in the unity of the Holy Spirit,
one God, now and for ever.

Reflection by **Kate Bruce**

Psalms **42**, 43 *or* 113, **115**   **Thursday 14 March**
Jeremiah 6.9-21
John 6.1-15

Jeremiah 6.9-21

'Your burnt-offerings are not acceptable ...' (v.20)

Jeremiah describes a situation in which the external performance of religious ritual continues alongside political, social and moral corruption. No one is listening to God's call to penitence, 'their ears are closed'. There seems to be no desire to 'ask for the ancient paths, where the good way lies'. The people's understanding of life's meaning seems to have shrunk down to mere materialism. Relationship with God has been forgotten. Temple ritual continues but has become empty religious platitude, little more than *Songs of Praise* on low in the background. Worse still, those tasked with tending the spiritual health of the people have left the wound to fester. The nation is rank with infection, but her illness has been normalized. Jeremiah alone knows the raging temperature of the people; he faithfully calls her back to health. Her spiritual illness is grave, but she is mulishly resistant to Jeremiah's ministry. Jeremiah holds out the possibility of rest, hope and healing, repentance and renewal, a return to the deep, loving security of the covenant. But, his plea falls on deaf ears.

Lent is an invitation to the surgery where Jeremiah examines us like a physician of the soul: ask for the ancient paths; seek God in his ways; don't just go through the motions; God doesn't want empty praises, he desires your heart ... will you give it?

Heavenly Father,
your Son battled with the powers of darkness,
and grew closer to you in the desert:
help us to use these days to grow in wisdom and prayer
that we may witness to your saving love
in Jesus Christ our Lord.

COLLECT

Reflection by **Kate Bruce**   97

Friday 15 March

Jeremiah 6.22-end

'O my poor people, put on sackcloth' (v.26)

Jeremiah's compassion is deep and striking, particularly since no one listens to him and he is mocked and pilloried. Taking the plight of the people seriously, he speaks with passion and integrity.

Jeremiah prophesies against a backdrop of political instability. Assyria had held Judah in thrall, but as their power waned, Babylon loomed. King Josiah had wiped out pagan practices, and restored temple worship, but with his death the people flirted with foreign gods once more and forgot the covenant. Jeremiah reads the complex politics with clear sight, discerning God's hand in the midst of it all. The people's decision to forsake the covenant will bring God's judgement upon them, and Jeremiah sees the coming exile in this light.

His cry for their repentance is expressed with deep anguish, a reflection of God's fierce desire for his people to turn back to him. In spite of their refusal to listen, Jeremiah mourns for them and for the disaster that is coming because they have abandoned God.

The prophet's compassion for those who reject God speaks into our Lenten journey. Do we react with indifference to those who turn aside from God, or dismiss his ways, or have never heard of him? In what way do we demonstrate compassion, particularly for those who will not listen?

COLLECT

Almighty God,
whose Son Jesus Christ fasted forty days in the wilderness,
and was tempted as we are, yet without sin:
give us grace to discipline ourselves in obedience to your Spirit;
and, as you know our weakness,
so may we know your power to save;
through Jesus Christ your Son our Lord,
who is alive and reigns with you,
in the unity of the Holy Spirit,
one God, now and for ever.

Reflection by **Kate Bruce**

Saturday 16 March

Jeremiah 7.1-20

'My anger and my wrath shall be poured out on this place ...' (v.20)

The wrath of God is not a popular theme; it's much easier to preach a message of grace and love. However, when we edit out God's anger at the human heart bent on evil, we create a toothless idol, a dashboard-sized, nodding godlet, graceless and loveless: 'Oh well, my people are stealing, murdering, destroying each other's relationships, and baking cakes for some Canaanite fertility goddess in an attempt at magic, but humans will be humans.' Such idolatry is an insult to all who have suffered injustice. God's rage is a mark of the depth of his love for the alien oppressed, the orphan abused, the widow uncared for and the innocent maimed. God's anger is against the hypocrisy of his people who serve themselves and their idols whilst performing set religious practice as a 'holy' veneer.

Divine wrath comes with a call to repentance, and co-exists with divine patience that reaches out again and again. In the terrifying sermon 'Sinners in the hands of an angry God' (1741) Jonathan Edwards writes: 'The wrath of God is like great waters that are dammed for the present; they increase more and more, and rise higher and higher, till an outlet is given ...' The dam bursts when Babylon invades, the temple is destroyed and the chosen people are exiled because when God called, they did not answer.

Heavenly Father,
your Son battled with the powers of darkness,
and grew closer to you in the desert:
help us to use these days to grow in wisdom and prayer
that we may witness to your saving love
in Jesus Christ our Lord.

COLLECT

Reflection by **Kate Bruce** 99

Monday 18 March

Psalms 26, **32** *or* 123, 124, 125, **126**
Jeremiah 7.21-end
John 6.41-51

Jeremiah 7.21-end

'... walk only in the way that I command you' (v.23)

As a child, when I first decided to try to pray, I thought I had to pray in a certain order or God would be cross and not hear me. My religious practice pointed to a faulty image of God. Jeremiah's temple sermon challenges us to think about what our religious practice says about the god we believe in. Rather than staying true to the path God had chosen for them, the people cut their own furrow, blending temple offering with alien religious practice. What did sacrificing children in fire at the high place of Topheth suggest about the god they believed in? Their theology had split apart from religious practice; failure to dwell on the true nature of God always leads to distorted, and often dangerous, religious practice.

What does our religious practice suggest about God? If church is little more than an hour's commitment on a Sunday, rather than a daily attitude of heart, mind and action, then perhaps god is little more than a golf buddy?

Is church a place where you have to look smart and speak right? Perhaps god is a corporate director of a middle-class company? Does our worship point to the glorious, loving, life-giving freedom of God, known in Christ, full of the Spirit – generous, open and accepting of all comers? If it doesn't... who or what are we worshipping?

COLLECT

Almighty God,
you show to those who are in error the light of your truth,
that they may return to the way of righteousness:
grant to all those who are admitted
    into the fellowship of Christ's religion,
that they may reject those things
    that are contrary to their profession,
and follow all such things as are agreeable to the same;
through our Lord Jesus Christ,
who is alive and reigns with you,
in the unity of the Holy Spirit,
one God, now and for ever.

| *Reflection by* **Kate Bruce**

Psalms 25, 147.1-12
Isaiah 11.1-10
Matthew 13.54-end

Tuesday 19 March
Joseph of Nazareth

Matthew 13.54-end

'Is not this the carpenter's son?' (v.55)

We leave Jeremiah aside in this reflection; today the Church remembers Joseph, the earthly father of Jesus. The question, 'Is not this the carpenter's son?' might well have been asked with a knowing smirk as no doubt there were rumours about Jesus' parentage. The question is dismissive: Joseph reduced to a trade. There is incredulity and offence that the local boy speaks with wisdom and deeds of power.

Where did his wisdom and power come from? The obvious answer is 'from God' – but God works through ordinary and extraordinary means. What did Christ learn from Joseph? He was a man who is described as 'righteous' and 'unwilling to expose [Mary] to public disgrace' (Matthew 1.19). He is kind and considerate, as well as spiritually open. Obedient to the angelic voice in the dream (Matthew 1.20-24), he takes Mary to be his wife, in spite of the strange circumstances around the conception. There is confidence here. Joseph is also a man of considerable courage; the flight into Egypt with a wife and young child would have been taxing. Alert to the spiritual and obedient to divine guidance, Joseph proves himself a worthy, earthly father, and plays his role in shaping the wisdom of Jesus. He is far more than a carpenter.

Meanwhile I sense Jeremiah nodding ruefully as Jesus comments 'Prophets are not without honour except in their own country.'

COLLECT

God our Father,
who from the family of your servant David
raised up Joseph the carpenter
to be the guardian of your incarnate Son
and husband of the Blessed Virgin Mary:
give us grace to follow him
in faithful obedience to your commands;
through Jesus Christ your Son our Lord,
who is alive and reigns with you,
in the unity of the Holy Spirit,
one God, now and for ever.

Reflection by **Kate Bruce**   101

Wednesday 20 March

Psalm **35** *or* **119.153-end**
Jeremiah 8.18 – 9.11
John 6.60-end

Jeremiah 8.18 – 9.11

'Is there no balm in Gilead?' (8.22)

Jeremiah's original audience did not listen to his words. However, those who read the prophecies after the exile would have been able to identify with his anguish. What does it mean to be God's people when the temple lies ruined and the land is in thrall? What does it mean to follow God from the ruins of failure? As we read of the fall from grace of a minister splashed across the news; or hear the revelations of historic abuse; or look at the empty pews and boarded-up chapels, we might cry out with Jeremiah's earlier readers 'Is there no balm in Gilead? Is there no physician there?'

When Jesus ate in the house of Levi the tax collector, the scribes and Pharisees complained at his choice of friends. Jesus said, 'Those who are well have no need of a physician, but those who are sick; I have come to call not the righteous but sinners to repentance' (Luke 5.31-32). Jesus is the divine physician who tends those who have wounded themselves by their own actions or been hurt by the behaviour of others. Here is hope for all who are exiled, all who know they are steeped in sin, and trapped in the corruptions of the heart. God is found in the places of darkness and failure. There is a balm in Gilead; his name is Jesus.

COLLECT

Almighty God,
you show to those who are in error the light of your truth,
that they may return to the way of righteousness:
grant to all those who are admitted
    into the fellowship of Christ's religion,
that they may reject those things
    that are contrary to their profession,
and follow all such things as are agreeable to the same;
through our Lord Jesus Christ,
who is alive and reigns with you,
in the unity of the Holy Spirit,
one God, now and for ever.

| *Reflection by* **Kate Bruce**

Psalm **34** *or* **143**, 146*
Jeremiah 9.12-24
John 7.1-13

Thursday 21 March

Jeremiah 9.12-24

'... in these things I delight, says the Lord' (v.24)

The plumb line for holy living is to live in harmony with God's character. The Lord acts 'with steadfast love, justice, and righteousness in the earth', for in these things he delights. The goal of seeking to delight God in the ways we think and live is deeply appealing. However, most of us often fail, and it is easy to feel disheartened. St Paul was familiar with the gap between our best intentions and the frequent results, writing in Romans 'I do not do what I want, but I do the very thing I hate' (Romans 7.15).

Lent beckons us into deep self-examination, allowing us to reset the compass course of our hearts, naming the ways we have failed 'through negligence, through weakness', as well as 'through our own deliberate fault', as the confession puts it. A good Lenten discipline is to make a confession with another person; it is easy to beat ourselves up for trivial things and miss the failings that are most insidious. Formal confession with a priest in the Sacrament of Reconciliation includes having the words of absolution spoken over you. Spiritual direction also offers safe space to explore the areas of perceived failure and to allow someone else to see something of our inner world and help us to live in ways that delight God.

Almighty God,
by the prayer and discipline of Lent
may we enter into the mystery of Christ's sufferings,
and by following in his Way
come to share in his glory;
through Jesus Christ our Lord.

COLLECT

Reflection by **Kate Bruce** | 103

Friday 22 March

Psalms 40, **41** or 142, **144**
Jeremiah 10.1-16
John 7.14-24

Jeremiah 10.1-16

'... he is the living God and the everlasting King' (v.10)

Elijah stands on top of Mount Carmel, mocking the prophets of Baal for their absent god as they cry out in vain (1 Kings 18.27-29). He sets the stage for the God of Abraham, Isaac and Jacob to act with spectacular power. Why would anyone choose Baal over the King of the Nations? Jeremiah wrestles with the same question. The idols are blocks of wood, prettified by artistry, mere 'scarecrows in a cucumber field'. God cannot be compared to these dumb and lifeless imposters. God is incomparable, great in name and might, 'the living God and the everlasting King'. Jeremiah uses language skilfully, layering up his argument for God's creative majesty in contrast to the nothingness of the idols. Why would anyone choose a lump of painted wood over the King of the Nations?

The dangerous thing about an idol is that you can make it say what you want; it's like a religious nodding dog. If we shrink-wrap our conception of God, we can slip it into our back pocket and whip it out in a tight spot. We have mastery over the idol: worthless mastery.

The Lenten journey invites us to look again at our images of God. A reduced god reduces our vision and limits our dreams. A small god means a small life. We were created for so much more.

COLLECT

Almighty God,
you show to those who are in error the light of your truth,
that they may return to the way of righteousness:
grant to all those who are admitted
    into the fellowship of Christ's religion,
that they may reject those things
    that are contrary to their profession,
and follow all such things as are agreeable to the same;
through our Lord Jesus Christ,
who is alive and reigns with you,
in the unity of the Holy Spirit,
one God, now and for ever.

| *Reflection by* **Kate Bruce**

Saturday 23 March

Jeremiah 10.17-24

'... mortals as they walk cannot direct their steps' (v.23)

Jeremiah is a man with a deep understanding of humanity. He sees that, left to our own devices, we remain unschooled in the ways of God and stumble onto destructive pathways, mired in stupidity and sin. Like sheep without a shepherd, his people have gone astray. For all Jeremiah's calling and chiding, they remain scattered, lost on the dark side of the mountain, oblivious to Babylon the stalking wolf, unaware of the great gulf between them and the safety of their true sheepfold.

We never find God; God always finds us. Jesus is the shepherd who teaches his sheep to recognize his voice, who knows them, names them and leads them out.

This Lent we are invited to draw nearer to our Shepherd, to attend more closely to his instruction and direction. Left to our own devices, we soon become lost, as Jeremiah observed. However, we are not left *alone*: 'the sheep follow him because they know his voice' (John 10.4). Knowing his voice means spending time in his company. He is the shepherd who guides with rod and staff, comforting and corralling. He is the Good Shepherd who 'lays down his life for the sheep' (John 10.11). In his presence there is safety, comfort, protection, guidance and salvation. 'Mortals as they walk cannot direct their steps', but Christ can.

Almighty God,
by the prayer and discipline of Lent
may we enter into the mystery of Christ's sufferings,
and by following in his Way
come to share in his glory;
through Jesus Christ our Lord.

COLLECT

Reflection by **Kate Bruce** | 105

Monday 25 March

Annunciation of Our Lord
to the Blessed Virgin Mary

Psalms 111, 113
1 Samuel 2.1-10
Romans 5.12-end

1 Samuel 2.1-10

'… no Rock like our God' (v.2)

Hannah's song, recorded in 1 Samuel after the birth of Samuel himself, is so, distractingly, like Mary's Magnificat that it can be hard to focus on it in its own right. Even if we manage to do so, the song throws up for us such a lot of questions, such as whether this was Hannah's original creation and if it was, who her enemies were that her 'mouth derides'. It is, however, worth persevering through these many barriers to the gem beyond.

This song, attributed here to Hannah, is a song of profound trust in God. In the space of ten short verses, it speaks movingly of the power of God. He is a rock – the word used refers to a large boulder – and is utterly reliable. The song explores poetically the extent of God's power – he rules over the battlefield, the dinner table, birth, death and wealth. He is also the God of reversals, turning the world's order on its head, so that those sitting in the 'ash heap' (which could also be translated as dunghill) are raised to sit, direct from the dunghill, among princes.

This was the God of Hannah. This was also the God of Mary. This reliable, subversive God remains the same today, turning our world – with all its status and wealth – on its head and challenging us to do the same.

COLLECT

We beseech you, O Lord,
pour your grace into our hearts,
that as we have known the incarnation of your Son Jesus Christ
    by the message of an angel,
so by his cross and passion
we may be brought to the glory of his resurrection;
through Jesus Christ your Son our Lord,
who is alive and reigns with you,
in the unity of the Holy Spirit,
one God, now and for ever.

Tuesday 26 March

Jeremiah 11.18 – 12.6
'Why do all who are treacherous thrive?' (12.1)

Jeremiah's heartfelt cry in this passage could as easily be uttered today as it was then. We are all born with a sense of innate justice and the expectation that good things should happen to good people; yet as we look around us, this belief appears to have little if any foundation in reality. Now, as then, 'the way of the guilty' seems to prosper.

If there were an easy answer to this age-old problem, theologians would have found it years ago, and at first glance, this passage offers us little in the way of help. In it, Jeremiah, who felt like a gentle lamb led to the slaughter, remonstrated with God for a sign that he was about to act to overturn the wicked. The phrase he used to describe them is evocative: those for whom God is 'near in their mouths yet far from their hearts'. In other words, they talked the talk but had not allowed God to shape who they really were (in Hebrew thought, the heart was the seat both of emotion and of decision making).

What is striking, however, is that Jeremiah remained confident in who he knew God to be and protested when he saw no evidence of God's action in the world. This is the essence of intercessory prayer: remaining confident that God is the God of justice and remonstrating relentlessly at the injustice we see all around us.

Almighty God,
whose most dear Son went not up to joy
but first he suffered pain,
and entered not into glory before he was crucified:
mercifully grant that we, walking in the way of the cross,
may find it none other than the way of life and peace;
through Jesus Christ your Son our Lord,
who is alive and reigns with you,
in the unity of the Holy Spirit,
one God, now and for ever.

COLLECT

Reflection by **Paula Gooder** | 107

Wednesday 27 March

Psalm **38** *or* **119.1-32**
Jeremiah 13.1-11
John 8.12-30

Jeremiah 13.1-11

'... they would not listen' (v.11)

Jeremiah is famous for his prophetic actions – visual enactments of the message he came to proclaim. For the most part they are evocative and rich, explaining in ways that words alone could not the message he was called to proclaim. For the twenty-first-century reader, however, this particular enactment is harder to work out: loincloths not dipped in water and buried in a gap of a rock communicate little to our modern minds.

A little explanation might help: the loincloth was the underwear of the ancient world. Wrapped around the waist it hung down to around the middle of the thigh. The command not to put it in water probably means that Jeremiah is not to wash it. He was then told to take his rank underwear and bury it in the East (the Euphrates was in Babylon, modern Iraq) where it would have been very hot indeed. The rest can now be left to the imagination!

Here, then, as elsewhere, Jeremiah's prophetic action illustrated his message powerfully. God's people, who simply would not listen to his words, would become like an unwashed piece of underwear left to fester in sweltering heat. We may not wish to proclaim messages quite like this one today, but there is much to be learnt more widely from Jeremiah's prophetic actions – sometimes actions can speak louder than words.

COLLECT

Almighty God,
whose most dear Son went not up to joy but first he suffered pain,
and entered not into glory before he was crucified:
mercifully grant that we, walking in the way of the cross,
may find it none other than the way of life and peace;
through Jesus Christ your Son our Lord,
who is alive and reigns with you,
in the unity of the Holy Spirit,
one God, now and for ever.

| *Reflection by* **Paula Gooder**

Thursday 28 March

Jeremiah 14

'Let my eyes run down with tears night and day' (v.17)

This section of Jeremiah (indeed much of the book) can be grim reading: condemnation follows condemnation, the fate of God's people laid out in uncompromisingly harsh terms. In the midst of this misery, Jeremiah reports that there were prophets who were prophesying words of hope, that there would be 'true peace' in this place.

Our instinct is to welcome such messages – surely the God of love would want people to be reassured, calmed and given hope? It is interesting, therefore, to discover that God did not support the message of hope that they were offering. In fact, the false prophets were to be singled out for a particular punishment of their own. We see, in contrast, God's reaction to the state of his people – he wept night and day for the state that they were in and in knowledge of what would happen to them.

It is natural human nature to shy away from suffering and pain and to look forwards for hope and reassurance. This passage seems to suggest, however, that this is not always the right reaction. The false prophets, who elsewhere in Jeremiah were criticized for proclaiming peace when there was no peace (Jeremiah 8.11), tried to rush from pain to peace, from suffering to comfort. Sometimes we are called to stay with the pain, to weep with God for it and all that it means, and to speak even though it is neither welcome or comforting.

Eternal God,
give us insight
to discern your will for us,
to give up what harms us,
and to seek the perfection we are promised
in Jesus Christ our Lord.

COLLECT

Friday 29 March

Jeremiah 15.10-end

'Why is my pain unceasing ...?' (v.18)

It is easy to imagine that the biblical characters found following the call of God to be far easier and less taxing than we do ourselves. It is easy to imagine this ... but only if we have never really read the stories about them in the Bible. We love to read and linger over the call narratives, the noble responses summed up in Isaiah's words 'Here am I, send me' (Isaiah 6.8), but forget to read on to discover how very hard it has always been to live up to God's call.

These verses in Jeremiah 15 are a classic example of this kind of passage. Sometimes called 'Jeremiah's second lament', here we find Jeremiah sunk into a pit of gloom and self-pity. He has lived a good and upright life, but the whole land cursed him; he has suffered insults for his faithfulness to God; he has avoided the company of 'merrymakers', but his pain is unceasing.

It is, perhaps, mildly alarming to discover that God's response was far from sympathetic. We might imagine a warm embrace, a gentle listening, a bit of comfort and hope. Instead, God challenged him to utter what is precious rather than what is worthless. Jeremiah's despair had caused him to turn from God and to seek, instead, the approval of those he was called to serve. Following God's call has never been easy, but it is comforting to discover that even the 'biblical greats' struggled too.

COLLECT

Almighty God,
whose most dear Son went not up to joy but first he suffered pain,
and entered not into glory before he was crucified:
mercifully grant that we, walking in the way of the cross,
may find it none other than the way of life and peace;
through Jesus Christ your Son our Lord,
who is alive and reigns with you,
in the unity of the Holy Spirit,
one God, now and for ever.

Reflection by **Paula Gooder**

Psalms **31** *or* 20, 21, **23**
Jeremiah 16.10 – 17.4
John 9.1-17

Saturday 30 March

Jeremiah 16.10 – 17.4

'... the days are surely coming' (v.14)

It is hard, in this section of Jeremiah, to find any glimmers of hope. God's anger at the people's sin is presented as burning so strong that it is difficult to uncover any kind of inspiration in the passage at all. Jeremiah's message here is that Judah's sin had become so deeply ingrained – written with an iron stylus or a diamond pen on their hearts – that only the most radical action on God's part – hurling them out of their land – would bring them back to him.

In the midst of this, there is hope, even if it flickers with a dim glow. God may hurl the people out of their land, but he remains the God who brought his people out of Egypt. It is in God's nature to bring his people out of bondage in a foreign land and so he will act in this way again. He will, Jeremiah declared, become as known for bringing his people out of the lands to which he drove them as he was for bringing them out of Egypt.

Faint hope though this may be, it reminds us that the God who brought his people out of slavery in Egypt was the same God who brought his people out of exile in Babylon. This God remains the same, summoning us into lives of freedom, healing and wholeness, even if the slaveries in which we find ourselves are entirely self-inflicted.

Eternal God,
give us insight
to discern your will for us,
to give up what harms us,
and to seek the perfection we are promised
in Jesus Christ our Lord.

COLLECT

Reflection by **Paula Gooder** | 111

Monday 1 April

Jeremiah 17.5-18

'... like a tree planted by water' (v.8)

We have a scrubby bush in our garden that has never grown very well; it is stunted, small and, in the middle of the summer, turns brown at the edges.

It is this bush that comes to mind when I read Jeremiah 17. We may not have a full-blown wilderness in our garden, but we do have a patch of soil under a large conifer tree that deprives the bush both of light and water. The bush struggles on year after year but it will never thrive because it has no access to the light and water it needs.

It is so easy, Jeremiah suggests, for our lives to be stunted and dry in a similar way. We, like bushes and trees, need nourishment to thrive and grow. Perhaps even more importantly than that, we need reserves: deep wells of enrichment that will continue to feed us in times of drought and famine. Putting our trust in human beings, rather than God, has the same effect on us as it does on my stunted bush in the garden. We might survive and even grow a little, but without the nourishment of a living stream we cannot thrive.

Jeremiah's evocative image here reminds us of the importance of developing deep roots that can access the resources we need in times of drought. It is trusting in God that sends our roots deep, helping to live and grow no matter what our lives bring.

COLLECT

Merciful Lord,
absolve your people from their offences,
that through your bountiful goodness
we may all be delivered from the chains of those sins
which by our frailty we have committed;
grant this, heavenly Father,
for Jesus Christ's sake, our blessed Lord and Saviour,
who is alive and reigns with you,
in the unity of the Holy Spirit,
one God, now and for ever.

| *Reflection by* **Paula Gooder**

Psalms 54, **79** *or* 32, **36**
Jeremiah 18.1-12
John 10.1-10

Tuesday 2 April

Jeremiah 18.1-12

'... like the clay in the potter's hand' (v.6)

There is something mesmerizing about watching a potter making a pot: slowly but surely a ball of clay turns from an amorphous blob into an elegant pot or bowl. Then, in the blink of an eye, one false move or twitch can cause the pot to collapse in on itself, causing the potter to reshape it once more.

In this passage, Jeremiah reminds the people of Israel that the God who created Adam from the clay of the ground can just as easily collapse their country, their lives and their welfare and begin again in exactly the same way as a potter can collapse the pot she or he is working on. Our world – and the structures we build within it – can feel so concrete, stable and secure, but to the God who created it in the first place, it is as fragile as a piece of clay.

Some see this passage as a symbol of the way in which God would crush his people just as a potter would crush a pot gone wrong before remoulding them again; others see in it a much gentler image of the potter God taking a flawed pot and reshaping it into something altogether more beautiful. Either way, the image of God creating and recreating the world, and everything in it, as a potter does the clay, is an image that, deservedly, sticks richly in the mind.

Merciful Lord,
you know our struggle to serve you:
when sin spoils our lives
and overshadows our hearts,
come to our aid
and turn us back to you again;
through Jesus Christ our Lord.

COLLECT

Wednesday 3 April

Psalms 63, **90** *or* **34**
Jeremiah 18.13-end
John 10.11-21

Jeremiah 18.13-end

'... my people have forgotten me' (v.15)

The story of the Old Testament is the story of God's people hearing God's call of love but struggling to live up to that calling. All these years later, it can be easy to look on with a certain level of superiority: at best wondering at their stupidity; at worst despising them for getting things so very wrong.

It is language such as is used in this passage that should bring us up short in our superiority. Although their actions are nonsensical (as nonsensical as snow leaving the permanently snow-capped mountains of Lebanon), it is not hard to see how they got there. They began to make offerings to 'a delusion' – the word used refers to something vapid or empty that has no substance – and have stumbled from the highway onto side roads and into cul-de-sacs.

Before we find ourselves too dismissive of the people of Jeremiah's day, it might be worth asking ourselves what God might want to say to us too. What in our world and our churches has so distracted us that we focus more on a delusion than on the one who is substance itself? When have we stumbled off the highway to become lost in labyrinthine side roads of irrelevance? Such self-examination, while being potentially depressing, will ensure that our judgement of the people of Jeremiah's day will be much more generous and understanding.

COLLECT

Merciful Lord,
absolve your people from their offences,
that through your bountiful goodness
we may all be delivered from the chains of those sins
which by our frailty we have committed;
grant this, heavenly Father,
for Jesus Christ's sake, our blessed Lord and Saviour,
who is alive and reigns with you,
in the unity of the Holy Spirit,
one God, now and for ever.

| *Reflection by* **Paula Gooder**

Psalms 53, **86** *or* **37***
Jeremiah 19.1-13
John 10.22-end

Jeremiah 19.1-13

'... the ears of everyone who hears of it will tingle' (v.3)

One of the most evocative phrases in Jeremiah can be found in this passage – the disaster that is coming on God's people will be so catastrophic that it will make the ears of everyone who hears of it tingle or quiver. Although we might describe it differently these days, this is not an unfamiliar idea – that we are so struck by news that we hear about other people that we are affected physically by it.

As the passage unfolds, it is easy to see why the ears of those hearing would quiver. The disaster coming on God's people is so great that words cannot capture the extent of the desolation. This string of passages from Jeremiah are not an easy read but, if anything, I find this one more bleak than any of the others so far. This is probably because of the symbolic prophecy that accompanies it. Words alone cannot capture the desolation that is coming to God's people, but an action can.

Jeremiah's shattering of the potter's vessel into such tiny pieces that it cannot be salvaged speaks so powerfully of devastation that it almost takes your breath away. This was Jeremiah's message to God's people – bleak, miserable and hopeless – and still they did not listen. It makes you wonder what God is trying to say to us today that, in the same way, we find ourselves unable to hear.

Merciful Lord,
you know our struggle to serve you:
when sin spoils our lives
and overshadows our hearts,
come to our aid
and turn us back to you again;
through Jesus Christ our Lord.

COLLECT

Friday 5 April

Psalm **102** *or* **31**
Jeremiah 19.14 – 20.6
John 11.1-16

Jeremiah 19.14 – 20.6

'... carry them captive to Babylon' (20.4)

In this passage, Jeremiah's message in all its awfulness becomes one step clearer. So far, his message of gloom and destruction has been of the devastation of the land, of the horrors that God's people would suffer in pain and torment, but this passage takes it further. Not only are all those things going to happen but then they will be ripped out of that land and taken, in captivity, to a land far away.

One of the questions that arises as we read these terrible passages is, if God's people had listened to Jeremiah, what might they have done? By this point in Jeremiah's message, there is no doubt that the future was fixed; Jeremiah was not, unlike some of the earlier prophets, offering the hope that they could avoid the disaster if they changed their behaviour. This suggests that what they needed to do was to look into the abyss, to recognize the disaster for what it was and seek to live faithfully through it.

It is human nature to want to avoid acting like this: to rush onto a happier future or to hope for something better. Jeremiah suggests that faithfulness requires us to look at the world and all that is happening in it unflinchingly, recognizing it for what it is, awful though it may be – to live through it step by step until a better future arrives.

COLLECT

Merciful Lord,
absolve your people from their offences,
that through your bountiful goodness
we may all be delivered from the chains of those sins
which by our frailty we have committed;
grant this, heavenly Father,
for Jesus Christ's sake, our blessed Lord and Saviour,
who is alive and reigns with you,
in the unity of the Holy Spirit,
one God, now and for ever.

| *Reflection by* **Paula Gooder**

Psalm **32** *or* 41, **42**, 43
Jeremiah 20.7-end
John 11.17-27

Saturday 6 April

Jeremiah 20.7-end

'I must cry out ...' (v.8)

I don't know about you, but sometimes I wonder why certain people keep on 'making a nuisance of themselves': speaking when we would prefer them to be silent; making waves when we would prefer all to be calm. The reality is that we, like the people of Jeremiah's day, prefer our prophets to be biddable and not too irritating, to prophesy the kinds of messages we like to hear and not those that annoy or discomfort us.

Jeremiah 20 reminds us powerfully that this is not how prophets function. Jeremiah is so overcome with his sense of God and of his need to speak God's message in the world that he simply cannot keep quiet. No matter how badly people responded to him; no matter how much of a laughing stock he became, he simply had to speak. This is true of all prophets. Almost by their nature they cannot moderate their speech into something that we want to hear.

This is not to say that everyone who is annoying is a prophet. We need to sift what they say, listen carefully to their words and discern from them what, if anything, is from God. What it does mean, however, is that we dismiss those who irritate us, those who go on and on about what they believe to be true, at our peril. They may not be prophets ... but what if they are and we refuse to listen?

Merciful Lord,
you know our struggle to serve you:
when sin spoils our lives
and overshadows our hearts,
come to our aid
and turn us back to you again;
through Jesus Christ our Lord.

COLLECT

Monday 8 April

Jeremiah 21.1-10
'I myself will fight against you...' (v.5)

Traitor. Turncoat. Quisling. Fifth columnist. Spy. Collaborator. Judas.

These are all words we use to name those who betray us to our enemies. And in our readings, the prophet Jeremiah appears to take on this role. He looks like the worst kind of traitor to his people. Surrender to the empire attacking you – it's the only way to save your lives! For a British person, it would sound like someone telling us to surrender to Hitler and the Nazis in 1940, in the darkest days of the Second World War.

But here's the big difference. It is God himself who has become Judah's enemy because of their sin, and the only way to survive is to surrender. And just in case King Zedekiah and his people were in any doubt about God's attitude towards their past behaviour, his anger is named three times. God will fight against them in his anger, fury, and great wrath. But in his mercy he is not just presenting them with the way of death. He is offering a way of life in this appalling situation, even with the Babylonians at their gates.

We need to ask ourselves concerning any conflict in our lives: am I on God's side in this? Or am I in reality trying to fight him?

COLLECT

Most merciful God,
who by the death and resurrection of your Son Jesus Christ
delivered and saved the world:
grant that by faith in him who suffered on the cross
we may triumph in the power of his victory;
through Jesus Christ your Son our Lord,
who is alive and reigns with you,
in the unity of the Holy Spirit,
one God, now and for ever.

| *Reflection by* **Jeanette Sears**

Psalms **35**, 123 *or* **48**, 52
Jeremiah 22.1-5, 13-19
John 11.45-end

Jeremiah 22.1-5, 13-19

'Act with justice and righteousness ...' (v.3)

Every street near me seems to have a house doubling in size. It is not just a matter of a small extension to someone's home. It is like a duplicate house being tacked onto the side, taking up all the available space and leaving a wafer-thin gap between it and the next house. I wonder about the owners' motives as I walk past. Is it more space to care for relatives that's needed, or self-aggrandizement?

If anyone is allowed to have a huge beautiful home, you would think it ought to be a king. But in our reading today, King Jehoiakim is blasted by the prophet for his fancy house and luxurious decor. This is not because God is against beauty or even palaces. It is because King Jehoiakim has been building his house 'by unrighteousness ... and injustice', making people work for nothing, indulging his own appetites and fantasies of grandeur instead of being a real leader and protecting the weak. He needs to remember that he is on the throne of David and that carries responsibilities: to be God's heart for his people.

His fat cat complacency towards the poor and oppressed will end in him being treated like a dead donkey, dragged out of the city onto the rubbish tip.

If not you, King Jehoiakim (and us), then who will care for the alien, the orphan, the widow and the innocent?

COLLECT

Gracious Father,
you gave up your Son
out of love for the world:
lead us to ponder the mysteries of his passion,
that we may know eternal peace
through the shedding of our Saviour's blood,
Jesus Christ our Lord.

Reflection by **Jeanette Sears** | 119

Wednesday 10 April

Psalms **55**, 124 *or* **119.57-80**
Jeremiah 22.20 – 23.8
John 12.1-11

Jeremiah 22.20 – 23.8

'I will raise up for David a righteous Branch ...' (23.5)

Which do you want first – the good news or the bad news?

Jeremiah doesn't give his hearers the choice. It is a constant pattern of seriously bad news followed by major good news. But the good can only happen if they've gone through the bad experience first.

It will apply just as much to the royal house of David. This time it is King Jehoiachin who is being warned of the full displeasure of God over his behaviour. The imagery of God's rejection of his servant is deeply intimate and personal. Just as we might take off a wedding ring during a divorce, God tells the king that even if he were 'the signet ring on my right hand, even from there I would tear you off'. The signet ring is the symbol of royal power: Jehoiachin (or 'Coniah') has been rejected as king over God's people.

But then the good news. God will restore the Davidic line and his people. We know that Jehoiachin's grandson Zerubbabel will return with his people to be governor of Jerusalem in the restoration. Eventually God will tell Zerubbabel that he will be a signet ring on God's hand (Haggai 2.23). And we know that Jehoiachin's and Zerubbabel's Davidic line will lead us to the ultimate wise and just king, the Lord Jesus himself (Matthew 1.12).

Take time now to thank God for the restorations in your life after hard times.

COLLECT

Most merciful God,
who by the death and resurrection of your Son Jesus Christ
delivered and saved the world:
grant that by faith in him who suffered on the cross
we may triumph in the power of his victory;
through Jesus Christ your Son our Lord,
who is alive and reigns with you,
in the unity of the Holy Spirit,
one God, now and for ever.

| *Reflection by* **Jeanette Sears**

Psalms **40**, 125 *or* 56, **57** (63*)
Jeremiah 23.9-32
John 12.12-19

Thursday 11 April

Jeremiah 23.9-32
'I have heard what the prophets have said ...' (v.25)

God has certainly heard 'the prophets', but the question is, have they heard him?

The prophet's main task is to listen to God and then to report what they've heard. This listening can take the form of receiving auditory or visual stimuli from God, sometimes in very exact words, sometimes in dreams and symbols that need interpreting. The crucial question is whether these are from God or not. The fate of the whole nation depends on the answer.

Only those prophets who have 'stood in the council of the Lord' (23.18) are qualified to speak as if from him. Instead, the people are being deceived by self-styled prophets, communicating their own ideas. We should be particularly suspicious of those who tell us what we want to hear. Straw and wheat may seem similar but only one is really nourishing. You will need to look more deeply to know the difference. God's word to us can be as fierce as fire or as destructive as a hammer. It's not soft gloop.

Do you know God well enough to know when a message is authentically from God? Now that God has poured out his gifts on his whole Church, a prophet or prophetess could be a member of your own congregation or family. If you listen to God and open up your spirit and dreams to him, it could be you.

Gracious Father,
you gave up your Son
out of love for the world:
lead us to ponder the mysteries of his passion,
that we may know eternal peace
through the shedding of our Saviour's blood,
Jesus Christ our Lord.

COLLECT

Reflection by **Jeanette Sears** | 121

Friday 12 April

Psalms **22**, 126 *or* **51**, 54
Jeremiah 24
John 12.20-36*a*

Jeremiah 24

'I will build them up ... I will plant them' (v.6)

When I was first studying Theology I went through some difficult times. It could feel as though all my ideas of God and his ways were being torn down and uprooted, and for a while there was nothing left. But gradually I was built up again, and new ideas were sown and grew in their place, better than before.

Every idea we have of God is bound to be an idol; it is never God himself. And so having that old idol torn down and replaced with something more accurate is always a good thing, although it can feel like agony at the time. These words in Jeremiah became a cornerstone of my faith – that God is a God who tears down and then builds up, who uproots then plants again. To remember that it is God himself in the very process of destruction – that it is therefore therapeutic – is a tremendous help.

Jeremiah is being shown the people of God split into two camps. The 'bad figs' are no longer fit for purpose and will be revealed for the Godless group they have become and removed. But the 'good figs' have listened to God and surrendered to his will, even though it seemed counterintuitive at the time.

Can you see ways in which God has torn down or uprooted you, and you are waiting to 'return to God' with your 'whole heart'?

COLLECT

Most merciful God,
who by the death and resurrection of your Son Jesus Christ
delivered and saved the world:
grant that by faith in him who suffered on the cross
we may triumph in the power of his victory;
through Jesus Christ your Son our Lord,
who is alive and reigns with you,
in the unity of the Holy Spirit,
one God, now and for ever.

| *Reflection by* **Jeanette Sears**

Psalms **23**, 127 *or* **68**
Jeremiah 25.1-14
John 12.36*b*-end

Saturday 13 April

Jeremiah 25.1-14

'I will repay them according to their deeds ...' (v.14)

We say 'What goes around, comes around', as if there is some sort of impersonal karma that pays people for what they have done. But this is not what Jeremiah the prophet is saying here. For him, there is a highly personal God who sees and judges our inmost hearts and makes decisions about us, but on the basis of a love relationship.

The shock in this passage is that God intends to punish those whom he has used to punish his people. The Babylonians may have been used by God, but they are not perfect and are idolators in their turn. The ones who have punished sinners have sinned themselves; those who have made slaves of others will also become slaves.

It is impossible to avoid the thread of teaching that runs throughout Scripture, the golden rule: 'In everything do to others as you would have them do to you; for this is the law and the prophets' (Matthew 7.12) with its concomitant 'For with the judgement you make you will be judged, and the measure you give will be the measure you get' (Matthew 7.2). The people of Judah have learned this the hard way. Now it is the turn of their captors, the Babylonians.

Take some time now to let God show you if there is some person or group that you are holding to exacting standards, even though you are not keeping those standards yourself.

Gracious Father,
you gave up your Son
out of love for the world:
lead us to ponder the mysteries of his passion,
that we may know eternal peace
through the shedding of our Saviour's blood,
Jesus Christ our Lord.

COLLECT

Reflection by **Jeanette Sears** | 123

Monday 15 April

Monday of Holy Week

Psalm 41
Lamentations 1.1-12*a*
Luke 22.1-23

Luke 22.1-23

'When the hour came, he took his place at the table' (v.14)

Jesus says: 'I have eagerly desired to eat this Passover with you before I suffer.' This was something he was particularly keen to do with his disciples at this crucial moment. The Passover reminded the people of Israel who they were – those who had been rescued from slavery in Egypt, when the angel of death had passed over the Israelites during a deadly plague.

Jesus' recasting of the Passover in the light of his forthcoming passion is a similarly defining moment in the new community that will soon emerge after his death and resurrection. This meal, to be celebrated time and time again, tells the disciples of Jesus who they are. They are to be a community gathered around Jesus, called first and foremost to a holy communion with him. They are a community bound together by blood – not the blood of their enemies but the sacrificial blood of Christ who died to make them one. They are an imperfect community; among the twelve gathered around the table was Judas the betrayer – if we ever get too precious about those who take Communion alongside us we perhaps need to remember that. And they are a community dedicated to seeing the kingdom of God come.

At the heart of the meal, Jesus looks forward to the day when it is 'fulfilled in the kingdom of God', and we do the same every time we gather around his table at his invitation.

COLLECT

Almighty and everlasting God,
who in your tender love towards the human race
    sent your Son our Saviour Jesus Christ
to take upon him our flesh
and to suffer death upon the cross:
grant that we may follow the example of his patience and humility,
and also be made partakers of his resurrection;
through Jesus Christ your Son our Lord,
who is alive and reigns with you,
in the unity of the Holy Spirit,
one God, now and for ever.

| *Reflection by* **Graham Tomlin**

Psalm 27
Lamentations 3.1-18
Luke 22. [24-38] 39-53

Tuesday 16 April
Tuesday of Holy Week

Luke 22. [24-38] 39-53

'But Jesus said, "No more of this!"' (v.51)

The picture Luke paints of the disciples is far from flattering. They bicker over who is more important, just before Peter commits his shameful denial. A group of them fail miserably in their support of Jesus as they sink into despair ('sleeping because of grief'). Judas then informs on Jesus to the Roman authorities with the most infamous kiss in history. They then resort to violence in their defence of Jesus, perhaps out of shame over their failure to stay awake, or perhaps in anger at their friend Judas' betrayal.

In the midst of this catalogue of human failure stands Jesus, a picture of human grace and dignity, the light shining in this hour of darkness. He rebukes neither Peter nor Judas but simply lays bare their weakness and betrayal in the gentlest of ways. He refuses to incite violence but heals the ear of the very soldier who has come to arrest and crucify him.

There could hardly be a starker picture of the extremes of what humanity is capable of. The difference lies in Jesus' close identity with the mind and will of his Father: 'not my will but yours be done'. Our true humanity is found not in self-assertion or in independence from God – that way lies chaos; instead, submission to the divine law of love makes us more human and not less.

True and humble king,
hailed by the crowd as Messiah:
grant us the faith to know you and love you,
that we may be found beside you
on the way of the cross,
which is the path of glory.

COLLECT

Reflection by **Graham Tomlin** | 125

Wednesday 17 April

Wednesday of Holy Week

Psalm 102 [*or* 102.1-18]
Wisdom 1.16 – 2.1; 2.12-22
or Jeremiah 11.18-20
Luke 22.54-end

Luke 22.54-end

'But he denied it, saying, "Woman, I do not know him."' (v.57)

The remarkable thing about the story of the denial of Peter is that it was told at all. This was a small gathering of servants of the High Priest's household and Peter was the only follower of Jesus present. It is hard to know how this story ever would have got out unless Peter himself told it. It is, in fact, one of the few stories that makes it into all four Gospels, and so it seems it was particularly well known in the early Church. Presumably, Peter told the story to his friend and confidant, Mark, and then all the other Gospel writers picked it up as well.

Contradicting the advice of every political advisor in history, Peter, who was later to become the most prominent Christian of them all, chooses to trumpet the moment of his greatest shame and most catastrophic failure. Why? Is it because this was the key turning point in Peter's life? Having let Jesus down so drastically, Jesus simply looks at him, a look which, in the light of his later reinstatement of Peter (John 21.15-19) must have been a look that combined sorrow, compassion and forgiveness. Failure enabled Peter to learn something about himself that success could never do.

Failure can lead to despair, but handled wisely, can be the beginning of wisdom, as we learn to accept and live out of the forgiveness and grace of Christ.

COLLECT

Almighty and everlasting God,
who in your tender love towards the human race
    sent your Son our Saviour Jesus Christ
to take upon him our flesh
and to suffer death upon the cross:
grant that we may follow the example of his patience and humility,
and also be made partakers of his resurrection;
through Jesus Christ your Son our Lord,
who is alive and reigns with you,
in the unity of the Holy Spirit,
one God, now and for ever.

| *Reflection by* **Graham Tomlin**

Psalms 42, 43
Leviticus 16.2-24
Luke 23.1-25

Thursday 18 April
Maundy Thursday

Luke 23.1-25
'Jesus gave him no answer' (v.9)

As the story nears its climax, the storm rages around Jesus. He is handed around like a hot potato between Pilate, the governor of Judea, and Herod Antipas, who was responsible for the territory of Galilee, who happened to be in Jerusalem at the time. Pilate is portrayed as feeble, unable to secure evidence against Jesus, but unwilling to make the unpopular decision to release him. Herod is initially curious, but again fearful of making a decision, and hands him back as swiftly as possible. The crowd is swept along by the clamour for blood and someone to blame. And in the middle of all the noise and political dealing, Jesus is silent. As he appears before these two men who have the power of life and death over him he utters (in the Greek) just two words.

Where does power lie in this episode? Pilate and Herod both have the political power of decision making. The crowd has the power of a loud voice and public opinion. And yet somehow the figure who emerges with the most authority is the one who is most silent. After the struggles of Gethsemane, Jesus is the one who seems at peace, having accepted the path laid out for him.

The presence of Jesus, even when he is silent, facing death, yet secure in the hands of his Father, speaks more eloquently than any number of fear-filled human voices.

True and humble king,
hailed by the crowd as Messiah:
grant us the faith to know you and love you,
that we may be found beside you
on the way of the cross,
which is the path of glory.

COLLECT

Friday 19 April
Good Friday

Psalm 69
Genesis 22.1-18
John 19.38-end
or Hebrews 10.1-10

Hebrews 10.1-10

'... it is by God's will that we have been sanctified' (v.10)

The scene on the first Good Friday was messy, brutal and ugly. A small crowd gathered in a disused quarry, now used as an execution site, watched an assorted group of criminals and rebels savagely executed in a manner calculated to inspire fear and terror. Yet the writer to the Hebrews saw much more going on than met the eye. Death by sacrifice took place day after day in the temple, just a few hundred yards further east in the city, and was understood to cleanse the people from the defilement of sin. Those sacrifices could never bring 'closure' as we would say, as they only worked until further sins were committed that then required further sacrifice.

The death of Jesus however, was the offering to end all offerings, the final sacrifice that could 'make perfect' or 'sanctify' those for whom it was made. Human nature had been stained by the tragic story of human weakness, failure, betrayal, violence and injustice that we have watched over this past week as we have followed Jesus to the cross. Yet now, for once, by the power of the Spirit, Jesus the divine Son had been enabled to offer up a perfect, obedient, clean life, fully in harmony with the character of the God who gives himself to the world.

And so humanity is cleaned up, re-booted as it were, so that all who approach God in Christ can know that same cleansing of the conscience and renewal of life.

C O L L E C T

Almighty Father,
look with mercy on this your family
for which our Lord Jesus Christ was content to be betrayed
    and given up into the hands of sinners
    and to suffer death upon the cross;
who is alive and glorified with you and the Holy Spirit,
one God, now and for ever.

| *Reflection by* **Graham Tomlin**

Psalm 142
Hosea 6.1-6
John 2.18-22

Saturday 20 April

Easter Eve

John 2.18-22

'Destroy this temple, and in three days I will raise it up' (v.19)

In this reading, John recalls Jesus' prediction of the destruction of the temple in Jerusalem, an outburst that contributed to his conviction (Mark 14.58), and the bold assertion that in three days he would raise it up again. The saying produced some confusion at the time, with some thinking this was a prediction of violent insurrection, so that John had to clear it up by pointing out 'he was speaking of the temple of his body'. The temple was the place Israel went to meet God, the place of sacrifice and reconciliation, the place where God dwelt in the midst of his people. Now, however, the presence of God among his people was to be found not in a building but a person, and the ultimate final perfect sacrifice had been made. This is why the early Christians had no more place for the temple, seeing it as superseded, and its time expired.

Holy Saturday is a strange day, poised between death and life, crucifixion and resurrection, between destruction and rebuilding. It is a day which calls for faith, to 'believe the Scripture and the word that Jesus had spoken'. Today is a day for thankfulness for the perfect self-sacrifice of Christ, for the assurance of God's presence among us in him, and for patience and trust as we wait for his resurrection on that long-anticipated day when all things will be brought together in Christ.

Grant, Lord,
that we who are baptized into the death
of your Son our Saviour Jesus Christ
may continually put to death our evil desires
and be buried with him;
and that through the grave and gate of death
we may pass to our joyful resurrection;
through his merits,
who died and was buried and rose again for us,
your Son Jesus Christ our Lord.

COLLECT

Reflection by **Graham Tomlin**   129

Monday 22 April

Monday of Easter Week

Psalms 111, 117, 146
Song of Solomon 1.9 – 2.7
Mark 16.1-8

Mark 16.1-8

'Who will roll away the stone for us?' (v.3)

Nobel prizewinner William Golding ended his 1984 novel *The Paper Men* mid-word. This unusual conclusion vividly connects the reader to the fate of the narrator who dies mid-thought. This passage of Mark's Gospel seems to end similarly mid-story. We may never know if this is how Mark intended his account to end, but it is very striking.

The emphasis is on the very human responses of the women to an event that overwhelmed them. The three women are depicted as powerless, as they approach the tomb discussing how they might gain entry. They had seen for themselves how Joseph rolled the stone over the entrance. Their discussion of the problem emphasizes the arrival of a new age when they discover the stone has been removed.

News of Jesus' resurrection, and instructions on what to do next, are given to them by an angel. Mark uses a rare Greek word, not used elsewhere in the New Testament, *ekthambeisthai*, to describe their alarm. The word expresses a strong sense of awe and shock in the face of the inexplicable. The women's terror gets the better of them and they depart in fear without telling their story.

Though we know they must have told it eventually or we would never have heard it, we have become so used to it that we miss the terror and power of it. Thank God for Mark's account that reconnects us to the overwhelming experience of discovering Jesus raised from the dead.

C O L L E C T	Lord of all life and power,
	who through the mighty resurrection of your Son
	overcame the old order of sin and death
	to make all things new in him:
	grant that we, being dead to sin
	and alive to you in Jesus Christ,
	may reign with him in glory;
	to whom with you and the Holy Spirit
	be praise and honour, glory and might,
	now and in all eternity.

| *Reflection by* **Libby Lane**

Psalms 112, 147.1-12
Song of Solomon 2.8-end
Luke 24.1-12

Tuesday 23 April

Tuesday of Easter Week

Luke 24.1-12

'Remember how he told you ...' (v.6)

Luke's resurrection account reminds us that women had been members of Jesus' close circle of followers during his ministry. They had witnessed at close hand his public actions and they had heard him speak about the central purpose of that ministry. Indeed, we can assume from the angel's words that Jesus had taught these women alongside his male disciples and would expect them to understand that the moment of fulfilment of all that Jesus had said and done had now come to pass.

The angel's words reflect those found in Mark's Gospel at 9.31. In verse 32, Mark goes on to tell us that 'they did not understand what he was saying and were afraid to ask him'. Here is a case of unconscious denial, in contrast to Peter's all too conscious later betrayal: the disciples could not hold on to the meaning of Jesus' words because they were focused on the victories that they saw Jesus winning each day. They did not want to recognize the work of God in Jesus' difficult words.

This denial continues into this moment when the women return from the tomb to report their news. Jesus had included the women in his life's work and chose them to be the first bearers of the good news of his resurrection. God's action and purpose is rejected all over again as the men dismiss the women's account as nonsense.

What opportunities and possibilities of God do we risk missing because we fail to hear God's voice from unexpected people?

God of glory,
by the raising of your Son
you have broken the chains of death and hell:
fill your Church with faith and hope;
for a new day has dawned
and the way to life stands open
in our Saviour Jesus Christ.

COLLECT

Reflection by **Libby Lane** | 131

Wednesday 24 April
Wednesday of Easter Week

Psalms 113, 147.13-end
Song of Solomon 3
Matthew 28.16-end

Matthew 28.16-end

'... to the end of the age' (v.20)

Matthew tells us, in Matthew 10, that the first time Jesus sent out his disciples on mission, it was specifically to 'the lost sheep of the house of Israel'. Matthew, unlike Luke, does not record the return of this first mission, nor its results. Now, though, the disciples are to embark on a greater, more difficult task – the evangelization of the world. This is not to be a short-term mission. This is to last until the very end of time itself. Matthew articulates that the natural, constant state for the Church, and for the individual Christian, is to be on mission.

The resurrection has transformed the Christ-mission from a local matter defined by particular cultic identity into a global movement transcending all differences of culture. The modern Anglican Church describes this calling to perpetual mission in its 'Five Marks of Mission', summed up as proclaiming the Good News of the Kingdom, and to include teaching, baptizing and nurturing believers; responding to human need in loving service; transforming unjust structures of society, challenging violence of every kind and pursuing peace and reconciliation; and safeguarding the integrity of creation, sustaining and renewing the life of the earth.

Whatever our particular gifts and circumstances, each of us, like those first disciples, individually and together, is called to our place in this great mission and to act on it.

COLLECT

Lord of all life and power,
who through the mighty resurrection of your Son
overcame the old order of sin and death
to make all things new in him:
grant that we, being dead to sin
and alive to you in Jesus Christ,
may reign with him in glory;
to whom with you and the Holy Spirit
be praise and honour, glory and might,
now and in all eternity.

| *Reflection by* **Libby Lane**

Psalms **114**, 148
Song of Solomon 5.2 – 6.3
Luke 7.11-17

Thursday 25 April
Thursday of Easter Week

Luke 7.11-17
'... he had compassion for her' (v.13)

The woman's future is bleak. Already widowed, now she has lost her only son, her last source of support, income and comfort. She is precisely the sort of person Deuteronomy's injunctions to the people of Israel are intended to protect from destitution. She is a test case of her neighbours' commitment to righteousness under the law of Moses. At best this was a precarious position. For the moment, she is surrounded by the local community, supporting her in her grief, but crowds can be fickle.

1 Kings 17 and 2 Kings 4 tell the stories of how the prophets Elijah and Elisha revived from death the only sons of two women, one of them a widow. Whilst these prophets laid their bodies over the expired young men and prayed elaborate prayers, Jesus revives the widow's son with a few words. The crowd would have had no difficulty in recognizing that a prophet even greater than Israel's greatest prophets had come among them.

Yet Jesus is not just a link in a theological pattern. He is a man of passions. He responds to the widow's tears out of deep feeling. The fact that the boy, once revived, immediately speaks confirms that his mind and spirit have been restored, and that in restoring him, Jesus has brought restoration to the woman as well. He has brought the kingdom of righteousness near, a kingdom of which he will soon reveal himself to be Lord.

God of glory,
by the raising of your Son
you have broken the chains of death and hell:
fill your Church with faith and hope;
for a new day has dawned
and the way to life stands open
in our Saviour Jesus Christ.

COLLECT

Reflection by **Libby Lane** | 133

Friday 26 April
Friday of Easter Week

Psalms **115**, 149
Song of Solomon 7.10 – 8.4
Luke 8.41-end

Luke 8.41-end
'... and she will be saved' (v.50)

Two interfolded stories provide us with insight into Jesus' dismantling of empty religious ritual. Jairus is a public official at risk of serious censure from Jesus' pious adversaries when he humbles himself before Jesus. With the crowd pressing round, Jesus starts to respond but experiences a strange, sudden loss of power, pivoting the story in a new direction.

An unknown woman's private shame has driven her to touch Jesus from behind under the cover of the jostling crowd. Her heavy menstruation has rendered her ritually unclean and therefore an outcast. Does Jesus simply intend to identify her by calling out? Or does he grasp an opportunity to show the power of the kingdom of God in action?

Rather than shrinking away with her private cure, the woman imitates Jairus and falls down in front of Jesus. Now her healing can become the gateway to a deeper encounter with God's saving action.

Has the woman's intervention – her 'stolen touch' – disrupted the ongoing drama of the dying girl, causing untold harm to an innocent? It appears so. The arrival of a man who bluntly delivers his dreadful news makes it look as if it is Jairus who will slip away from view, claimed again by the world of conventional ritual as the only comfort in the face of death. However, Jesus offers him a new world. By faith in Jesus, he too will encounter God in ways far beyond those falsely promised by ritual righteousness for its own sake.

COLLECT

Lord of all life and power,
who through the mighty resurrection of your Son
overcame the old order of sin and death
to make all things new in him:
grant that we, being dead to sin
and alive to you in Jesus Christ,
may reign with him in glory;
to whom with you and the Holy Spirit
be praise and honour, glory and might,
now and in all eternity.

| *Reflection by* **Libby Lane**

Psalms 116, 150
Song of Solomon 8.5-7
John 11.17-44

Saturday 27 April
Saturday of Easter Week

John 11.17-44
'I am the resurrection and the life' (v.25)

The raising of Lazarus is placed right in the middle of John's Gospel, the centrepiece of John's design. This pivotal point pitches us from the teaching, the performance of various signs and the gathering reaction to them, into the narrative of the Passion, preparing us for the resurrection itself. We are in the middle of a messy, emotional situation, but we know at the outset that this is an opportunity for the in-breaking of God's glory.

Lazarus has been in the tomb for four days. His death is irreversible. Martha's response to Jesus' consoling words tell us that her recognition of Jesus as Messiah, as Son of God and as the Coming One, is a deep moment of full-sightedness, of faith *as* seeing.

Jesus too soon will die. His resurrection, however, will not be a resuscitation. It will be the crowning moment of his glorification, which has suffering at its heart.

Mary's encounter with Jesus brings us back firmly to earth. Her distress and the grief of the community move him deeply. Jesus is disturbed by death. The death of Lazarus propels us towards Jesus' own Passion: not the shielded, formulaic and ritual suffering of a divine being, of one who is not actually suffering. Jesus' death will be the suffering of a God who is fully human.

COLLECT

God of glory,
by the raising of your Son
you have broken the chains of death and hell:
fill your Church with faith and hope;
for a new day has dawned
and the way to life stands open
in our Saviour Jesus Christ.

Reflection by **Libby Lane** | 135

Monday 29 April

George, martyr,
patron of England

Psalms 5, 146
Joshua 1.1-9
Ephesians 6.10-20

Ephesians 6.10-20

'... the cosmic powers of this present darkness' (v.12)

The stories of St George are often associated with the exercise of power for good. It is appropriate today, therefore, to reflect on Paul's image of the 'armour of God'. If Paul had simply given a list of noteworthy spiritual words – truth, gospel, righteousness, peace, faith, salvation, Scripture – his letter might have ended quietly with a useful summary of Christian themes on which his readers could reflect. Instead, he gives us a vivid picture that provides a culmination to the theme he has seeded throughout his letter: the cosmic power and sovereignty of God working in Christ. The Greek name for rhetorical devices such as this was *energeia* ('energy', usually translated as 'working') and it was used in order to present an audience with a powerful description of something as if they were actually present to see it. Paul indeed uses precisely this word three times in his letter to the Ephesians: first at 1.19, 'according to the *working* of his great power'; second at 3.7, 'the *working* of his power'; and finally at 4.16, 'as each part is *working* properly'. His point is that the Church, a body equipped with the whole armour of God, with Christ as its head, participates in the working of God's sovereign power over all other powers in the cosmos.

Paul's climax to the letter transports us all to this spiritual realm, all the while emphasizing that, as a body, we can protect ourselves from the evil that threatens us only by committed use of all the gifts of grace God has given us.

COLLECT

God of hosts,
who so kindled the flame of love
in the heart of your servant George
that he bore witness to the risen Lord
by his life and by his death:
give us the same faith and power of love
that we who rejoice in his triumphs
may come to share with him the fullness of the resurrection;
through Jesus Christ your Son our Lord,
who is alive and reigns with you,
in the unity of the Holy Spirit,
one God, now and for ever.

| *Reflection by* **Libby Lane**

Psalms 37.23-end, 148
Isaiah 62.6-10
or Ecclesiasticus 51.13-end
Acts 12.25 – 13.13

Tuesday 30 April
Mark the Evangelist

Acts 12.25 – 13.13

'... will you not stop making crooked' (13.10)

Quietly, St Mark is introduced into the narrative of the Acts of the Apostles. As a companion to Paul, Mark bears witness to the transforming work of Christ to set people on the path of life.

Many who had scattered from Jerusalem at the time of Stephen's martyrdom, at which Saul had been present and of which Saul had approved, had gone north, establishing a Church in Antioch which attracted large numbers of gentile converts. Into this Church comes Saul, its former persecutor, along with Barnabas and Mark. Now those whom he had persecuted are commissioning him to begin his missionary life.

The practice of 'magic' evokes the kind of angry passion so evident in Saul (hereafter known as 'Paul') before his conversion. We see this again later in Acts 19.18-19 when Paul is in Ephesus. Practising magic was prohibited in Deuteronomy 18.10-14. The invocation of spirits in order to interfere in the lives of others was the chief end of magic – the Greek word *perierga* used in Acts 19.19 is also used in 1 Timothy 5.13 to refer to 'busybodies'.

Paul cannot allow a 'busybody' like Elymas to interfere with the Lord's work, and his rebuke brings upon the magician a blindness similar to that experienced by Paul himself on the Damascan road. That darkness enlightened Paul to see and embark upon the Way, and Paul now lends his passion to ensure that others are not diverted from it.

Almighty God,
who enlightened your holy Church
through the inspired witness of your evangelist Saint Mark:
grant that we, being firmly grounded in the truth of the gospel,
may be faithful to its teaching both in word and deed;
through Jesus Christ your Son our Lord,
who is alive and reigns with you,
in the unity of the Holy Spirit,
one God, now and for ever.

COLLECT

Reflection by **Libby Lane** | 137

Wednesday 1 May

Philip and James, Apostles

Psalms 139, 146
Proverbs 4.10-18
James 1.1-12

James 1.1-12

'... whenever you face trials of any kind' (v.2)

As we celebrate Philip and James, we consider the emphasis in the letter of James on repentance. The mention of 'Dispersion' in the prescript to James' letter indicates an underlying purpose to exhort his readers to repentance. Dispersion was punishment for Israel's failure to honour its covenant with God. Older 'Diaspora letters' (e.g. Jeremiah 29.1-23) were sent by authoritative figures in Jerusalem to Diaspora communities with the expectation of repentance followed by restoration. James understands that followers of Christ were the new Israel. He also believes that, like Israel of old, they have fallen prey to sins of various kinds. His letter identifies, for example, neglect of the poor, a servile kowtowing to the rich, gossip and the judgement of others, and a failure to put faith into action.

James, though, considers it a matter for joy when Christians are tempted. The summary explanation James gives of this in his first paragraph is unpacked in the rest of his letter. Temptation, the testing of faith, leads to endurance, which in turn leads to completion. Completion, says James, is to be without lack. He gives two examples of those who lack: doubters who are too unstable to receive from the Lord; and the rich who put their trust elsewhere than Christ. We may lack in other ways.

Only God can provide the completion that enables us to resist such temptation. Growing in our trust of God, in all circumstances, is a cause for joy. Indeed, it is through such growth comes 'the crown of life'.

COLLECT

Almighty Father,
whom truly to know is eternal life:
teach us to know your Son Jesus Christ
as the way, the truth, and the life;
that we may follow the steps of your holy apostles Philip and James,
and walk steadfastly in the way that leads to your glory;
through Jesus Christ your Son our Lord,
who is alive and reigns with you,
in the unity of the Holy Spirit,
one God, now and for ever.

| *Reflection by* **Libby Lane**

Psalms **28**, 29 *or* 14, **15**, 16
Deuteronomy 4.1-14
John 21.1-14

John 21.1-14

'Come and have breakfast' (v.12)

This scene is replete with the sheer physicality of resurrection life: the business of fishing, a charcoal fire, cooked fish, bread. It is also alive with symbols: the untorn net, the number of fish, the fish themselves. However, it is feeding, and being fed, that is at the heart of the story. In common with the other resurrection appearances in John's Gospel, the disciples recognize Jesus only gradually. The emphasis in this chapter though is on Jesus' invitation to a meal, rather than on the need to open the eye of faith.

While the tone of the story is 'eucharistic', it lacks the features of the institution of the Lord's Supper found in the other Gospels. Jesus feeds the disciples with bread and fish. Although there are already fish cooking on the fire when the disciples land their catch, some of their haul is added to the meal. This recalls the miracle of the feeding of the 5,000, in which a small boy contributes the initial elements, a link established when Jesus calls the disciples 'children'. The bulging nets after a night of futile toil reflect not only the miraculous plenty that Jesus provides but also remind us of the calling of the disciples, as told in Luke's Gospel.

As disciples, we are called and nourished by Jesus. We, too, need to take the time to sit and eat with him, and each other, so that we also may be fed and nourished for the work of the kingdom of God.

COLLECT

Almighty Father,
you have given your only Son to die for our sins
and to rise again for our justification:
grant us so to put away the leaven of malice and wickedness
that we may always serve you
in pureness of living and truth;
through the merits of your Son Jesus Christ our Lord,
who is alive and reigns with you,
in the unity of the Holy Spirit,
one God, now and for ever.

Reflection by **Libby Lane**

Friday 3 May

Psalms 57, **61** *or* 17, **19**
Deuteronomy 4.15-31
John 21.15-19

John 21.15-19

'... he said to him, "Follow me."' (v.19)

With breakfast over, the details of the setting slip away. The focus now is on an intimate moment between Jesus and Peter. The three-fold questioning of Peter by Jesus cannot help but echo the prediction of Peter's three-fold denial of Jesus as told earlier in John's Gospel (John 13.38). On that occasion, Jesus had prophesied, obliquely, that Peter would one day follow him into a martyr's death, and Peter had avowed that he would be willing to lay down his life for Jesus. Peter's words then echoed the language used to describe the Good Shepherd, in John 10.11, who 'lays down his life for the sheep'.

Before such a destiny will be realized, however, Peter has work to do. There are sheep in need of tending and feeding. They need to be pastored. John's shaping of the story of Peter's rehabilitation becomes a meditation upon the meaning of discipleship. In bringing Peter back into the fold after his denial of him during his trial, Jesus searches the depths of Peter's soul. He wants to know that Peter's words and actions are united in their focus on Jesus as the bedrock for the future Church.

Those who are to be fed by Peter belong not to him but to Jesus and are therefore highly precious. As a true leader of others, Peter holds a sacred trust, exercised only by virtue of his obedience to Jesus' invitation to follow him.

COLLECT

Almighty Father,
you have given your only Son to die for our sins
and to rise again for our justification:
grant us so to put away the leaven of malice and wickedness
that we may always serve you
in pureness of living and truth;
through the merits of your Son Jesus Christ our Lord,
who is alive and reigns with you,
in the unity of the Holy Spirit,
one God, now and for ever.

| *Reflection by* **Libby Lane**

Psalms 63, **84** *or* 20, 21, **23**   **Saturday 4 May**
Deuteronomy 4.32-40
John 21.20-end

John 21.20-end

'... the disciple whom Jesus loved' (v.20)

The 'beloved disciple' is a mysterious figure, attested as the writer and witness to 'these things'. He is not named in the list of seven disciples identified as present for this early morning encounter with the risen Jesus, but appears in the narrative at verse 7 as the one who recognizes the Lord from the boat.

The theme of this brief exchange between Peter and Jesus concerning the beloved disciple returns to the theme of discipleship, which appears throughout the Gospel. It highlights a contrast between two different models: the bold, dramatic style of Peter, with its passionate responses, brave undertakings, misunderstandings and abject failures set beside the quiet intimacy and mutuality between Jesus and the beloved disciple. In this latter model there is no vested authority, no designated responsibility of leadership, no crisis, no dramatic end; just an enduring and humble witness to the reality of the risen Lord. Neither is to be reckoned superior. They recognize different personalities within the body of Christ.

All this is compressed into Peter's question and Jesus' answer. Peter needs to be reminded that his turbulent energy and boundless passion must be disciplined and focused on Jesus. That is to be the shape of his discipleship. Others' faithfulness will take a different shape. What gifts and personality do we bring to our obedience to Jesus' call, 'Follow me'?

Risen Christ,
for whom no door is locked, no entrance barred:
open the doors of our hearts,
that we may seek the good of others
and walk the joyful road of sacrifice and peace,
to the praise of God the Father.

COLLECT

Reflection by **Libby Lane**   141

Monday 6 May

Ephesians 1.1-14

'Blessed be the God and Father of our Lord Jesus Christ' (v.3)

In some ways, Paul's letter to the Ephesians is a difficult letter to fathom. Its sentences are long (verses 3 to 14 are a whole sentence in the Greek!), and the exact purpose of the letter is hard to ascertain. Taken at face value, however, this first half may be described as a proclamation of the salvation experienced by both the writer and his readers – and, of course, by us too. So, take a deep breath and enter into this ancient text with its timeless words of praise.

In order to look forward, we need to reflect backwards. The invocation of blessing is there to remind us of what God has done so that we might be ready to accept the teaching that will follow. The consequence of God's intervention in the world through Jesus Christ means that every aspect of Christian living needs to be refracted through that lens. We cannot move forward unless we accept the absolute certainty of what God has done; this becomes the guiding light for all our lives.

One of the reasons why Paul is often both liked and disliked is that he has a canny knack of reminding us of the basics. Stepping out with the words of this letter means that we hold that foundation of blessing with one hand and with the other reach forward in hope.

COLLECT

Almighty Father,
who in your great mercy gladdened the disciples
 with the sight of the risen Lord:
give us such knowledge of his presence with us,
that we may be strengthened and sustained by his risen life
and serve you continually in righteousness and truth;
through Jesus Christ your Son our Lord,
who is alive and reigns with you,
in the unity of the Holy Spirit,
one God, now and for ever.

Reflection by **Helen-Ann Hartley**

Psalms **98**, 99, 100 *or* 32, **36**
Deuteronomy 5.22-end
Ephesians 1.15-end

Ephesians 1.15-end

'I do not cease to give thanks for you as I remember you in my prayers' (v.16)

Here we have Paul's prayer for his readers (or listeners as the case may be), and it is one that is grounded in ceaseless thanks. I once knew a person who at any available opportunity would say 'thank you'. This was to the point where I began to get a bit irritated by it. So I asked, 'Why do you always say "thank you"?', to which the reply was, 'Why not? If we all said thank you a bit more, we might all get along better.'

At times I struggle with words that may be forced or appear empty of true meaning, but Paul's thanksgiving for his audience – his companions in faith – was a genuine extension of his love for them. From the blessing of the previous verses, the thanksgiving now given here connects praise to practice: God's blessing leads to a response of praise, which in turn leads to a thanksgiving for all that God has done.

The purpose these verses serve is to emphasize the glory and power of God, which is poured out upon the Church: Christ's Body. This is a startling reminder of the responsibility of the Church to be that dynamic, living reflection of Christ in our communities and in our world. Christ himself is beyond all earthly powers; the challenge for the Church is not to get caught up in power but rather to reflect that higher authority of God.

COLLECT

Risen Christ,
you filled your disciples with boldness and fresh hope:
strengthen us to proclaim your risen life
and fill us with your peace,
to the glory of God the Father.

Reflection by **Helen-Ann Hartley**   143

Wednesday 8 May

Ephesians 2.1-10

'... by grace you have been saved' (v.5)

The picture painted by Paul in these verses is not particularly edifying. Reflective of the general complex mess of life, Paul is realistic about the ways in which our behaviour can place us outside God's realm. Yet the utterly remarkable thing about the story of redemption is the power of God's grace alone. Grace is the only thing that brings about salvation.

Paul's language here is blunt and absolute: 'dead', 'children of wrath' – it's all rather gloomy and foreboding, almost as if Paul has to stress the worst in order then to give us the best news. This news changes everything for the reader, because Christ's resurrection was completely transformative of the world order. This transformation lifts us into a new realm, but, as before, this is not without consequence. Paul seems to be drumming the point home to make it stick. It's a classic teaching tool; we aren't meant to forget what the implications of this are for our lives.

Grace is free. What we do does not merit its reward, and yet, because this has happened, our lives are framed in response. God expects us to act as a result of this grace, treating ourselves and others around us in the light of this overwhelming gift. That is both a challenge and an immense opportunity. How will we respond today?

COLLECT

Almighty Father,
who in your great mercy gladdened the disciples
    with the sight of the risen Lord:
give us such knowledge of his presence with us,
that we may be strengthened and sustained by his risen life
and serve you continually in righteousness and truth;
through Jesus Christ your Son our Lord,
who is alive and reigns with you,
in the unity of the Holy Spirit,
one God, now and for ever.

| *Reflection by* **Helen-Ann Hartley**

Psalm **136** *or* **37***
Deuteronomy 7.1-11
Ephesians 2.11-end

Thursday 9 May

Ephesians 2.11-end
'So then you are no longer strangers and aliens ...' (v.19)

Whenever we make an excursion to a new country, there comes a point when we begin to feel more 'at home'. Sometimes this is simply because we have got used to our new environment for however long we are to be there, but at other times it is as a result of a new relationship. We are in that moment no longer considered 'foreign' but 'part of the furniture' (as the well-known song from *Oliver!* goes). That can be an incredibly powerful experience. Even if it is just a fleeting glimpse of recognition, all the same it can change who we are and how we feel about where we are.

One of the recurring themes of Paul's letters is the relationship between Jews and gentiles, and how the unity that Paul proclaims is now possible because of Christ. Although a tension remains, Paul is anxious to remind his readers that Christ's death and resurrection have changed the landscape of how identity is built. The Holy Spirit plays a vital role in this new reality, which suggests an ongoing dynamic and fluid structure, not one that is fixed for all time.

Could this suggest a radical sense of inclusion beyond that which we can at present imagine? These verses would suggest it can. To be a dwelling place for God offers a renewed hope of hospitality for everyone. Put simply: all are welcome.

Risen Christ,
you filled your disciples with boldness and fresh hope:
strengthen us to proclaim your risen life
and fill us with your peace,
to the glory of God the Father.

COLLECT

Friday 10 May

Psalm 107 *or* 31
Deuteronomy 7.12-end
Ephesians 3.1-13

Ephesians 3.1-13

'This is the reason that I Paul am a prisoner for Christ Jesus for the sake of you Gentiles' (v.1)

Some of the most profound and humbling experiences of God's love I have ever had have been in the company of persecuted Christians. It may be a cliché, but such experiences can radically shift your perspective on your own 'problems'. Interestingly enough, at the heart of such narratives of hope is a strong desire to give thanks to God. This then connects us back to a major theme of this whole letter: thanksgiving for what God has done and for what this new reality means for our lives.

Paul (as he does elsewhere in his letters) tells his audience of his commissioning by God to be an apostle, while emphasizing his *lack* of credentials. All the more so remarkable, then, is his capacity to unfold the mystery of God. Yet again, this is not simply for the sake of keeping things in secret but somehow so that by grasping its possibility, the Church (and we) can enable that transformation to take place in our lives and in the lives of those around us.

That 'wave effect' of faith is one that enabled the early Church to grow rapidly. Lives were transformed, and people renewed in the hope of this most ancient of stories made real in their lives. Paul had certainly experienced that in his own life. Who better then to speak words of resurrection to those yet to hear the good news?

COLLECT

Almighty Father,
who in your great mercy gladdened the disciples
    with the sight of the risen Lord:
give us such knowledge of his presence with us,
that we may be strengthened and sustained by his risen life
and serve you continually in righteousness and truth;
through Jesus Christ your Son our Lord,
who is alive and reigns with you,
in the unity of the Holy Spirit,
one God, now and for ever.

| *Reflection by* **Helen-Ann Hartley**

Psalms 108, **110**, 111 *or* 41, **42**, 43
Deuteronomy 8
Ephesians 3.14-end

Saturday 11 May

Ephesians 3.14-end

'Now to him who by the power and work within us is able to accomplish abundantly far more than all we can ask or imagine' (v.20)

Sometimes you know a verse so well that hearing it in its context brings fresh meaning. I have a colleague who always uses these words as a blessing at the end of a service. Her own life over the past few years has been incredibly stressful, at times harrowing, and almost always full of uncertainty. Whenever I hear these words, I think of my friend and her leadership in a place of despair, and the constant faithfulness of God to uphold and renew. This I think is what drives Paul in this letter, particularly in the light of his imprisoned location.

Another aspect of these verses that catches me unawares is the notion that the love of Christ transcends knowledge. This surely is an invitation for us to dwell with the word. We cannot comprehend the enormity of God's love in Jesus Christ, nor should we even try to do so. Paul's prayer here reminds us that the Spirit gives us an inner strength, that Christ is present in our hearts, and that the relationship of the love of God gives us a firm foundation. All of these elements are present in the lives of those who believe, and we would do well to be reminded of them. When we are tossed and turned by life's events, God's love holds us steady.

Risen Christ,
you filled your disciples with boldness and fresh hope:
strengthen us to proclaim your risen life
and fill us with your peace,
to the glory of God the Father.

COLLECT

Reflection by **Helen-Ann Hartley** | 147

Monday 13 May

Ephesians 4.1-16

'The gifts he gave were that some would be apostles, some prophets, some evangelists, some pastors and teachers' (v.11)

The letter switches gear at this point towards exhortation for practical action, demonstrated by the verse above. The significance of this, however, is the somewhat radical idea that it is Jesus who gives gifts having triumphantly entered heaven.

But what is the purpose of all of this? Paul tells us, again stressing the importance of unity; while it is important to recognize that the Spirit binds those who believe together in unity, it is up to us to make that a reality. In other words, we have to work that out in our own context. What does unity look like? The answer is all around us (which of course may also tell us what unity is not like!).

Paul doesn't talk about 'gifts of the Spirit' but rather the ways in which the Spirit inspires individuals to certain tasks for the purpose of building up the whole Body. This is neatly phrased by Paul as a 'growing up', a maturing away from child-like interest in all things shiny and new, towards a more considered fullness of life.

It's not all simple of course, because those who purport to be 'mature' are often not, while those who seem 'simple' can tell forth the profoundest of truths. So, it would seem, a wise discernment is needed to join all the parts of the body together.

C
O
L
L
E
C
T

Almighty God,
whose Son Jesus Christ is the resurrection and the life:
raise us, who trust in him,
from the death of sin to the life of righteousness,
that we may seek those things which are above,
where he reigns with you
in the unity of the Holy Spirit,
one God, now and for ever.

Psalms 16, 147.1-12
1 Samuel 2.27-35
Acts 2.37-end

Tuesday 14 May
Matthias the Apostle

Acts 2.37-end

*'They devoted themselves to the apostles' teaching and fellowship,
to the breaking of bread and the prayers' (v.42)*

According to Acts, Matthias was the apostle chosen to replace Judas Iscariot. Matthias was (uniquely) not chosen by Jesus himself, and he became an apostle before the outpouring of the Holy Spirit at Pentecost. These verses offer us a broader context into which we can place Matthias' ministry, that of the continuity of discipleship: devotion to teaching and gathering together, breaking bread and praying. You could easily say, then, that the life of the Church today closely mirrors that of the early Church. Even if we don't baptize three thousand in one day, we can make a difference to the lives of an infinite number of people, if we choose to engage.

A lot is said in contemporary narratives about growth of the Church – often couched in ways that can lead to anxiety and/or to despair. But this is an unhelpful perspective because it fails to recognize that the life of the early Church was (as it is today) a complex bundle of highs and lows. So, talk of growth is meant to inspire because the need for growth never expires or passes its 'use-by' date.

If we talk about growth, we are actually talking about the expansion of God's kingdom – that was the very life-blood of the early Church, and the work of the apostles that we remember today. The challenge for us is to see our own participation in this grand narrative as one that makes a difference, however large, however small. God is in it all.

Almighty God,
who in the place of the traitor Judas
chose your faithful servant Matthias
to be of the number of the Twelve:
preserve your Church from false apostles
and, by the ministry of faithful pastors and teachers,
keep us steadfast in your truth;
through Jesus Christ your Son our Lord,
who is alive and reigns with you,
in the unity of the Holy Spirit,
one God, now and for ever.

COLLECT

Reflection by **Helen-Ann Hartley** | 149

Wednesday 15 May

Psalm **135** *or* **119.57-80**
Deuteronomy 10.12-end
Ephesians 5.1-14

Ephesians 5.1-14

*'Entirely out of place is obscene, silly, and vulgar talk; but instead,
let there be thanksgiving' (v.4)*

Sometimes I wonder what Paul would have made of social media? While I wouldn't want to hazard a guess, I suspect he might have found a way of using it to his advantage. Yet it is true that this particular verse tends to make for uncomfortable reading. We are reminded again of the central theme of thanksgiving that drives the whole of Ephesians, thanksgiving that both drives right behaviour and is the result of it.

There is a real sense in this passage of a life before and a life after, a life of darkness and a life now lived in the light. This is sometimes reflected in the way Christians speak about their faith journeys, but it isn't always the case that we have a clear before and after. The boundaries can sometimes be blurry. What is important, however, is the real sense of a life newly lived that stands in contrast to the old.

However we choose to describe that, there are surely points of change and transformation when we make a conscious decision to act differently. Paul's own narrative of faith is a good example of this, and gives us what German theologian Jürgen Moltmann describes as a 'wayfaring character of hope'.

If we turn our attention this day to how we present ourselves to the world as Christians, what is there in our words and in our manner of speech that enables Christ to be known?

COLLECT

Almighty God,
whose Son Jesus Christ is the resurrection and the life:
raise us, who trust in him,
from the death of sin to the life of righteousness,
that we may seek those things which are above,
where he reigns with you
in the unity of the Holy Spirit,
one God, now and for ever.

Reflection by **Helen-Ann Hartley**

Psalm 118 *or* 56, 57 (63*)
Deuteronomy 11.8-end
Ephesians 5.15-end

Thursday 16 May

Ephesians 5.15-end

'Wives, be subject to your husbands as you are to the Lord' (v.22)

There is no escaping the discomfort of this verse, and the subsequent verses, in our contemporary age. Nor can we deny the way in which these verses have been used – and continue to be used – to promulgate violence against women, and the oppression of girls and younger women in particular. The 'household code' (for this is an example of such a literary type) can be a tricky passage to interpret. Surely this is a prime example of the need to read biblical passages very carefully indeed, taking full account of context.

It is also an invitation to look more carefully at what Paul is saying as a whole here, because Paul turns it back on those who would ordinarily not have considered themselves liable for their behaviour. So, husbands are to love their wives. There is a deeper obligation of relationship; it is not a one-sided endeavour.

Perhaps at the heart of Paul's words is a call to re-examine the social order (certainly we need to take this passage and the rest of the letter into account here). What might the implications of that be for us today?

If texts like this are going to be of any use to us today, we need to be able also to challenge them, and to challenge the way in which they are misused. Paul's call to thanksgiving is done to enable a life to be lived in its fullness. Where many are denied that fullness today, we have a duty to speak up.

Risen Christ,
faithful shepherd of your Father's sheep:
teach us to hear your voice
and to follow your command,
that all your people may be gathered into one flock,
to the glory of God the Father.

COLLECT

Reflection by **Helen-Ann Hartley** | 151

Friday 17 May

Psalms **33** *or* **51**, 54
Deuteronomy 12.1-14
Ephesians 6.1-9

Ephesians 6.1-9

'And, fathers, do not provoke your children to anger, but bring them up in the discipline and instruction of the Lord' (v.4)

This verse is a good example of the radical nature of Paul's instructions. The notion that parents should not make their children angry is what a friend of mine describes as 'daring'. Similarly, masters of slaves are told not to threaten their slaves, who are themselves fully part of the household. All are under the authority of God, who doesn't put labels on people according to their particular status.

But let's take a moment to consider what else Paul is advocating here, namely some Christian education at home. Education in a home-based context was not a particularly innovative injunction, but extending that to teaching in the faith was new. Paul is saying that the responsibility for instruction in Godly ways lies at home.

Have we lost this in our 'there's surely an app for that' mindset? A friend of mine whose daughter has a young child recently showed me such an online facility for toilet-training! The danger of outsourcing everything means that we become more and more removed from our own capacity to contribute to one another's development, whether that means bearing with potty-training or anything else!

If we are to have any hope of helping to educate the next generation in the faith, then we ourselves need to commit to ongoing learning and growth. If we do that, then we can participate in the radical re-envisioning of relationships that lie at the heart of these challenging verses.

COLLECT | Almighty God,
whose Son Jesus Christ is the resurrection and the life:
raise us, who trust in him,
from the death of sin to the life of righteousness,
that we may seek those things which are above,
where he reigns with you
in the unity of the Holy Spirit,
one God, now and for ever.

| *Reflection by* **Helen-Ann Hartley**

Psalm **34** *or* **68**
Deuteronomy 15.1-18
Ephesians 6.10-end

Saturday 18 May

Ephesians 6.10-end

'Finally, be strong in the Lord and in the strength of his power'
(v.10)

For some, the overtly militaristic tone of these concluding verses of the letter can be uncomfortable or embarrassing. Yet they come out of a context in which military might was ever-present. Again, as with so much of this letter, Paul is encouraging his audience to look and look again, to see and reimagine what life might be like if we are clothed with Christ.

Paul is also speaking into a context where there was a strong sense of a battle against evil, and I wonder if we have lost awareness of what that looks and feels like? Having experience of places where there is a tangible presence of evil forces us to equip ourselves with what can be described as armour, even if that is of light. The narrative of our faith is full of such imagery, so we should not be so reluctant to embrace its potential.

This concluding section clearly places the whole of the Christian life in a context of a struggle between good and evil. This was fundamental to Paul, so much so that we cannot ignore it without rejecting the entirety of his message, so passionately and keenly delivered.

As we take our leave of this letter, perhaps you have been struck again by the fervour of its words? There is no doubt that it confronts us with a lived context far in time from our own, yet very present in its tone and challenges. What, we might well ask, has changed for us today?

COLLECT

Risen Christ,
faithful shepherd of your Father's sheep:
teach us to hear your voice
and to follow your command,
that all your people may be gathered into one flock,
to the glory of God the Father.

Reflection by **Helen-Ann Hartley** | 153

Monday 20 May

Psalm **145** *or* **71**
Deuteronomy 16.1-20
1 Peter 1.1-12

1 Peter 1.1-12

'To the exiles .... grace and peace be yours in abundance' (vv.1-2)

This letter is written to 'the exiles'. The word variously means 'sojourner', 'migrant', 'refugee' or 'resident alien'. It seems to have been a name the first Christians chose for themselves. An exile is an outsider. The exiles are far from home – and where they are they do not belong. This appears to be a circular letter written to widely scattered Christian communities across a huge area covering modern-day Turkey and beyond. Nothing more is known about them except the faith they share.

Believers today might well be surprised to be greeted as 'exiles' on a Sunday morning. But when the first Christians turned to the Old Testament to help them reflect on their call and identity, they were drawn to, and quoted from, the periods of exodus wandering and exiled living more than any other part of the scriptures.

So one of the earliest self-chosen names for the Christian church reflects a life shaped by the experience of enforced or chosen mobility, vulnerable exile, worldly powerlessness and disorientating change. And within this was found the vocation to live and hope in a land that is far from home. It was a call to sing the Lord's song in a strange land.

Christian discipleship is always a call to a certain kind of homelessness. We are to grow wherever we find ourselves.

COLLECT

Almighty God,
who through your only-begotten Son Jesus Christ
have overcome death and opened to us the gate of everlasting life:
grant that, as by your grace going before us
you put into our minds good desires,
so by your continual help
we may bring them to good effect;
through Jesus Christ our risen Lord,
who is alive and reigns with you,
in the unity of the Holy Spirit,
one God, now and for ever.

| *Reflection by* **David Runcorn**

Psalms **19**, 147.1-12 *or* **73**
Deuteronomy 17.8-end
1 Peter 1.13-end

Tuesday 21 May

1 Peter 1.13-end
'All flesh is like grass ...' (v.24)

Visiting a very ancient church on holiday, I noticed from the gravestones and memorial plaques how brief life had been for so many. Those generations (like communities in many parts of the world today) knew only too well how fragile and short this earthly life could be.

That life is brief and impermanent – as fleeting as the meadow grasses – is a repeated stress in the Bible. Human existence is a passing thing. This is not stressed to make us depressed. An honest acceptance of the finitude of things and the presence of death changes everything. It asks what we are living for. It helps us shape our priorities. After all, without death nothing would have any more importance than anything else. Life would have no direction or importance.

By contrast, Peter never tires of spelling out in his letter how a Christian is one who has been born into a life that is *im*perishable. This is the new life God makes his gift.

Peter returns to this again and again. He urges his readers to make sure they are living for something lasting and enduring – a life founded on something so much more than our income level, the vagaries of history, the luck of the draw, accident of birth, good looks, or the happy accident of being in the right time and the right place.

COLLECT

Risen Christ,
your wounds declare your love for the world
and the wonder of your risen life:
give us compassion and courage
to risk ourselves for those we serve,
to the glory of God the Father.

Reflection by **David Runcorn** | 155

Wednesday 22 May

Psalms **30**, 147.13-end *or* **77**
Deuteronomy 18.9-end
1 Peter 2.1-10

1 Peter 2.1-10

'The stone that the builders rejected' (v.7)

On the north coast of Cornwall a now abandoned quarry has been cut deep into the sheer sea cliffs. Standing alone and battered in the middle of the quarry floor is a tall pillar of rock. To the expert eye of quarriers and builders it was flawed. They could not use it so they simply cut round it into purer seams. There were similar stumps and columns, but none so large.

Jesus was crucified in a quarry outside Jerusalem by a stone similarly rejected by builders – one that by awful irony had the look of a skull. There is evidence that the Christians celebrated Easter there. Peter may have that stone in mind in this passage.

'Come to him', says Peter. Build your lives on him. Peter's first readers knew what it was to feel on the edge of what society thought important and valuable. They knew what it was to be mocked and treated as irrelevant. So did Jesus, says Peter. But who would have believed it? – the stone rejected is revealed as the foundation stone of life itself.

To build with materials that have been rejected by professionals as flawed and unsuitable is not only foolish, it is surely dangerous. But this is exactly what God can do with us. So, borrowing the image of the temple, Peter invites us to build our lives on Christ. Like living stones.

COLLECT

Almighty God,
who through your only-begotten Son Jesus Christ
have overcome death and opened to us the gate of everlasting life:
grant that, as by your grace going before us
    you put into our minds good desires,
so by your continual help
we may bring them to good effect;
through Jesus Christ our risen Lord,
who is alive and reigns with you,
in the unity of the Holy Spirit,
one God, now and for ever.

| *Reflection by* **David Runcorn**

Psalms **57**, 148 *or* **78.1-39***
Deuteronomy 19
1 Peter 2.11-end

Thursday 23 May

1 Peter 2.11-end

'Conduct yourselves honourably among the Gentiles' (v.12)

There is much in a plain reading of today's passage to baffle or even offend modern ears and beliefs. What is Peter thinking teaching Christians to accept uncritically the authority of every human authority? Or telling slaves to accept and submit to the authority of their owners however harsh their treatment?

It helps to understand this as a practical strategy for those living for Christ in an uncomprehending and hostile world. This was a mission strategy for Christians who found themselves living as vulnerable minorities in the midst of societies that did not share their faith or values. 'Conduct yourselves honourably among the Gentiles'. When you are living as sojourners within social regimes that give you no voice or means of negotiating, the wisest option may be to live in such a way that your quality of life commends the faith you hold and leaves those watching curious and perhaps attracted. And for their comfort and inspiration, Peter reminds them they have Jesus himself for company, who submitted to suffering and abuse without retaliating or repaying evil for evil. The reality is that there are Christian communities in today's world who are living just like that.

If we have never had to work out faithful living in such a context, then perhaps we might pause and pray today for those who have costly experience of doing just that.

Risen Christ,
your wounds declare your love for the world
and the wonder of your risen life:
give us compassion and courage
to risk ourselves for those we serve,
to the glory of God the Father.

COLLECT

Friday 24 May

Psalms **138**, 149 *or* **55**
Deuteronomy 21.22 – 22.8
1 Peter 3.1-12

1 Peter 3.1-12

'... love for one another, a tender heart, and a humble mind' (v.8)

The ancient Greek had what were called 'Household Codes'. These were written to the man of the household to guide him in the ordering of the home. The codes assumed a patriarchal and hierarchical world with the man at the centre, ruling over his household. He was to exercise absolute unilateral authority over his subordinate wife, children and slaves: 'A husband and father rules over wife and children' (Aristotle); 'The woman is in all things inferior to the man' (Josephus).

In Peter's letter is one of several examples of early Christian versions of these. Western society today starts from such different assumptions, it is easy to miss how radically those first Christians had begun to rewrite those codes in the light of their new-found faith – a task still continuing today. Quite simply, Jesus changes everything. One example is the way Peter addresses wives, slaves and children directly rather than just the man. Though there are still cultural differences in the world described here, Peter urges a community in which all participate freely in a spirit of mutual honour that reflects and imitates the love they have received in Christ.

He calls all followers of Christ to live in humility and mutual respect. The example is Jesus, who time and again willingly chose to place himself in a position of submission and taught his followers to do the same.

COLLECT

Almighty God,
who through your only-begotten Son Jesus Christ
have overcome death and opened to us the gate of everlasting life:
grant that, as by your grace going before us
    you put into our minds good desires,
so by your continual help
we may bring them to good effect;
through Jesus Christ our risen Lord,
who is alive and reigns with you,
in the unity of the Holy Spirit,
one God, now and for ever.

| *Reflection by* **David Runcorn**

Psalms **146**, 150 *or* **76**, 79
Deuteronomy 24.5-end
1 Peter 3.13-end

Saturday 25 May

1 Peter 3.13-end
'Do not fear what they fear' (v.14)

'Always be ready to make your defence', says Peter. It takes a certain confidence to initiate conversation with someone about the Christian faith. But Peter is talking about being ready and prepared when the response of others to us is aggressive or hostile. We have already noted that Peter is writing to communities where being too active or vocal about what they believe might be a dangerous thing to do. This is more than a matter of sensitivity. In some parts in the world today it is actually illegal. It is not insignificant that these words of Peter are offered alongside repeated observations about the likelihood that they will be suffering for what they believe.

Peter describes the surrounding society of his day as fearful. Anxious and insecure societies are often dangerous places for minority groups. Blaming and scapegoating others is a familiar way of bolstering our own need to feel in control.

In such a world, a community found living with a quiet security that has nothing to do with its actual status or power in the world will surely make an impact. When people notice and ask you why you are hopeful and living without fear, be ready to tell them. Be able, gently and courteously, to put it into words. Tell them about Jesus. Can you do that?

Risen Christ,
your wounds declare your love for the world
and the wonder of your risen life:
give us compassion and courage
to risk ourselves for those we serve,
to the glory of God the Father.

COLLECT

Reflection by **David Runcorn** | 159

Monday 27 May

1 Peter 4.1-11

'The end of all things is near' (v.7)

Another prediction about the end of the world came and went recently. We are still here. These days it is an idea more easily mocked than believed. But the first Christians lived with an intense sense that they were living on the threshold of a new world – one as yet unseen but very near. It was a belief that shaped all their priorities and choices in life. Of course it does.

A criticism is that end-of-world beliefs are simply 'other worldly' and therefore of no earthly use. There are certainly escapist versions of this belief. But here in Peter's letter the vision of the future adds depth and urgency to the way the believer lives in the here and now. Our hope is for this world – not of an escape to another one. Furthermore, we are accountable to God for our earthly lives.

In another era, Lord Shaftesbury, the great English social reformer, would say at the end of his life how powerfully motivated he was, daily, by the conviction that Christ was going to return. He knew he needed to live in readiness and to be accountable.

It may be that one of the things that leaves contemporary living so impoverished is our loss of a sense of eternity – and with it a vision for our part in a bigger, in-breaking story. What if, after all the jokes, it really is very near?

COLLECT

God our redeemer,
you have delivered us from the power of darkness
and brought us into the kingdom of your Son:
grant, that as by his death he has recalled us to life,
so by his continual presence in us he may raise us
    to eternal joy;
through Jesus Christ your Son our Lord,
who is alive and reigns with you,
in the unity of the Holy Spirit,
one God, now and for ever.

| *Reflection by* **David Runcorn**

Psalms 124, 125, **126**, 127
or 87, **89.1-18**
Deuteronomy 28.1-14
1 Peter 4.12-end

Tuesday 28 May

1 Peter 4.12-end

'... rejoice in so far as you are sharing Christ's sufferings' (v.13)

When life treats us unjustly – and especially when we were seeking to do what was right and good – it is tempting to ask: 'Why me?' It's not fair. We may also expect that as a follower of Christ, God might have offered us some protection. This is not a new question. It sounds as if Peter was being asked this very question by hard-pressed believers. Peter reminds them they follow one who did no wrong but who suffered and was rejected by the world. The Christian discipleship is a call, at times, to share in the sufferings of Christ. If the world rejected him, it will reject his followers. We are called to take up our cross and follow him.

This is a daunting teaching. But Peter is speaking about something more than just enduring the hardship and persecution when it comes. He stresses the sheer honour of being identified with Jesus in this way. Rejoice in this!

General Booth, the founder of the Salvation Army, once took some of his uniformed recruits into a pub. When one of them tried to engage someone in conversation the man angrily spat in his face. Shaken, he reached for his handkerchief, but before he could wipe his face, Booth shouted: 'Don't wipe it off. It is your badge of honour!'

COLLECT

Risen Christ,
by the lakeside you renewed your call to your disciples:
help your Church to obey your command
and draw the nations to the fire of your love,
to the glory of God the Father.

Wednesday 29 May

Psalms **132**, 133 *or* **119.105-128**
Deuteronomy 28.58-end
1 Peter 5

1 Peter 5

'... clothe yourselves with humility' (v.5)

Peter calls himself an 'elder'. He may be of older years at the time he is writing. He may also be one of a dwindling group of believers still alive who actually followed Jesus on earth through his life, death and resurrection.

What does he remember most at this point as he looks back over all he witnessed? He writes here about humility. He speaks of it as being like a garment we must fasten on and wear. Some translations speak of putting on the 'apron of humility'. This would be the clothing of slaves at work. And it may be a particular memory of Peter's. At the last supper, in a way that shocked all the disciples, Jesus clothed himself and served them as a slave, washing their feet. This humble serving love of Jesus was beneath his own sense of dignity and pride, and he refused it at first. It is easy to imagine this memory burning in him even now.

Humility is the quality that shapes all relationships in the fellowship of believers – across ages, gender and hierarchy. This humility of mutual honouring and loving submission is not just the way we serve Christ in one another. It is always the way he chooses to serve us. The love of God is always beneath us.

COLLECT

God our redeemer,
you have delivered us from the power of darkness
and brought us into the kingdom of your Son:
grant, that as by his death he has recalled us to life,
so by his continual presence in us he may raise us
    to eternal joy;
through Jesus Christ your Son our Lord,
who is alive and reigns with you,
in the unity of the Holy Spirit,
one God, now and for ever.

| *Reflection by* **David Runcorn**

Psalms 110, 150
Isaiah 52.7-end
Hebrews 7. [11-25] 26-end

Thursday 30 May
Ascension Day

Hebrews 7. [11-25] 26-end
'You are a priest for ever' (v.17)

The dramatic scene of the ascension of Jesus to heaven brings to glorious completion the story that began with one who emptied himself of all his heavenly identity and honour to be born of Mary, in the manger, in Bethlehem. A too literal imagination does not help us here. Christ has not actually left us. He is not now 'somewhere else', further away. In fact he is *nearer*. In his ascension he ascends to 'fill all things' with his presence (Ephesians 4.10).

In a complex passage, the writer to the Hebrews seeks to spell out the uniqueness of Christ – and so the uniqueness of what he has done for us. He had no sin and so no need to be reconciled or make recompense. That means that in his incarnation, suffering and cross he can choose, regardless of personal cost, to make a free gift of himself for our sake. He is, in the imaginative language of Hebrews, the high priest who makes a perfect sacrifice. And in that moment, the whole debt economy of sin, guilt and punishment collapses. It becomes irrelevant. The whole religious industry of prayer, sacrifice and priesthood becomes irrelevant – though it never achieved the job anyway. This is not the basis on which God chooses to know us, accept us or love us. It is all gift.

COLLECT

Grant, we pray, almighty God,
that as we believe your only-begotten Son our Lord Jesus Christ
to have ascended into the heavens,
so we in heart and mind may also ascend
and with him continually dwell;
who is alive and reigns with you,
in the unity of the Holy Spirit,
one God, now and for ever.

Reflection by **David Runcorn** | 163

Friday 31 May

Visit of the Blessed Virgin Mary
to Elizabeth

Psalms 85, 150
1 Samuel 2.1-10
Mark 3.31-end

1 Samuel 2.1-10

'My heart exults in the Lord' (v.1)

On the day we remember the visit of Elizabeth to the pregnant Virgin Mary, this reading recalls events from much earlier in Israel's history. The song of Mary is based upon the much earlier song of a woman called Hannah.

Mary understood that if she, a woman, a virgin, an unknown village girl, had been chosen and honoured by God, a new world was surely beginning: a social revolution that turns everything upside down. For the Lord has looked on *me*, she sings. Mary has been described as 'the first of the little people'. She is the first sign of a coming kingdom in which the poor, voiceless and marginalized have an honoured place and actually minister and declare the ways of God in the world.

Hannah was not a virgin. She was barren. But virginity and infertility in the Bible are symbols of human powerlessness. They are states that can only become gifts of life if God wills it.

Hannah's story is found at the beginning of the huge saga of Samuel. Spanning two volumes, it tells of the journey of Israel from tribes to nation and kingdom and of the towering male figures of Samuel and David. But rather than being an affecting little story about where the 'real' leaders of that era came from, Hannah's testimony is the theological key to all that follows. Her song is a subversive celebration of this.

COLLECT

Mighty God,
by whose grace Elizabeth rejoiced with Mary
and greeted her as the mother of the Lord:
look with favour on your lowly servants
that, with Mary, we may magnify your holy name
and rejoice to acclaim her Son our Saviour,
who is alive and reigns with you,
in the unity of the Holy Spirit,
one God, now and for ever.

| *Reflection by* **David Runcorn**

Psalms 21, **47** or 96, **97**, 100
Numbers 11.16-17, 24-29
1 Corinthians 2

Saturday 1 June

1 Corinthians 2

'But we speak God's wisdom, secret and hidden' (v.7)

It seems that Paul, the man remembered as the great, founding Church leader and teacher, was not impressive to look at or to listen to. His colleague Peter confessed to finding him hard to understand at times. In this reading he seems very aware he is not a compelling speaker. We know one his sermons was so long that a young man sitting on a windowsill fell asleep and dropped to his death in the street below (Acts 20.9)!

We know Paul had regular health problems – possibly a speech impediment? The very honest reference here to 'fear' and 'much trembling' suggests genuine vulnerability. We know he struggled at times to exercise the leadership that he was called to and that the early churches needed. Some in the churches found it hard to respect him. There were others who looked and sounded more inspiring.

We are a society preoccupied with leaders and leadership. We like them to be strong and look impressive. But it means we are drawn to image rather than content – and we are never crueller than when leaders fail or appear weak. Paul's message, based on his own experience, is that God works most powerfully through what is weak and is revealed through what society despised and rejects. Paul's only priority was to point people to Christ crucified. Then, as now, it is never the way to popularity.

Grant, we pray, almighty God,
that as we believe your only-begotten Son our Lord Jesus Christ
to have ascended into the heavens,
so we in heart and mind may also ascend
and with him continually dwell;
who is alive and reigns with you,
in the unity of the Holy Spirit,
one God, now and for ever.

COLLECT

Reflection by **David Runcorn** | 165

Monday 3 June

Psalms **93**, 96, 97 *or* **98**, 99, 101
Numbers 27.15-end
I Corinthians 3

1 Corinthians 3

*'So neither the one who plants nor the one who waters is
anything, but only God who gives the growth' (v.7)*

When I was an undergraduate student, I famously spent the best part
of a term faithfully watering a plant in the stairwell of the house I
shared. I was quite pleased with how well the plant was thriving until
I discovered that it was, in fact, not real! I blamed the dim light of
that part of the house, but then of course never thought to wonder
why any plant would 'grow' so enthusiastically in poor lighting. It
was somewhat embarrassing to have to admit, but in hindsight it
taught me an important lesson, one that is helpfully illuminated by
Paul in this extended reflection on church growth and leadership.

As biblical scholar Nicholas King points out in his translation of the
New Testament, it is significant that Paul uses two metaphors for
unity in this chapter: a garden and a building. This suggests an
interesting confluence of organic and human-made involvement. We
can plan and strategize for growth, but we often cannot predict
where the growth will take place. More often than not it happens in
the most unlikely of locations and with the most unlikely people.
And growth can look different too, depending on the context. As is
so often the case, Paul draws the focus back to God as a way of
reminding the Corinthians (and us) where the true foundation lies.

COLLECT

O God the King of glory,
you have exalted your only Son Jesus Christ
with great triumph to your kingdom in heaven:
we beseech you, leave us not comfortless,
but send your Holy Spirit to strengthen us
and exalt us to the place where our Saviour Christ is gone before,
who is alive and reigns with you,
in the unity of the Holy Spirit,
one God, now and for ever.

| *Reflection by* **Helen-Ann Hartley**

Psalms 98, **99**, 100 *or* **106*** (*or* 103)
1 Samuel 10.1-10
1 Corinthians 12.1-13

1 Corinthians 12.1-13

'Now there are varieties of gifts, but the same Spirit' (v.4)

With the advent of so many modern technologies to help us do practically anything we can imagine, it is a frequent 'badge of honour' to be able to say how well we can multi-task. Similarly, it is often helpful to be able to use the self-description 'a good all-rounder'. Such is the pressure on many people, particularly young people setting out in the world of job applications, that an apparent inability to cope with more than one thing at any give time can be a source of despair.

Quite the opposite is found in Paul's well-known reflection on the spiritual gifts. Again, Paul calls his audience back to the foundation that is God and God's Holy Spirit. There are many gifts, but they aren't all given to one person; they are shared out in such a way that many make up the whole, which is the Body of Christ.

Perhaps this is a helpful reminder to us to celebrate one or two things that we know we can do well, and not to feel bad about not doing everything? Perhaps this is an invitation to encourage others to do likewise – to reflect on even the one thing that they can bring to the table?

It is vital that all work together; the call to unity is of paramount importance.

Risen, ascended Lord,
as we rejoice at your triumph,
fill your Church on earth with power and compassion,
that all who are estranged by sin
may find forgiveness and know your peace,
to the glory of God the Father.

COLLECT

Reflection by **Helen-Ann Hartley** | 167

Wednesday 5 June

Psalms 2, **29** *or* 110, **111**, 112
1 Kings 19.1-18
Matthew 3.13-end

Matthew 3.13-end

'Then Jesus came from Galilee to John at the Jordan' (v.13)

If we look back on our lives, we can often identify key turning points when something significant happened to mark the beginning or ending of a particular season. Christian discipleship is sometimes referred to with the imagery of a journey or pilgrimage, and it can be helpful to imagine various marking posts along the way. The gospel story works a bit like that too, and this passage is one of those occasions.

All four Gospels connect the start of Jesus' public ministry with the figure of John the Baptist. This is significant because it continues to root Jesus' own story in that of the wider narrative of Israel. John the Baptist is presented as an Old Testament prophetic forerunner, and Jesus begins his own proclamation of the kingdom of God with an awareness of that greater narrative. So we bear this in mind when we read through the Gospel as a whole.

At the same time, this passage ensures that we recognize John's status in relation to that of Jesus: while John was the forerunner, Jesus is the main player on the stage. Jesus, however, submits himself to John and marks his own baptism as being in accordance with 'righteousness', which – in Matthew at least – means doing God's will by obeying the commandments. Jesus' authority comes from that of his Father, and it is thus God's voice and God's Spirit that manifests itself at this crucial moment.

C O L L E C T

O God the King of glory,
you have exalted your only Son Jesus Christ
with great triumph to your kingdom in heaven:
we beseech you, leave us not comfortless,
but send your Holy Spirit to strengthen us
and exalt us to the place where our Saviour Christ is gone before,
who is alive and reigns with you,
in the unity of the Holy Spirit,
one God, now and for ever.

| *Reflection by* **Helen-Ann Hartley**

Psalms **24**, 72 *or* 113, **115**
Ezekiel 11.14-20
Matthew 9.35 – 10.20

Thursday 6 June

Matthew 9.35 – 10.20

'Then he said to his disciples, "The harvest is plentiful, but the labourers are few"' (9.37)

If you look at a field ready to be harvested, it seems vastly greater than the sum of the people that could be sent out to bring in the harvest. God's creation overflows with abundance: there is always more to gather in; there is always more to do. I wonder if it is fear that sometimes holds us back, that makes the harvest look overwhelming. Why bother, it's all too much? This narrative of anxiety disrupts the gospel message of hope in the resurrection. Jesus' words are meant to encourage us into action, not to inaction.

I wonder when you listen to this passage, do you see the harvest and the labourers as separate? As though the harvest represents the mission field into which we are sent? How would it be to see the labourers as themselves *part* of the harvest? Could this perspective be what Jesus is getting at? We are ourselves part of the harvest in which we 'labour'. The one thing we can do to enable the harvest is to accept change in ourselves – to let ourselves be transformed.

If we are willing to allow ourselves to be part of the harvest too, as we are transformed inwardly, our lives as disciples become more fully formed in the likeness of Christ. This is not a self-improvement programme, rather a process whereby our own formation encourages that of our neighbour's.

Risen, ascended Lord,
as we rejoice at your triumph,
fill your Church on earth with power and compassion,
that all who are estranged by sin
may find forgiveness and know your peace,
to the glory of God the Father.

COLLECT

Friday 7 June

Matthew 12.22-32

*'Whoever is not with me is against me, and whoever does not
gather with me scatters' (v.30)*

One of the defining features of Matthew's Gospel is its apocalyptic
tone. Far from inspiring fear, however, this is meant to galvanize us
into action based on hope and an abiding sense of the power and
love of God. There is a strong sense of 'either/or' in the Gospel
message, which can be startling and catch us unawares. At the heart
of this passage is a question about Jesus' identity; astonishment on
the part of the crowds who witnessed this miracle; fear and
scepticism among his opponents.

This contrast between good and evil powers – and a looming sense
of a battle between them – is the context for Matthew's community
of followers of Jesus, who themselves were struggling with questions
of identity and relationship. Often these struggles have been
presented in a way that does not understand the diversity of the first-
century Jewish context in which this Gospel was written. Great
damage has been done to Jewish-Christian relationships as a result.
Judaism was full of diversity in the first century, and this passage is
indicative of that feature.

Is this an invitation to us to think about our diversity today, within
Christianity? Where are the points of discussion and debate, and how
do we seek to resolve questions not just of *who* we are but, more
importantly, *whose* we are? We belong to God, and that is the root
of all that matters.

COLLECT

O God the King of glory,
you have exalted your only Son Jesus Christ
with great triumph to your kingdom in heaven:
we beseech you, leave us not comfortless,
but send your Holy Spirit to strengthen us
and exalt us to the place where our Saviour Christ is gone before,
who is alive and reigns with you,
in the unity of the Holy Spirit,
one God, now and for ever.

| *Reflection by* **Helen-Ann Hartley**

Psalms 42, **43** *or* 120, **121**, 122
Micah 3.1-8
Ephesians 6.10-20

Ephesians 6.10-20

'Put on the whole armour of God, so that you may be able to stand against the wiles of the devil' (v.11)

Among the long checklists for numerous school camps I have been on is the line 'remember appropriate clothing and footwear'. There is no point setting out on a trek across a mountain wearing flip-flops. I once attempted to learn to surf with a group of students and failed miserably before I had even got near the water by putting on my wetsuit back to front (who knew the zip goes at the back and not the front?).

Paul concludes his letter to the Ephesians with this call to action. It may sound uncomfortably militaristic to some, but it may helpfully be read in the context of life in the Roman Empire. If there is one thing Rome did well, it was to demonstrate military might. If Rome wanted to assert its authority, it could put on a show of strength to intimidate the most defiant of opponents. Paul often plays on this and subverts the message to demonstrate that it is really God who is in charge.

For Paul, the struggle between good and evil was a daily reality, and he wanted his audience to remember that at the conclusion of this letter. He finishes with prayer and reminds them that for him, although the cost of discipleship was imprisonment, its overwhelming joy and hope was confidence in the Lord.

Risen, ascended Lord,
as we rejoice at your triumph,
fill your Church on earth with power and compassion,
that all who are estranged by sin
may find forgiveness and know your peace,
to the glory of God the Father.

COLLECT

Reflection by **Helen-Ann Hartley** | 171

Monday 10 June
Psalms 123, 124, 125, **126**
2 Chronicles 17.1-12
Romans 1.1-17

Romans 1.1-17

'... a servant of Jesus Christ' (v.1)

We never have a second chance to make a good first impression. Paul, no slouch when it comes to rhetorical skills, seems well aware of this as he begins his letter to the Christians in Rome, whom he has never met.

The letter has various objectives. Paul wants to sign them up to the network of those who support him both prayerfully and materially. He asks their intercessions now, and hints at anticipating more tangible assistance when he visits on his planned travels to Spain (15.24-30). He also wants to share advice on contentious issues among the young churches (chapters 14,15). So he needs to establish a basis for their trust. And while it helps for him to list many friends in common as he ends his letter, it's the first impression that matters most.

Yet he begins not merely by listing helpful credentials but also by naming what really counts. His identity comes from God's initiative, in calling him to be an apostle of the gospel of Jesus Christ, whose servant he is. He is not ashamed of that gospel, he says. And he points to the heart of his manifesto, the dominant theme of the letter: the revelation of God's righteousness through faith, for faith.

But more of that later. To begin at the beginning: what do you understand as the fundamental basis of your identity? What first impression do you aim to make?

COLLECT	O Lord, from whom all good things come:
	grant to us your humble servants,
	that by your holy inspiration
	we may think those things that are good,
	and by your merciful guiding may perform the same;
	through our Lord Jesus Christ,
	who is alive and reigns with you,
	in the unity of the Holy Spirit,
	one God, now and for ever.

| *Reflection by* **Sarah Rowland Jones**

Psalms 100, 101, 117
Jeremiah 9.23-24
Acts 4.32-end

Tuesday 11 June

Barnabas the Apostle

Acts 4.32-end

'Barnabas (which means "son of encouragement")' (v.36)

I have a fridge magnet that says: 'If you can't be a good example, you'll have to be a terrible warning.' Barnabas is the epitome of the good example, being an encouragement both to individuals and to the wider Christian community.

At the heart of his encouraging lies his willingness to stick his neck out and take the initiative. He's prepared to take a step – possibly the first step – forward and start the ball rolling.

We find it in this passage, where he is commended for selling a field and bringing the proceeds to the apostles. Later in Acts, we read how Paul, after conversion, came to Jerusalem and 'attempted to join the disciples; and they were all afraid of him, for they did not believe he was a disciple'. But Barnabas has the courage to seek him out, and then, telling Paul's story for him, brings him into their company (Acts 9.26-27).

It takes courage to be the first to act, but, whether by an action or a word, it can so often become a channel through which God's remarkable, creative and redemptive grace can flow. It may set an example to others so that what seemed impossible becomes readily possible. It can break deadlocks and bring about new beginnings.

Where might God's grace be calling you to stick your neck out, take a step forward, and set a ball rolling, as an encouragement to others?

Bountiful God, giver of all gifts,
who poured your Spirit upon your servant Barnabas
and gave him grace to encourage others:
help us, by his example,
to be generous in our judgements
and unselfish in our service;
through Jesus Christ your Son our Lord,
who is alive and reigns with you,
in the unity of the Holy Spirit,
one God, now and for ever.

COLLECT

Reflection by **Sarah Rowland Jones**   173

Wednesday 12 June

Psalm **119.153-end**
2 Chronicles 18.2 – end of 19
Romans 2.1-16

Romans 2.1-16

'God's kindness is meant to lead you to repentance' (v.4)

Having introduced himself as called to share the gospel, the good news, of 'the power of God for salvation to everyone who has faith, to the Jew first and also to the Greek' (Romans 1.16), Paul then starts spelling out how this works, and why both Greek and Jew are in need of such salvation and why none of us are in a fit position to judge others.

But before we become focused on the consequences – and they are serious – of remaining under God's judgement, Paul wants us to get our context right. Why does God judge us? His truth-based assessment of our lives calls us to turn our backs on everything that leads away from him and consequently into harm; we are called instead to turn (which is what repent means) towards a life lived his way. His kindness, patience and forbearance implore us to act for our own good.

Have we grasped this? Too often we get the message back to front, as the Franciscan spiritual writer Richard Rohr says in his *Essential Teachings on Love*, 'Most of us were taught that God would love us if and when we change. In fact, God loves you so you can change.'

'Do you not realize', says Paul, the gospel of salvation is powered by the engine of God's redeeming love. Pray that he will reveal more of the riches of this kindness and love to you.

COLLECT

O Lord, from whom all good things come:
grant to us your humble servants,
that by your holy inspiration
we may think those things that are good,
and by your merciful guiding may perform the same;
through our Lord Jesus Christ,
who is alive and reigns with you,
in the unity of the Holy Spirit,
one God, now and for ever.

| *Reflection by* **Sarah Rowland Jones**

Thursday 13 June

Romans 2.17-end

'... real circumcision is a matter of the heart' (v.29)

A few years ago, the British author and playwright Alan Bennett claimed in an interview 'what I think we are best at in England, better than all the rest, is hypocrisy'. He caused a bit of a stir, no doubt intending to be wittily provocative while naming a few home truths.

But hypocrisy is no laughing matter. Any apparent espousal of virtuous character, or moral or religious beliefs or standards, that is belied by words or actions is worse than duplicitous. Jesus' fiercest ire is directed at hypocrisy among the religious leaders of his day, who fail to practise what they preach and whose distorted teaching misleads others.

Paul says that to boast in the law of God while bending and breaking that law is akin to blaspheming God in public. When the media calls out churches for some act or attitude of hypocrisy, we stand charged with betraying not merely our principles, but God's own self. It's not surprising that perceived hypocrisy so powerfully undermines our witness to the good news of Jesus Christ.

We're challenged to ask what might be our equivalent of the assumptions Paul condemns here, of reliance upon circumcision as 'a certain passport to salvation' as biblical scholar C. K. Barrett put it. Do we promote markers for Christian belonging that owe more to arbitrary cultural practices than our spiritual calling? Paul is returning us to the earlier question of the true foundations of our identity.

O Lord, from whom all good things come:
grant to us your humble servants,
that by your holy inspiration
we may think those things that are good,
and by your merciful guiding may perform the same;
through our Lord Jesus Christ,
who is alive and reigns with you,
in the unity of the Holy Spirit,
one God, now and for ever.

COLLECT

Reflection by **Sarah Rowland Jones** | 175

Friday 14 June

Romans 3.1-20

'… so every mouth may be silenced' (v.19)

Paul is still setting up his argument. Two apparently competing, even contradictory, perspectives are being lined up in opposing corners, ready for the show-down.

On the one hand, we have the assertion with which Paul began his letter: the quote from the prophet Habakkuk, 'The one who is righteous will live by faith' (Romans 1.17).

But over against this, Paul has been piling up mounting evidence for an apparently opposite view of the state of humanity before God. In the first two chapter of Romans, he has warned that we are in no position to pass judgement on others, and that humanity has the propensity to be hypocrites and liars. Now he offers a string of condemnatory quotes that draw on Psalms in the Greek translation known as Septuagint: no one is righteous; all have turned aside and become worthless.

Paul quotes more from the Jewish scriptures in this than any other letter, expecting his recipients to share with him in the context they offer. There is nothing here to justify the sort of thinking often popular today, which has more in common with Islam, that we should ensure our good deeds outweigh our bad deeds.

God is faithful, God is true – but before him we haven't got a leg to stand on. Silence can be our only response, as we wait for the God of love to provide the answer to our predicament.

COLLECT
O Lord, from whom all good things come:
grant to us your humble servants,
that by your holy inspiration
we may think those things that are good,
and by your merciful guiding may perform the same;
through our Lord Jesus Christ,
who is alive and reigns with you,
in the unity of the Holy Spirit,
one God, now and for ever.

| *Reflection by* **Sarah Rowland Jones**

Psalm **147**
2 Chronicles 24.1-22
Romans 3.21-end

Saturday 15 June

Romans 3.21-end

'... the righteousness of God through faith in Jesus Christ' (v.22)

'But now ...' humanity's predicament is finally solved, Paul now declares, by God in Jesus Christ acting decisively in history to change everything. This redemption in Christ Jesus is both the heart of Paul's letter and the hinge on which all history turns.

The pivotal point of all this is faith, trust – the Greek *pistis* and related words. God, who alone is righteous, is faithful and worthy of trust. God entrusts the redeeming sacrifice of atonement to Jesus Christ, who, trusting in God's faithfulness, proves himself faithful, laying down his life for our sakes. His faithfulness draws out our trust, our faith, in this trustworthy one, and so through him we find redemption, as we are caught up in cascading righteousness.

Thus, we should understand Paul's term 'faith in Christ' as operating in two directions. First comes the faith within Christ shown in his relationship with his heavenly Father: he is faithful to God and worthy of God's trust in him. And second, in consequence, we can know Christ trustworthy and so can have trust – have faith – in him. In this way we find ourselves caught up and drawn into the overflow of righteousness from God to Christ.

Paul spends the next chapters unpacking this dense argument. The good news is that God in Jesus Christ has done all that is required for our salvation, offering it to us as a free gift of grace.

COLLECT

O Lord, from whom all good things come:
grant to us your humble servants,
that by your holy inspiration
we may think those things that are good,
and by your merciful guiding may perform the same;
through our Lord Jesus Christ,
who is alive and reigns with you,
in the unity of the Holy Spirit,
one God, now and for ever.

Reflection by **Sarah Rowland Jones** | 177

Monday 17 June

Romans 4.1-12

'Faith was reckoned to Abraham as righteousness' (v.9)

'What then are we to say?' How do we who were rendered speechless, respond to God's answer? I suspect I'm prone to responding 'Yes, but ...' rather too often, especially with my nearest and dearest. It's an addiction to self-justification. Whatever the issue, my ego says my own reasoning, intentions or excuses should count in the mix.

That won't do here, not for me nor anyone else. Even the first and greatest of the patriarchs, Abraham himself, stands before God on the sole basis of offering nothing of his own achievements; instead, he entrusts himself utterly to the mercy of God, who freely imputes and gifts his own righteousness. The first and greatest of kings, David, similarly understood that righteousness is reckoned irrespective of works.

As for 'works', so closely linked here to circumcision, theologian John Barclay in his Grove Booklet *Paul and the Subversive Power of Grace* explains that Paul is not just objecting to reliance upon those 'works of the law' that became markers of Jewish identity, of belonging to God's covenant people. More astounding to Paul's readers would be his insistence that God's gift of righteousness in Christ is given without regard to any system by which we, Jew or gentile, attempt to measure a recipient's worth. Nothing we might measure counts!

The only route open to us is to 'follow the example of the faith that our ancestor Abraham had before he was circumcised'.

C O L L E C T	Almighty and everlasting God, you have given us your servants grace, by the confession of a true faith, to acknowledge the glory of the eternal Trinity and in the power of the divine majesty to worship the Unity: keep us steadfast in this faith, that we may evermore be defended from all adversities; through Jesus Christ your Son our Lord, who is alive and reigns with you, in the unity of the Holy Spirit, one God, now and for ever.

| *Reflection by* **Sarah Rowland Jones**

Tuesday 18 June

Romans 4.13-end

'It will be reckoned to us who believe …' (v.24)

Have you ever taken part in the team-building exercise where you just let yourself fall backwards, trusting that your colleagues will catch you safely? It's intended to help build your trust in them.

Onora O'Neill, often described as a philosopher of trust, argues, however, that to talk of the need in contemporary society to build or restore trust, in everything from management training to politics and international relations, is to start in the wrong place. She points out that it's only worth putting trust in what truly is trustworthy; therefore, we should begin by asking what constitutes trustworthiness, and who practises it.

We know that the 'God in whom [Abraham] believed' is the God 'who gives life to the dead and calls into existence the things that do not exist', and who is 'able to do what he had promised'. As Paul has already written, the God of Abraham, of us all, is righteous, kind, faithful and proven true. God's trustworthiness is not in doubt.

Yet knowing this in our heads is not the same as laying down our ego and letting go. It can be difficult to fall back and surrender ourselves to God. But if we do, we will discover there is no greater source of relief from all the painful efforts of self-justification, as we find ourselves not falling into oblivion, but caught, held, received, in eternal arms of infinite, redemptive love.

Holy God,
faithful and unchanging:
enlarge our minds with the knowledge of your truth,
and draw us more deeply into the mystery of your love,
that we may truly worship you,
Father, Son and Holy Spirit,
one God, now and for ever.

COLLECT

Wednesday 19 June

Psalm **119.1-32**
2 Chronicles 29.1-19
Romans 5.1-11

Romans 5.1-11

'... since we are justified by faith' (v.1)

It's worth remembering that the chapter and verse breaks in Scripture were added many centuries after biblical times. So we have to read Paul's opening 'therefore' with what comes before: 'It will be reckoned to us who believe in him who raised Jesus our Lord from the dead, who was handed over to death for our trespasses and was raised for our justification'.

The nature of the faith by which we are justified and made righteous – and thus have peace with God and access to grace – then becomes clearer. It is not merely a question of how much faith we can muster – and thank goodness for that, as I think I would find it worse than daunting if it depended on the strength and consistency of whatever faith I could muster. It is rather the practice of the trustworthiness and faithfulness between God and Christ that engenders trust and faith between Christ and the faithful. Christ's faith and faithfulness are particularly seen, says Paul, in his readiness to die for us, the ungodly, while we were still sinners and enemies of God.

All this God does in Christ, proving his love for us, a love in which we should in turn believe and trust. So we can readily say, with Corrie ten Boom, the Dutch Christian who helped many Jews escape the Nazi Holocaust: 'Never be afraid to trust an unknown future to a known God.'

COLLECT

Almighty and everlasting God,
you have given us your servants grace,
by the confession of a true faith,
to acknowledge the glory of the eternal Trinity
and in the power of the divine majesty to worship the Unity:
keep us steadfast in this faith,
that we may evermore be defended from all adversities;
through Jesus Christ your Son our Lord,
who is alive and reigns with you,
in the unity of the Holy Spirit,
one God, now and for ever.

| *Reflection by* **Sarah Rowland Jones**

Psalm 147
Deuteronomy 8.2-16
1 Corinthians 10.1-17

Thursday 20 June

Day of Thanksgiving for the
Institution of the Holy Communion
(Corpus Christi)

1 Corinthians 10.1-17

'... we who are many are one body' (v.17)

One reason I sometimes turn to the King James Version of the Bible is to clarify who is being addressed, especially by Jesus in the Gospels, or by the Epistle writers. There, the use of 'thee' and 'thou', alongside 'you', makes it clear whether it is one person or several.

In today's individualistic societies, the risk is that on reading 'you', we tend to think 'me', even when Scripture intends 'us'. This can make a great difference to how we understand God's actions, purposes and calling, and so to how we live as Christians.

This day of Thanksgiving for the Institution of the Holy Communion (Corpus Christi) is for each of us, and for all of us together, as we share in Christ's body broken, his blood shed, as he was 'lifted up' to 'draw all people' to himself (John 12.32). Though our churches may be divided over the Eucharist, we can pray and believe that we are united with everyone else embraced by his arms of love spread wide on the cross, no matter how great our differences now seem. There was one Last Supper to which we look back; there is one Wedding Feast of the Lamb, to which we look forwards. And we are all invited.

If you need reminding, then sometimes when you're reading your Bible you might put on your mental stetson and spurs, slide into Texan and try saying 'y'all' whenever it says 'you'.

COLLECT

Lord Jesus Christ,
we thank you that in this wonderful sacrament
you have given us the memorial of your passion:
grant us so to reverence the sacred mysteries
of your body and blood
that we may know within ourselves
and show forth in our lives
the fruits of your redemption;
for you are alive and reign with the Father
in the unity of the Holy Spirit,
one God, now and for ever.

Reflection by **Sarah Rowland Jones**   181

Friday 21 June

Psalms 17, 19
2 Chronicles 30
Romans 6.1-14

Romans 6.1-14

'... baptized into Christ Jesus' (v.3)

When the Victorians redeveloped a church where I once served, they sank a large baptistry into the floor. It's now hidden under carpeting, and most people don't know it's there. It was such a disappointment that I never got to use it!

In fact, it hasn't been used for baptisms in living memory, but it proved invaluable in the Second World War when it was kept full of water that was put to good use to extinguish an incendiary bomb that fell through the roof in 1941.

Our old self is extinguished by the waters of baptism – that at least should be in our minds, even if we're more familiar with water being poured on the forehead of a child or adult. But we mustn't lose sight of the powerful symbolism that total immersion has: of being buried with Christ and, as we resurface, also being raised with Christ.

Even if our mortal life still has years to run, and even though we're still fallible, we're no longer enslaved by sin, and resurrection life has begun. Whatever form of baptism we follow, it leaves us utterly drenched, and saturated through and through, with Jesus Christ. And from that point, we'll find his death and resurrection starting their work within us, steadily destroying death and bringing renewed, redeemed, overflowing life in every part of our being.

COLLECT

Almighty and everlasting God,
you have given us your servants grace,
by the confession of a true faith,
to acknowledge the glory of the eternal Trinity
and in the power of the divine majesty to worship the Unity:
keep us steadfast in this faith,
that we may evermore be defended from all adversities;
through Jesus Christ your Son our Lord,
who is alive and reigns with you,
in the unity of the Holy Spirit,
one God, now and for ever.

| *Reflection by* **Sarah Rowland Jones**

Psalms 20, 21, **23**
2 Chronicles 32.1-22
Romans 6.15-end

Saturday 22 June

Romans 6.15-end

'... enslaved to God, the advantage you get is sanctification' (v.22)

Benjamin, my spaniel, loves attention, and if he's bored, any attention is better than none. This leads to such naughtiness as stealing my hanky and prancing just out of reach in the hope I'll chase him. He knows all too well that I'll respond, and, once he's caught, make a fuss of him: there's more grace than law at work in our house.

Unlike spaniels, our experience of the triumph of grace over law leads us to desire greater obedience and holiness of life. And like faith itself, this comes to us as a gift, as we hand ourselves over to become 'slaves to righteousness'. Sanctification follows: it is the 'advantage' we then receive. All this is the free gift that comes to us, fully and unrestricted, once and for all, through faith.

I'm intrigued that the New Testament Greek word, translated here as 'advantage', is *karpon*, which primarily means fruit, though it could also be used for interest on a financial transaction. This sets images of time spent in growth, alongside the idea of the payback that comes from giving ourselves to God. So while we cannot earn faith by works, faith goes to work in us.

I'm also reminded of Jesus' words in John 15, that bearing fruit comes from abiding in him. One thing that Benjamin can do is sit and stay – it's a reminder I must do the same.

COLLECT

Holy God,
faithful and unchanging:
enlarge our minds with the knowledge of your truth,
and draw us more deeply into the mystery of your love,
that we may truly worship you,
Father, Son and Holy Spirit,
one God, now and for ever.

Reflection by **Sarah Rowland Jones** | 183

Monday 24 June
Birth of John the Baptist

Psalms 50, 149
Ecclesiasticus 48.1-10
or Malachi 3.1-6
Luke 3.1-17

Malachi 3.1-6

'See, I am sending my messenger to prepare the way before me' (v.1)

Eight days after the birth of the child, his family came together for the naming ceremony. His father cannot speak. They bring Zechariah a tablet to name his child: 'His name is John' he wrote (Luke 1.63). Then Zechariah is filled with the Holy Spirit and sings aloud his great shout of praise to God: 'Blessed be the Lord God of Israel' (Luke 1.68).

As Luke tells the story, Zechariah has spent nine months in silence pondering the message of the angel. As Elizabeth has grown a child in her womb, so Zechariah has conceived a prophecy, weaving together the story of salvation in the Scriptures and celebrating the good news of God's love.

Today's reading is a cornerstone of that prophecy, one of the key texts in Zechariah's silent reflection. The very name 'Malachi' means 'my messenger'. The passage introduces clearly the idea of the forerunner: the one who will come to prepare the way of the Lord.

The messenger will bring a severe mercy. The images of refiner's fire and fullers' soap are among the simplest and best in the books of the prophets. This is powerful cleansing, but cleansing for a purpose: to make the people of God ready to receive the one who will come. At the heart of that cleansing is the 'tender mercy of our God' (Luke 1.78). In the birth of this child, a new day has dawned.

COLLECT

Almighty God,
by whose providence your servant John the Baptist
    was wonderfully born,
and sent to prepare the way of your Son our Saviour
by the preaching of repentance:
lead us to repent according to his preaching
and, after his example,
constantly to speak the truth, boldly to rebuke vice,
and patiently to suffer for the truth's sake;
through Jesus Christ your Son our Lord,
who is alive and reigns with you,
in the unity of the Holy Spirit,
one God, now and for ever.

| *Reflection by* **Steven Croft**

Psalms 32, **36**
2 Chronicles 34.1-18
Romans 7.7-end

Tuesday 25 June

Romans 7.7-end
'For I do not do what I want ...' (v.15)

One of Paul's great gifts is introspection. He has been given the capacity to know himself and the condition of his inner being. He has been given the ability then to describe the state of his heart honestly and truthfully in words that are fresh in each generation. In those words he describes a universal human tension that points to God's grace.

The picture Paul paints is not a passive landscape but a battleground full of tension. This is much more helpful. 'For I do not do what I want, but I do the very thing I hate.' The more I understand what is good, the more clearly I see how far from good I truly am. The closer I come to a vision of holiness, the further I feel myself to be from that vision. We are, all of us, a bundle of tensions and mixed motives in everything we attempt.

Paul's courage in laying bare his own heart and ours comes from the stunning and glorious truth that, in the light of the grace of God, this knowledge of ourselves is good news. God knows already, of course, exactly what we are like. Knowing this, God comes in Jesus Christ to rescue us from this body of death and to bring peace even to that tension within. Only when we have reached the level of honesty of Romans 7 can we begin to appreciate the level of grace in Romans 8.

COLLECT

O God,
the strength of all those who put their trust in you,
mercifully accept our prayers
and, because through the weakness of our mortal nature
we can do no good thing without you,
grant us the help of your grace,
that in the keeping of your commandments
we may please you both in will and deed;
through Jesus Christ your Son our Lord,
who is alive and reigns with you,
in the unity of the Holy Spirit,
one God, now and for ever.

Reflection by **Steven Croft**

Wednesday 26 June

Romans 8.1-11

'... you are in the Spirit, since the Spirit of God dwells in you' (v.9)

Paul has unfolded the story of salvation in the first seven chapters of Romans. In Romans 8, he now lays out the consequences for human life and flourishing. We are set free first of all from condemnation. This will be a theme throughout this glorious chapter: nothing in all creation can separate us from the love of God.

But in the gospel there is even more. Christ by his death has set us free from death. Now the Holy Spirit of God has come to dwell in us and we in him. In the first seven chapters of Romans, Paul mentions the Holy Spirit just four times; there are 21 references to the Spirit in Romans 8.

One by one, Paul explores the layers of meaning in this mutual indwelling of the Spirit and the believer. The first is in reconciliation and peace of mind; our mental health is immeasurably strengthened: 'to set the mind on the Spirit is life and peace'. Reconciliation is first with God but then with the rest of God's creation.

From reconciliation Paul moves to resurrection. Resurrection is often left out of our theology of the Spirit's work. For Paul, it is by God's Spirit that Jesus is raised from the dead. The same Spirit dwells in us. Therefore, the Spirit is closely involved in our daily resurrection and being made new.

COLLECT

O God,
the strength of all those who put their trust in you,
mercifully accept our prayers
and, because through the weakness of our mortal nature
we can do no good thing without you,
grant us the help of your grace,
that in the keeping of your commandments
we may please you both in will and deed;
through Jesus Christ your Son our Lord,
who is alive and reigns with you,
in the unity of the Holy Spirit,
one God, now and for ever.

| *Reflection by* **Steven Croft**

Psalm **37***
2 Chronicles 35.1-19
Romans 8.12-17

Thursday 27 June

Romans 8.12-17

'... heirs of God and joint heirs with Christ' (v.17)

The Spirit's work and presence in us should shape the way we live and the daily decisions of our lives. Later in the letter, in Romans 12, Paul will explore further what that means, expanding the idea of debt into the image of a living sacrifice. Those daily decisions are marked by putting to death the deeds of the body. Death and resurrection is not only about the end of our lives on earth; for a Christian, dying to self is a daily decision and possible only because of the Spirit's life in us.

Those daily decisions have an eternal perspective: Paul's fourth theme. As we are led by the Spirit of God, so we grow into the immensity of our vocation as the children of God. That vocation is first and foremost about a relationship of love: we speak to God intimately and tenderly as Abba, Father. But next our vocation is about our inheritance: as children of God we are heirs of God with Christ. Our daily dying to self and experience of suffering will give way to a new glory that has not yet been revealed.

The Spirit's work in our lives is reconciliation, resurrection, realignment of our wills and restoring our inheritance as children of God. Take some time this morning to welcome the Holy Spirit once again into the depth of your identity in Christ as an active partner in salvation.

God of truth,
help us to keep your law of love
and to walk in ways of wisdom,
that we may find true life
in Jesus Christ your Son.

COLLECT

Reflection by **Steven Croft** | 187

Friday 28 June

Romans 8.18-30

'For in hope we were saved' (v.24)

Take a little extra time this morning to read to the end of the chapter. The lectionary omits verses 31-39 because of St Peter tomorrow. Let your mind rest for a while on the wonder and the glory of God's love and purpose for creation.

This world is glorious. Human beings are fearfully and wonderfully made. Yet we know we see a creation that is less than God intends it to be: blighted by death and decay, groaning and in labour. We know our lives also are marred by suffering, hardship, distress and death.

The whole story has not yet been revealed to us. In faith and in hope, because of Jesus, through the work of the Spirit in our lives, Paul invites us to look forward and see the present in the perspective of eternity. The suffering of this present time is not worth comparing to the glory that is to be revealed (v.18); the creation itself will be set free from bondage (v.21); nothing will be able to separate us from the love of God (v.39).

Hope is the most slender and the most powerful of virtues. Paul's aim in Romans 8 is to nurture and rekindle hope in the Christian community when we are at our lowest and most hard pressed. We will not find ways forward through clever plans and schemes but by returning to the gospel and catching a fresh vision of God's work. That vision will bear fruit in prayer and, ultimately, in the transformation of the earth.

COLLECT

O God,
the strength of all those who put their trust in you,
mercifully accept our prayers
and, because through the weakness of our mortal nature
we can do no good thing without you,
grant us the help of your grace,
that in the keeping of your commandments
we may please you both in will and deed;
through Jesus Christ your Son our Lord,
who is alive and reigns with you,
in the unity of the Holy Spirit,
one God, now and for ever.

| *Reflection by* **Steven Croft**

Psalms 71, 113
Isaiah 49.1-6
Acts 11.1-18

Saturday 29 June

Peter the Apostle

Acts 11.1-18

'... the circumcised believers criticized him' (v.2)

The story of Cornelius and Peter is told with great care in Acts. We read first of the vision of Cornelius; then of Peter's. We follow Peter's journey to Caesarea. We see Peter's words interrupted by the Spirit that falls on the Gentiles. Then in Acts 11, Peter tells the whole story again for the benefit of the apostles and believers in Judea.

Here and in Acts 15, the early Church makes its most critical decisions: that the grace of God given in Jesus Christ is given not only to the Jews but also to the Gentiles. Christianity is to become a faith for the whole world, not a sect of Judaism. In the centurion's story, Cornelius is received into the Church, but it is Peter who is converted.

Peter's name is at least partly ironic. He is rocky more than he is a rock. He denies Christ. He is a leader who is open to having his mind and heart changed by the grace of God. His real strength and resilience comes from his ability to be restored and rise up again despite his very public failure and then to be secure enough to discern what God is doing.

Peter's day invites us to reflect on our own ability to live with failure, to rise up again as wounded leaders and lead with courage. His day invites us to reflect on the way we lead bravely in the face of criticism and discern the purposes of God.

Almighty God,
who inspired your apostle Saint Peter
to confess Jesus as Christ and Son of the living God:
build up your Church upon this rock,
that in unity and peace it may proclaim one truth
and follow one Lord, your Son our Saviour Christ,
who is alive and reigns with you,
in the unity of the Holy Spirit,
one God, now and for ever.

COLLECT

Monday 1 July

Ezra 1

'... the Lord stirred up the spirit of King Cyrus of Persia' (v.1)

There is more going on in the world than we can see. Some of what we do see is really important, but it's sometimes hard to know which part.

The book of Ezra is centred on the return of the exiles from Babylon to Jerusalem and the rebuilding of the city and the temple. The return forms a key part of the Old Testament story. Ezra is in a close (but complicated) relationship with 1 and 2 Chronicles and with the book of Nehemiah. The book is named after the scribe Ezra, who appears in Chapter 7.

The return from exile is an historical event. The prophets and the writings attribute this great event to God acting through Cyrus, King of Persia. Cyrus is not, of course, part of the people of Israel. He is not a loyal worshipper of the Lord. Yet God acts through 'his anointed' Cyrus (Isaiah 45.1). Israel's horizons are broader after the exile: more open to seeing God at work beyond its own borders.

The Church is a community in exile (1 Peter 1.1). Like Israel, we need to keep our horizons broad in every generation. Where is God at work today in my own community but beyond the life of the Church? Where is God stirring up the spirit of politicians or business leaders or leaders of other faiths to bring freedom and justice and peace?

COLLECT

Lord, you have taught us
that all our doings without love are nothing worth:
send your Holy Spirit
and pour into our hearts that most excellent gift of love,
the true bond of peace and of all virtues,
without which whoever lives is counted dead before you.
Grant this for your only Son Jesus Christ's sake,
who is alive and reigns with you,
in the unity of the Holy Spirit,
one God, now and for ever.

| *Reflection by* **Steven Croft**

Tuesday 2 July

Ezra 3

'... old people who had seen the first house on its foundations'
(v.12)

One of the great lessons of Ezra is that rebuilding a community is backbreaking work. The returning exiles have a foothold only in Jerusalem. There are no city walls. There is no temple or public buildings. The returning exiles are few in number for so great a task. Yet they persist in this impossible dream of restoring their community based around the worship of the temple.

For that reason the two first great milestones are the restoration of worship at a simple altar and then, a year later, the laying of the foundation for the new temple. Each is bittersweet. The second event especially calls out mixed emotions: joy at the progress made combined with tears at the contrast with the temple of Solomon.

There will be much heartache and many setbacks for the Jerusalem community, yet still they persevere. They are not building a nation any longer, though that dream will come and go. They are attempting a new thing: building a community defined by its worship and religion in the midst of a foreign empire. That community has endured to this day in the Jewish people scattered across the earth.

What is the great task in which you are engaged in your life and in this generation? What will be the milestones of progress this year? What will be the bitter moments in those milestones? And where is the sweetness?

Faithful Creator,
whose mercy never fails:
deepen our faithfulness to you
and to your living Word,
Jesus Christ our Lord.

COLLECT

Wednesday 3 July
Thomas the Apostle

Psalms 92, 146
2 Samuel 15.17-21
or Ecclesiasticus 2
John 11.1-16

John 11.1-16

'Let us also go, that we may die with him' (v.16)

The story of the death and resurrection of Lazarus stands at the very centre of John's Gospel, looking back and looking forward. It is a long story that extends through Mary's anointing of Jesus to his entry into Jerusalem. Thomas is given one of the key lines that help us see the meaning in the story and unlock its interpretation: 'Let us also go, that we may die with him.'

Thomas is often understood as a pessimistic cynic. But his words can be read as a statement of faith and grit and as a prophetic commentary on what is happening.

In John's understanding of the story, for Jesus even to travel to Bethany is an act of great courage. For him to raise Lazarus from the dead leads directly to his own crucifixion. The miracle is followed directly by the plot to kill Jesus and then by Mary's anointing for death at Bethany. Thomas' speech is the opening of John's passion narrative.

Thomas sees the road ahead with open eyes. Yet, such is his love for Jesus that he wants still to travel with him and, if necessary, to die with him. He is not a model for cynics and doubters within us; he is a model of faith and love and courage in discipleship.

COLLECT

Almighty and eternal God,
who, for the firmer foundation of our faith,
allowed your holy apostle Thomas
    to doubt the resurrection of your Son
till word and sight convinced him:
grant to us, who have not seen, that we also may believe
and so confess Christ as our Lord and our God;
who is alive and reigns with you,
in the unity of the Holy Spirit,
one God, now and for ever.

Thursday 4 July

Ezra 4.7-end

'At that time the work on the house of God in Jerusalem stopped'
(v.24)

Ezra 4 to 6 is like a short play in several acts. There is opposition to the rebuilding of the temple from the other peoples settled in Israel. At first, this opposition is successful and the building work is halted. Haggai and Zechariah strengthen the people so that building begins again. The opponents write again, this time to Darius. Darius finds the original decree of Cyrus, and the situation is turned round. Darius issues a new and supportive decree. The building of the temple is completed. The Passover is celebrated for the first time by the exiles.

Over the coming generations, this small community gathered around the temple will face many trials. After the exile, Jerusalem no longer exists in a world of small kingdoms each with their local gods. Jerusalem can thrive only as one distinctive part of a large empire. There will often be tensions between the different parts of the empire, wary of this city with a powerful history. Sometimes the empire will support the Jerusalem community; sometimes it will side with the opposition.

The exiles teach the Church in every generation how to live as a minority community where our faith and practice is contested. The key discipline is quiet, determined perseverance: holding fast to what we believe, building when we can build and enduring when the building has to cease. What are the lessons the Church in our generation needs to learn from the book of Ezra?

Lord, you have taught us
that all our doings without love are nothing worth:
send your Holy Spirit
and pour into our hearts that most excellent gift of love,
the true bond of peace and of all virtues,
without which whoever lives is counted dead before you.
Grant this for your only Son Jesus Christ's sake,
who is alive and reigns with you,
in the unity of the Holy Spirit,
one God, now and for ever.

COLLECT

Reflection by **Steven Croft** | 193

Friday 5 July

Psalms **51**, 54
Ezra 5
Romans 11.1-12

Ezra 5

'We are the servants of the God of heaven and earth' (v.11)

The God of the exiles is no longer one tribal deity among many, championing his own people as they establish a kingdom. Although Haggai and Zechariah prophesy at the beginning of the chapter 'in the name of the God of Israel', the letters make it clear that this house and temple are dedicated to 'the God of heaven and earth', the creator and sustainer of all humankind.

This temple and the people who gather there have still an important place in the purposes of God, providing a place for worship without idols and according to God's own decree. This is despite the past failings of the people. This universal calling and distinctive identity both need to be preserved and nurtured.

The communities of Ezra and Nehemiah and the exiles who follow them will wrestle with their vocation and place in the purposes of God. They worship the God of the whole earth and therefore their calling is universal, in some sense for all people. They are a people with a special vocation and therefore their calling is particular and distinctive.

The Church inherits this tension and lives with it in every generation. How much do we focus on our inner life and purity and worship? How much do we look to the needs of the world around us to shape our life?

COLLECT

Lord, you have taught us
that all our doings without love are nothing worth:
send your Holy Spirit
and pour into our hearts that most excellent gift of love,
the true bond of peace and of all virtues,
without which whoever lives is counted dead before you.
Grant this for your only Son Jesus Christ's sake,
who is alive and reigns with you,
in the unity of the Holy Spirit,
one God, now and for ever.

| *Reflection by* **Steven Croft**

Psalm **68**
Ezra 6
Romans 11.13-24

Saturday 6 July

Ezra 6

'With joy they celebrated the festival of unleavened bread for seven days' (v.22)

The rebuilding of the temple is an immense labour, stretching across a generation. It has involved danger, division in the community, facing opposition, diplomacy, difficult journeys, cost, gathering materials, skilled and unskilled labour and above all perseverance. The rebuilding of the temple is the cornerstone of the life of the community. The temple connects the exiles with past glories. It gives an identity and purpose to the nation. It is a sign and guarantee of a good future. The lives of every person in the community are connected to something larger than themselves.

The endpoint of all of this labour is joy and celebration: a Passover. The temple traditions that go back to David and Solomon are connected with the even older tradition of the Exodus. A new rhythm of life and worship is established to sustain the Jerusalem community through all that is to come.

The Passover looks forward as well as back. It is a sign that the end of our labours on earth is meant to be joy and celebration. As Christians we read Ezra's Passover as a sign of another Passover that will be celebrated in Jerusalem, by Jesus, the lamb who was slain. As Christians we read Ezra's Passover, because of his death, as a sign and foretaste of a richer banquet in heaven, when all of our labours are ended and we are with Christ in joy for ever.

Faithful Creator,
whose mercy never fails:
deepen our faithfulness to you
and to your living Word,
Jesus Christ our Lord.

COLLECT

Monday 8 July

Ezra 7

'I took courage, for the hand of the Lord my God was upon me'
(v.28)

Ezra was one of Israel's most important spiritual leaders, the founder of the form of Judaism that we know today. His vocation was to lead a national and spiritual revival, re-establishing the ancient faith of God's people on the basis of a restored temple and a fresh zeal for God's law.

Ezra's qualification for this task was that he had applied himself to study. Over the years he has, as Thomas Cranmer's collect might put it, heard, read, marked, learnt and inwardly digested God's law. This gives him authority in the eyes of the Persian king, who generously provides for the establishment of temple worship and the maintenance of the temple clergy. Ezra also needs to ensure there are judges steeped in the law and qualified to give sound rulings.

As we pursue our daily calling, we reflect on what might qualify us to be agents of God's will. First would be a readiness to be instructed in the faith, to dig deep into the Bible and into the collective experience of the Church. Then, second, comes a willingness to offer ourselves generously to God, letting our time and talents be used for his purposes.

Ezra combines boldness with humility, and they together make a good combination.

COLLECT

Almighty God,
you have broken the tyranny of sin
and have sent the Spirit of your Son into our hearts
    whereby we call you Father:
give us grace to dedicate our freedom to your service,
that we and all creation may be brought
    to the glorious liberty of the children of God;
through Jesus Christ your Son our Lord,
who is alive and reigns with you,
in the unity of the Holy Spirit,
one God, now and for ever.

| *Reflection by* **Angela Tilby**

Tuesday 9 July

Ezra 8.15-end

'... he listened to our entreaty' (v.23)

Ezra cannot fulfil God's will on his own. His first task is to recreate a dedicated community, a people-in-waiting ready to reinhabit the land of promise. After years of false starts and disappointed hopes, this return of exiles to Jerusalem has to be definitive. So the journey is invested with solemn significance. The entry is described in such a way as to resemble the original conquest of Canaan. The gathering on the river bank and the three-day fast remind us of Joshua's crossing over the Jordan into the Promised Land.

The re-establishment of the Levites as the chosen priestly order also marks a new start based on sanctified memories: the Levites had carried the sacred vessels through the wilderness. Ezra also tests out the people's faith, refusing to rely on military protection from the Persian king, trusting in the power of God alone, and arriving safely in the holy city.

When we face a new challenge, it is often our memories of how God has sustained us in the past that give us strength. These memories are strengthened by communal ritual, and this is where frequent Holy Communion and the reaffirmation of Baptismal vows can be an enormous help. Sacred memories are meant to accompany us and also to generate fresh responses to God's work in our lives.

God our saviour,
look on this wounded world
in pity and in power;
hold us fast to your promises of peace
won for us by your Son,
our Saviour Jesus Christ.

COLLECT

Reflection by **Angela Tilby** | 197

Wednesday 10 July

Psalm **77**
Ezra 9
Romans 12.9-end

Ezra 9

'Here we are before you in our guilt' (v.15)

This chapter introduces a recurrent theme in the book of Ezra, the people's sin of intermarriage. This is a difficult topic for us because when it comes to marriage, we tend to prize personal choice above any communal considerations. But, as Ezra saw it, the choice of a marriage partner signified an alliance that went beyond the individual. For a faithful Jew to marry into a tribe that worshipped other gods was an act of profound disloyalty tantamount to abandoning faith in God. It is hardly surprising that Ezra displayed his horror so publicly; the discovery of such apostasy made his task seem virtually impossible.

At times of profound disappointment and challenge, honest prayer helps us to face reality. Ezra does not rush to prayer; he acts out the horror of what has been reported to him, sitting 'appalled' for many hours. Only later, at the time of the evening sacrifice does he break his fast and turn to God. In his prayer, he associates himself with the people's guilt and throws himself on God's mercy. His heartfelt plea contrasts the slavery the people still endure with the promise God still holds out to his people.

However badly we are let down, by our own folly or the faithlessness of others, God's face towards us is gracious, and we look to him (in Ezra's phrase) to 'brighten our eyes'.

COLLECT

Almighty God,
you have broken the tyranny of sin
and have sent the Spirit of your Son into our hearts
    whereby we call you Father:
give us grace to dedicate our freedom to your service,
that we and all creation may be brought
    to the glorious liberty of the children of God;
through Jesus Christ your Son our Lord,
who is alive and reigns with you,
in the unity of the Holy Spirit,
one God, now and for ever.

| *Reflection by* **Angela Tilby**

Thursday 11 July

Ezra 10.1-17
'Be strong, and do it' (v.4)

Ezra's public mourning attracts sympathy. Others follow his lead, picking up on his faith that there is still hope for Israel if the people channel their repentance into action. Ezra clearly believed that dismissing foreign wives and children was necessary to ensure God's future blessing. It is significant that he continued to fast even after the oath agreeing this had been taken.

Ezra then attempts to implement his demand for mass divorce, requiring all the returned exiles to report to Jerusalem and explain their domestic circumstances on pain of being excluded from the community. This was a demand too far, and the speed and the heavy rain forced a delay and a delegation of responsibility to appointed officials.

This is not an easy passage for us with our beliefs in equality and inclusivity. But it should remind us that limits and boundaries are sometimes necessary to ensure the health of communities. An example that faces us today is that of the speed of immigration as those with the means to escape flee from poverty and violence. There is a place for generosity and a place for restraint. As it happened, Ezra's rigour failed, and Judaism spread in gentile lands at least in part through intermarriage. Ezra tried to do the right thing. But sometimes God knows better. This should encourage, not discourage, us!

God our saviour,
look on this wounded world
in pity and in power;
hold us fast to your promises of peace
won for us by your Son,
our Saviour Jesus Christ.

COLLECT

Friday 12 July

Psalm **55**
Nehemiah 1
Romans 13.8-end

Nehemiah 1

'They are your servants and your people, whom you redeemed' (v.10)

The exact relationship between Ezra and Nehemiah has baffled commentators. In some versions, the two form one book, but how their testimonies connect historically is not at all clear. While Ezra is envisaging a revival of a holy community around the law, Nehemiah, still in exile, hears bad news from Jerusalem. Part of the city walls have been destroyed, and murder and mayhem are rife in the countryside. The holy land is lawless. Nehemiah is driven to prayer by this news, calling on God in language derived from Deuteronomy and the Psalms. God's people are oppressed as a result of their own sinfulness; the dire circumstances in Jerusalem can only be put right through God's forgiveness. His prayer recalls God's promises and pleads for God to remember his faithfulness. Surely his people are still precious to him!

Nehemiah's heartfelt contrition for communal sin is something that is hard for most of us to identify with. We tend to feel detachment from our political leaders and blame them, or society, for the flaws we see around us, as though they had nothing to do with us. Nehemiah, however, sees the hand of God in his own moment of history. His prayer plunges him into action.

We, too, should recognize that we are part of the events of our time, complicit in society's wrongs and responsible for our part in them.

COLLECT

Almighty God,
you have broken the tyranny of sin
and have sent the Spirit of your Son into our hearts
    whereby we call you Father:
give us grace to dedicate our freedom to your service,
that we and all creation may be brought
    to the glorious liberty of the children of God;
through Jesus Christ your Son our Lord,
who is alive and reigns with you,
in the unity of the Holy Spirit,
one God, now and for ever.

| *Reflection by* **Angela Tilby**

Saturday 13 July

Nehemiah 2

'The God of heaven is the one who will give us success' (v.20)

There is much talk of leadership in the Church these days; Nehemiah's testimony demonstrates the transition he makes from faithful servant to servant leader. For Nehemiah to confide in the king is not without risk, but his candour calls out the king's support. Trusting God, he puts himself at God's disposal and so comes to fulfil his own prayer in a way that reveals both his courage and his prudence.

He starts work immediately, but is wise enough to be discreet, conducting a secret survey of the walls by night. His project of restoration is bound to arouse opposition from those who are profiting from the city's misfortunes. Having assessed the extent of the damage, he proposes a programme of rebuilding the walls, which brings the opposition out into the open.

Nehemiah's leadership is courageous but not reckless. He knows when to speak and when to be silent. He also judges when he needs to keep his own counsel and when he needs to evoke a sense of common purpose. He confronts his enemies at a time and place of his own choosing and lays out his intention without compromise. We should be careful what we pray for – we too may find ourselves fulfilling our own prayers!

God our saviour,
look on this wounded world
in pity and in power;
hold us fast to your promises of peace
won for us by your Son,
our Saviour Jesus Christ.

COLLECT

Monday 15 July

Psalms **80**, 82
Nehemiah 4
Romans 14.13-end

Nehemiah 4

'Our God will fight for us' (v.20)

Nehemiah's attempt to reconstruct the city wall was bold to the point of audacity. Success depended on getting the practicalities right, but it also required him to maintain a defiant spirit among the workers. The enemy tried to undermine the restoration by mockery, and when this did not work, they resorted to violence. Nehemiah responded with urgent and heartfelt prayer and continued with the rebuilding, keeping his focus on the practical issues, ensuring that the workmen were guarded and that the builders had weapons.

Opposition is an inevitable part of the Christian life. God does not force us to obey him; he does not intervene to crush those who are opposing his will. Good leadership is both practical and spiritual. Nehemiah's oversight was characterized by constant encouragement. He knew how easy it is for those under verbal and physical threat to lose confidence – hence his constant assurance that God was supporting the work.

This passage invites us to consider how generous we are in our encouragement to those struggling for justice and for the spread of the gospel. We live at a time when the harshest mockery is regarded as acceptable social currency. The Church and the beliefs of Christianity are routinely rubbished and deeply misunderstood. What will we do today to 'rebuild the walls' of faith and to encourage a compassionate and civilized society?

COLLECT

O God, the protector of all who trust in you,
without whom nothing is strong, nothing is holy:
increase and multiply upon us your mercy;
that with you as our ruler and guide
we may so pass through things temporal
that we lose not our hold on things eternal;
grant this, heavenly Father,
for our Lord Jesus Christ's sake,
who is alive and reigns with you,
in the unity of the Holy Spirit,
one God, now and for ever.

| *Reflection by* **Angela Tilby**

Tuesday 16 July

Nehemiah 5

'The people did as they had promised' (v.13)

The account of the work on the wall is interrupted by Nehemiah's description of a wave of social unrest caused by the consequences of famine. People are hungry; households are in debt as they struggle to survive. Characteristically, Nehemiah does not rush impulsively into action but spends time in thought and reflection. This gives him time to analyse the situation, not only economically but morally. He is then in a position to shame the 'nobles and officials' who have demanded interest on loans at a time when no one can afford to pay. Nehemiah leads by example, pointing out that he has never sought to enrich himself and has never lorded it over those who worked with him.

The call to justice rings through scripture. Debt is not forbidden, but it is outrageous for the rich to exploit the poor. We have no authority to call others to live justly unless we are prepared to be fair in our dealings with others. The security that many crave in our society is not something that can be imposed; it requires everyone to live with an awareness of others' needs.

In the end, the outer security provided by the city will is connected to the establishment of a just community within. Christian leadership has many elements, but perhaps the most important is to lead by example.

Gracious Father,
by the obedience of Jesus
you brought salvation to our wayward world:
draw us into harmony with your will,
that we may find all things restored in him,
our Saviour Jesus Christ.

COLLECT

Reflection by **Angela Tilby**   203

Wednesday 17 July

Nehemiah 6.1 – 7.4

'Now, O God, strengthen my hands' (6.9)

As the work on the reconstruction of the wall comes near to completion, Nehemiah's enemies increase their attempts to remove him. This chapter describes a series of plots designed to rubbish his reputation and put him in physical danger. The plots are all foiled, and the wall is finally completed.

Nehemiah's courage and persistence continue to provoke those who have profited from the city's downfall. At first they had employed mockery and vague threats, but now they resort to downright lies and intimidation. Nehemiah needs to exercise the gift of discernment, teasing out the truth behind the false accusation that he is trying to set himself up as king, and the false warning that he is about to be murdered.

We might think that our context of 'fake news' and intimidation spread by social media is something new. Nehemiah's testimony assures us that such tricks are ancient and very human. In our daily life and prayer, we need to cultivate both resilience and humility. We cannot necessarily rely on others' goodwill, especially when circumstances require us to implement change. Nehemiah does not ask God to destroy his enemies, but to 'remember' what they did. It is sometimes difficult to find the truth when untruth is the currency of communication, but God remembers and knows and judges the intentions of all human hearts.

COLLECT

O God, the protector of all who trust in you,
without whom nothing is strong, nothing is holy:
increase and multiply upon us your mercy;
that with you as our ruler and guide
we may so pass through things temporal
that we lose not our hold on things eternal;
grant this, heavenly Father,
for our Lord Jesus Christ's sake,
who is alive and reigns with you,
in the unity of the Holy Spirit,
one God, now and for ever.

| *Reflection by* **Angela Tilby**

Thursday 18 July

Nehemiah 7.73*b* – end of 8

'... the joy of the Lord is your strength' (8.10)

Ezra and Nehemiah are now depicted together; the faithful scribe and the political reformer share a platform at this great gathering to read and interpret the law and to inaugurate the feast of booths. This whole part of the narrative reflects a major transition in Israel's history; the regathering of the community in the restored Jerusalem encountering God through the reading and reception of the law.

The initial response to the reading of the law is a deep sense of failure and inadequacy. But Nehemiah and Ezra respond that this is a holy day, a day of feasting and rejoicing. God has restored his people, and to mark his care for them from the time of the exodus until now, they are to celebrate the feast by living in temporary shelters, acting out their trust in God's protection and provision.

In John's Gospel, it is at the end of the feast of booths that Jesus calls on the thirsty to come to him and drink, and promises the gift of the Holy Spirit to those who believe in him (John 7.37-39). Through Christ, Christians inherit the promises of God to Israel. In spite of our sins and failures, God renews our life, revealing his love in the provision he makes for our survival, continuity and flourishing. There should be a place in our prayer today for joy and gratitude for all God's goodness.

Gracious Father,
by the obedience of Jesus
you brought salvation to our wayward world:
draw us into harmony with your will,
that we may find all things restored in him,
our Saviour Jesus Christ.

COLLECT

Reflection by **Angela Tilby**   205

Friday 19 July

Psalms **88** (95)
Nehemiah 9.1-23
Romans 16.1-16

Nehemiah 9.1-23

'You gave your good spirit to instruct them' (v.20)

Believers are formed by memories drawn both from history and from communal and individual experience. After the celebration of the feast of booths, the people enter another period of fasting, separating themselves from those not of Israelite descent who do not share the memory of Israel's ancient past. Ezra's prayer summarizes the whole Biblical story from creation 'until today'. It is a glorious and terrible story of promise, elections, conquest and betrayal. God's people have constantly fallen short, but God has remained faithful, renewing and restoring them.

Although this tells the history of Israel, it follows a pattern that Christians should recognize. We thank God as the General Thanksgiving puts it 'for our creation, preservation and all the blessings of this life', and, as we contemplate our failures and betrayals, we also thank God for 'the redemption of the world by our Lord Jesus Christ'. A lively faith is not always looking for something new and different but refreshes itself from within, by recalling what God has done for us and allowing that memory to shape our daily expectations.

This repeated cycle of memory and hope is the work of the Holy Spirit within us, instructing and transforming us into people who bear the fruit of holiness, kindness and goodness. Give thanks today 'for the means of grace and for the hope of glory'.

COLLECT

O God, the protector of all who trust in you,
without whom nothing is strong, nothing is holy:
increase and multiply upon us your mercy;
that with you as our ruler and guide
we may so pass through things temporal
that we lose not our hold on things eternal;
grant this, heavenly Father,
for our Lord Jesus Christ's sake,
who is alive and reigns with you,
in the unity of the Holy Spirit,
one God, now and for ever.

| *Reflection by* **Angela Tilby**

Psalms 96, **97**, 100
Nehemiah 9.24-end
Romans 16.17-end

Saturday 20 July

Nehemiah 9.24-end

'... do not treat lightly all the hardship that has come upon us'
(v.32)

The theme of God's goodness and human failure is reflected throughout the Hebrew Bible, especially in Deuteronomy and the prophetic books, and here this theme is the basis of Ezra's prayer. God's people are still trapped in the cycle of disobedience and disaster. The returned Jews, for all that had been promised, were still under foreign rule, 'slaves to this day'. God has kept his side of the covenant; the reason for the continued subjection of God's people is their continuing proneness to rebellion.

Christians can sometimes overstate their freedom from the constraints of the law and make light of the notion that suffering can arise from disobedience. But we do live in a society that has largely rejected the moral constraints that generations of Christians have lived by. In a general sense, some of the suffering that we observe about us and within us comes from our own behaviour – our greed and envy, vanity and pride.

It is sometimes hard to take a stand on good and evil; hard to recognize the potential for evil in ourselves. Every day we have the opportunity to contribute to society's wellbeing, or, if we choose, to its disintegration. Our Christian responsibility is to live from the love of God, and so to be a channel of God's blessing to those around us.

COLLECT

Gracious Father,
by the obedience of Jesus
you brought salvation to our wayward world:
draw us into harmony with your will,
that we may find all things restored in him,
our Saviour Jesus Christ.

Reflection by **Angela Tilby** | 207

Monday 22 July
Mary Magdalene

Psalms 30, 32, 150
I Samuel 16.14-end
Luke 8.1-3

Luke 8.1-3

'... some women ... provided for them' (vv.2-3)

Women of faith are not always recognized as prominent characters in the story of the Church. Our image of Mary of Magdala, shaped by centuries of iconographic (mis)representation, may be more of a pleading penitent than the woman of stature whom Luke describes as a key figure in the Jesus movement.

The extent of Mary's contribution is all the more remarkable because she was a woman of her times. Yet Luke presents her, alongside the twelve male disciples, as one of a group of leading women who supported Jesus and his ministry out of their own means. Not only was she a woman of substance, but she was also capable of significant initiative and influence to provide for this fast-growing movement out of her own means.

Each individual, in every generation, has to work out their vocation. What can I do? What is the particular gift I can offer, as one woman, one man, to take forward the good news? Whatever my place in society, I can trust that there is something unique for me to do that would otherwise not be done.

In a culture that worships celebrity status and ostentatious leadership, it is easy to undervalue the work of those pillars of the Church – many of them women – without whom the work of God in our own day would all too quickly falter and fail. What is the motive that drives your own unique contribution to the good news?

COLLECT

Almighty God,
whose Son restored Mary Magdalene to health of mind
　　and body
and called her to be a witness to his resurrection:
forgive our sins and heal us by your grace,
that we may serve you in the power of his risen life;
who is alive and reigns with you,
in the unity of the Holy Spirit,
one God, now and for ever.

| *Reflection by* **Margaret Whipp**

Psalms **106*** *(or* 103)
Nehemiah 13.1-14
2 Corinthians 1.15 – 2.4

Tuesday 23 July

Nehemiah 13.1-14

'Why is the house of God forsaken?' (v.11)

Nehemiah's memoirs paint a vivid picture of a fully three-dimensional character. Arguably not all of his passions and priorities would sit comfortably with the principles of a modern liberal society.

The loosely connected episodes in today's reading show a decisive leader consolidating his agenda with considerable force as he works to establish his ideal vision of a reformed Jerusalem.

What are we to make of Nehemiah's programme? Were the dangers of religious dilution so serious as to require strict policies of racial segregation (v.3)? Was the honour of God so compromised by the reallocation of living space in the temple precincts as to justify violent eviction of his one-time political opponent (v.8)? And how well founded were his allegations of corruption in the management of the Levites (v.10)?

As usual in the narration of reform movements, we are hearing only one side of a complex story. Who knows what motives of ethnic pride and religious fervour combined to drive Nehemiah's hard-line approach? Yet perhaps his reforming zeal was not entirely different from that which later drove Jesus to such a furious show-down in the temple that his disciples remarked, 'Zeal for your house will consume me' (John 2.17, cf. Psalm 69.9). However history may judge this fervent character, we recall that at the end of the day, he laid all of his efforts before God, praying humbly for mercy (vv.14,22,31).

COLLECT

Almighty and everlasting God,
by whose Spirit the whole body of the Church
is governed and sanctified:
hear our prayer which we offer for all your faithful people,
that in their vocation and ministry
they may serve you in holiness and truth
to the glory of your name;
through our Lord and Saviour Jesus Christ,
who is alive and reigns with you,
in the unity of the Holy Spirit,
one God, now and for ever.

Reflection by **Margaret Whipp** | 209

Wednesday 24 July

Psalms 110, 111, 112
Nehemiah 13.15-end
2 Corinthians 2.5-end

Nehemiah 13.15-end

'Did not your ancestors act in this way ...?' (v.18)

In today's final section, Nehemiah drives further down the road of vigorous reform. His programme of vehement cleansing and consolidation entails a crackdown on sabbath violations and mixed marriages, alongside a determined restoration of the order and sanctity of temple worship. After the humiliation of exile and the degradation of Jewish worship, it is hardly surprising that Nehemiah should feel so keenly for the honour of God's holy city and temple. It must have been unbearable to contemplate that the fragile remnant of God's covenant people, under pressure to assimilate into the dominant pluralism of the mighty Persian Empire, might gradually crumble or disappear. Against this background we may sympathize with Nehemiah's anxious desire to protect the signs of a distinctive Jewish identity. Perhaps above everything else he wanted to avoid any return to the complacency that had led his ancestors down the tragic road of disobedience and exile.

But is this always the best approach? Is holiness necessarily defined by distinctiveness and opposition to prevailing tides of religious or cultural identity? There are several telling counter-examples in the Old Testament – Joseph, Moses, Boaz, David – whose marriages to 'foreign wives' suggest a rather different vision of faithful leadership.

Nehemiah prays; for it is only through God's mercy that the best of human ideals, despite our inevitable blindspots, will yield any lasting blessing.

COLLECT

Almighty and everlasting God,
by whose Spirit the whole body of the Church
    is governed and sanctified:
hear our prayer which we offer for all your faithful people,
that in their vocation and ministry
they may serve you in holiness and truth
to the glory of your name;
through our Lord and Saviour Jesus Christ,
who is alive and reigns with you,
in the unity of the Holy Spirit,
one God, now and for ever.

Reflection by **Margaret Whipp**

Psalms 7, 29, 117
2 Kings 1.9-15
Luke 9.46-56

Thursday 25 July
James the Apostle

Luke 9.46-56

'... which one of them was the greatest' (v.46)

Today we celebrate the feast of Saint James. Known as James the Greater, he was one of the foremost of the twelve disciples, though our reading scarcely shows him in a complimentary light. Luke's glimpse into the everyday interactions among Jesus' disciples crackles with jealousy, self-importance and competitiveness. At the very moment when Jesus sought to confide in them, and to share the profound significance of his forthcoming passion (v.44f.), his closest friends were too preoccupied with their own internal squabbles to listen.

This rivalry amongst the inner band of disciples reflects a broader competitive spirit between the true followers of Jesus, as they saw themselves, and certain other people working in his name whom the disciples deemed to be unsound. Jesus' gnomic comment exposes the shallowness of their presumed superiority: 'whoever is not against you is for you'.

Such petty sectarianism between individual believers plays out on a still wider canvas in the deep-rooted suspicion between Jews and Samaritans. The Samaritans showed outright hostility towards pilgrims heading to Jerusalem who, from their point of view, worshipped God in the wrong way and in the wrong place.

It is sobering to recognize how people, entrusted in one way or another with God's favour, can fall into a sense of spiritual entitlement. We read that Jesus knew their thoughts. I wonder what he would make of ours?

Merciful God,
whose holy apostle Saint James,
leaving his father and all that he had,
was obedient to the calling of your Son Jesus Christ
and followed him even to death:
help us, forsaking the false attractions of the world,
to be ready at all times to answer your call without delay;
through Jesus Christ your Son our Lord,
who is alive and reigns with you,
in the unity of the Holy Spirit,
one God, now and for ever.

COLLECT

Reflection by **Margaret Whipp** | 211

Friday 26 July

Esther 2

'... the king loved Esther more than all the other women' (v.17)

The book of Esther gives a distinctive slant on the Persian period of Jewish experience. Unlike the broadly historical memoirs of Nehemiah, which centre on the holy city of Jerusalem, this diaspora folktale is set in the heart of the Persian capital of Susa, where geopolitical forces intersect with everyday racial and sexual power-play in a richly ironic and entertaining story.

Esther (her Persian name) is an orphan child who has been adopted into the home of her cousin Mordecai. Disadvantaged from every angle, she is a child without parents, a woman in a man's world, and – central to the main plot of the story – a Jew in an alien land where genocide threatens.

The tale of Esther's rise to the crown is a classic Eastern court romance – enchanting or appalling, depending on your point of view. From one perspective, Esther gains favour because of her outstanding loveliness: the Jewish 'beauty queen' who wins the most glamorous place in the imperial household. From another perspective, she is a submissive pawn in a world where young girls had little choice but to comply with the demands of sexually and politically all-powerful men.

Whichever reading you prefer, the story turns on the fact that there is much more to Esther than her sexual attractiveness to the Persian king. Through her artfulness and courage, her subtlety and initiative, we shall learn how this undercover Jewess becomes the unlikely saviour of her people.

COLLECT

Almighty and everlasting God,
by whose Spirit the whole body of the Church
    is governed and sanctified:
hear our prayer which we offer for all your faithful people,
that in their vocation and ministry
they may serve you in holiness and truth
to the glory of your name;
through our Lord and Saviour Jesus Christ,
who is alive and reigns with you,
in the unity of the Holy Spirit,
one God, now and for ever.

| *Reflection by* **Margaret Whipp**

Psalms 120, **121**, 122
Esther 3
2 Corinthians 5

Saturday 27 July

Esther 3

'... do with them as it seems good to you' (v.11)

King Ahasuerus needs loyal henchmen. Following an attempted plot on his life, this ineffectual Persian potentate elevates the villainous Haman to the position of his senior court official. It is a foolish appointment. Haman comes from the lineage of Hammedatha the Agagite, a descendant of the Amalekites who were historic arch-enemies of the people of Israel. The stage is set for some ugly interracial tensions to be inflamed by personal pique and jealousy.

When Mordecai, possibly for religious reasons, or perhaps simply as a matter of personal dignity, refuses to bow down in obeisance to his newly-exalted fellow courtier, the infuriated Haman smells blood. Here is his opportunity to enact a 'final solution' on the minority Jewish population.

What follows is a classic outworking of uncritical state-sponsored terrorism. Ahasuerus provides the necessary funding, and hands over his signet ring to Haman, in a fatal abdication of power to his murderous deputy. The secretaries, and satraps, and governors, each in their respective layer of unthinking bureaucracy, move to implement the horrific order that will exterminate all Jews, 'young and old, women and children, in one day'. Even as an exaggerated piece of pious fiction, this is a narrative to make anyone shudder.

Which is worse: the careless abdication of responsibility, the vindictive abuse of power, or the mindless compliance with wickedness in high places?

COLLECT

Almighty God,
send down upon your Church
the riches of your Spirit,
and kindle in all who minister the gospel
your countless gifts of grace;
through Jesus Christ our Lord.

Monday 29 July

Esther 4

'... for just such a time as this' (v.14)

How do God's people respond to a time of crisis? The psalmist prays for deliverance, trusting a guiding hand behind cruel or random dictates of fate. 'My times are in your hand; deliver me from the hand of my enemies and persecutors' (Psalm 31.15).

Esther, with her fellow Jews in terror for their lives, and the whole city of Susa in confusion, faces a time of crucial decision. Now that she is in a unique position of potentially enormous significance, she must decide where her loyalties lie. But Esther is astute enough to recognize the terrible risk to herself as she considers how best to navigate the complex and capricious regulations of palace life.

Strangely, the canonical book of Esther contains no explicit mention of God. Yet throughout its terrifying chronicle of events, we sense the outworking of a divine providence. It is left to an apocryphal tradition (chapter 14 of the Greek additions to the book of Esther) to fill in the background of heartfelt prayer through which faithful Esther entrusts these times into God's hand.

Esther steps up to her appalling moment of destiny, a woman of spiritual and moral courage gathering all the strength of solidarity in prayer and fasting to fulfil her unique vocation. To this day, in the festival of Purim on the thirteenth day of Adar, Jewish people still honour her remarkable faithfulness.

COLLECT

Merciful God,
you have prepared for those who love you
such good things as pass our understanding:
pour into our hearts such love toward you
that we, loving you in all things and above all things,
may obtain your promises,
which exceed all that we can desire;
through Jesus Christ your Son our Lord,
who is alive and reigns with you,
in the unity of the Holy Spirit,
one God, now and for ever.

Psalms **132**, 133
Esther 5
2 Corinthians 7.2-end

Tuesday 30 July

Esther 5

'Esther put on her royal robes' (v.1)

Esther rises from her knees to seize the initiative. Up to this point in the story, her character has been docile and passive, but now, at this critical moment, the mature woman steps forward to take command. Putting on her royal robes, Esther strides into the king's chamber as an archdiplomat for the Jewish people.

How does Esther know what to do? Until this juncture, she has been coached by Mordecai and cossetted by the king's eunuchs. Now she must stand alone to fulfil her vocation in a situation of utmost danger.

There are moments in every life when a unique calling comes sharply into focus. Often it takes a crisis to break open the opportunity that will galvanize our hidden gifts. For women, it can take a particular kind of courage to embrace the authority which God gives them for such a time.

There is no clever algorithm or magical formula for divining human vocation. Esther applied her intellect and her considerable social skills; she worked out a careful strategy and followed it through; she kept a cool head and a faithful heart, and seized the challenge which was laid before her. This was her defining opportunity to be of service to her people, and her God.

'I have done what was mine to do,' said the dying Saint Francis. 'May Christ teach you what you are to do.'

COLLECT

Creator God,
you made us all in your image:
may we discern you in all that we see,
and serve you in all that we do;
through Jesus Christ our Lord.

Reflection by **Margaret Whipp**   215

Wednesday 31 July

Psalm **119.153-end**
Esther 6.1-13
2 Corinthians 8.1-15

Esther 6.1-13

'... the king could not sleep' (v.1)

Who would imagine that the fate of the entire Jewish population would turn on the quality of King Ahasuerus' sleep? It is not uncommon in biblical narratives to find rulers facing questions of profound moral consequence in the small hours of the night (cf. Daniel 6.18-19; Matthew 27.19).

At this point in the story we would not be surprised to find Mordecai or Esther tossing and turning on their beds. Ruthless Haman has erected a gallows on which he plans to have his archenemy put to death the following morning. But, in a twist of supreme irony, the king's sleepless night marks the turning point towards Haman's destruction and the salvation of the Jews.

We are left marvelling at this outworking of providence. God moves in mysterious ways, and it is worth reflecting on some of these mysteries in the way that our story unfolds. Was providence at work in the choice of reading that the king's attendants selected for him? Did some inner voice remind them of the unshakable loyalty of Mordecai the Jew? Perhaps a guiding hand was at work in the chronicler's epic writing style that brought the integrity of Mordecai so engagingly to the king's consciousness. We can certainly marvel at the instinctive sense of timely restraint by which good Queen Esther had prepared the ground for this historic reversal.

God moves in mysterious ways – even in the depths of insomnia.

COLLECT

Merciful God,
you have prepared for those who love you
such good things as pass our understanding:
pour into our hearts such love toward you
that we, loving you in all things and above all things,
may obtain your promises,
which exceed all that we can desire;
through Jesus Christ your Son our Lord,
who is alive and reigns with you,
in the unity of the Holy Spirit,
one God, now and for ever.

| *Reflection by* **Margaret Whipp**

Psalms 143, 146
Esther 6.14 – end of 7
2 Corinthians 8.16 – 9.5

Thursday 1 August

Esther 6.14 – end of 7

'... as they were drinking wine' (7.2)

One of the striking motifs of the book of Esther is the repeated description of lavish banquets. Three are called by the king, the second in honour of Queen Esther (Esther 2.18); one is called by Vashti; two are called by Esther; and the book closes with joyful Jewish banquets foreshadowing the great festival of Purim (Esther 9).

Today's reading shows Esther using the social apparatus of the banquet to triumphant political effect. With an impeccable sense of timing, our heroine holds her nerve until the second day of her second banquet before disclosing her true identity as an imperilled Jewess.

By this stage the king is both curious and merry with wine. Seizing the moment to gain his ear, Esther speaks out boldly to reveal the genocidal plan that will not simply threaten her own life but, more tellingly as far as the king is concerned, bring shame and dishonour to his royal court (v.4).

It is this combination of shrewdness and audacity that plays so effectively into the purpose of a guiding providence. If we can speak of a theology in the book of Esther, then the working of the unnamed God of the Jews is decisively enacted through the astuteness and courage of his endangered people. Even with horrific consequences at stake, Esther appreciates that there is 'a time to keep silence, and a time to speak' (Ecclesiastes 3.7).

COLLECT

Creator God,
you made us all in your image:
may we discern you in all that we see,
and serve you in all that we do;
through Jesus Christ our Lord.

Reflection by **Margaret Whipp** | 217

Friday 2 August

Psalms 142, **144**
Esther 8
2 Corinthians 9.6-end

Esther 8

'... how can I bear to see the destruction of my kindred?' (v.6)

Evil Haman is dead. And honours are being piled upon faithful Mordecai. But the dreadful threat of state-sanctioned extermination still hangs over the Jewish people.

Reading the story of Esther in a post-holocaust world should be a disturbing experience. On one level we can enjoy the fabulously overdrawn characters, with their pantomime exaggerations of villainy and vengeance. In the spirit of good folklore, we know that the baddies will get their comeuppance in the end. However, real life and the unfoldings of human history are rarely so straightforward. Dark shadows of evil and chilling inhumanity threaten generation after generation. We need only place the name Hitler alongside the name of Haman to recall the horrific reiterations of megalomania and cruelty, especially towards diaspora or minority peoples.

Faced with unimaginable terror, Esther abandons her cool and falls at the king's feet in tears. Her weeping echoes the lament of countless victims of hatred down the centuries. For every Purim prayer giving thanks to God for his miraculous deliverances, believers are called to persist in prayer for the unfinished business of overcoming evil with good in this violent world.

As we pray in faith for deliverance from evil, God's people must often weep. 'How long, O Lord?' (Psalm 13.1)

COLLECT

Merciful God,
you have prepared for those who love you
such good things as pass our understanding:
pour into our hearts such love toward you
that we, loving you in all things and above all things,
may obtain your promises,
which exceed all that we can desire;
through Jesus Christ your Son our Lord,
who is alive and reigns with you,
in the unity of the Holy Spirit,
one God, now and for ever.

| *Reflection by* **Margaret Whipp**

Psalm 147
Esther 9.20-28
2 Corinthians 10

Saturday 3 August

Esther 9.20-28

'These days should be remembered and kept ...' (v.28)

In modern Judaism, the springtime festival of Purim is marked by exuberance and great good humour. It is often compared to Mardi Gras in its colourful, carnivalesque atmosphere. Children and adults dress up, taking the parts of Queen Esther, Uncle Mordecai, or the black-clad, villainous Haman. Gifts are exchanged; good causes are supported; and, following a preliminary fast ('the fast of Esther' Esther 4.16), a time of joyful feasting ensues.

Central to the festivities is the synagogue reading of the book of Esther (the *Megillah*), which is typically accompanied by raucous audience participation in the form of shouts, boos and rattles every time the name of evil Haman is pronounced.

Although scholars may question the historicity of the biblical story of Esther, there is no doubt about the deeply historical sense of identity that is rekindled with every Jewish celebration of Purim. Inheritors of this ancient tradition 'in every family, province, and city' spare no effort to re-enact the saga which turned them 'from sorrow into gladness and from mourning into a holiday'.

One of the great functions of religion is to bind communities together in acts of solemn and joyful remembrance. This is how we re-engage our deepest identity, and re-dedicate ourselves, for our own life and times, to the providential care of the High and Holy One who – at least in the book of Esther – remains the Great Unnamed.

Creator God,
you made us all in your image:
may we discern you in all that we see,
and serve you in all that we do;
through Jesus Christ our Lord.

COLLECT

Reflection by **Margaret Whipp** | 219

Monday 5 August

Jeremiah 26

'I may change my mind about the disaster that I intend to bring on them' (v. 3)

Jeremiah is given a straightforward message to proclaim publicly in the temple with the instruction not to delete a single word: walk in my law and heed my prophets or share the fate of Shiloh – destruction. It is an unenviable commission that carries with it the threat of personal danger. Predictably, it is received badly; this dreadful news stands counter to the reassurance given by false prophets that all will be well. But the harshness of Jeremiah's message is tempered by the possibility of an alternative outcome. *If* they turn from their evil ways, I *may* change my mind, says God. In many ways the conditional nature of the message makes it even more difficult to hear. Destruction is not a foregone conclusion, but avoiding it will require significant effort and a reversal of behaviour. Jeremiah makes it clear that responsibility for the future of the city lies with those he is addressing: the choice of the people will determine the action of God. The elders recognize elements from past prophecies. 'Ah, it's like what happened with Micah and Hezekiah: then, a great disaster was averted.' But their wisdom goes unheeded.

It is hard to hear a message that makes it clear that change is necessary, but real wisdom involves listening to unwelcome truths. We always get a choice with God and, if we seek it, help in choosing so that we may respond with humility and courage.

COLLECT

Lord of all power and might,
the author and giver of all good things:
graft in our hearts the love of your name,
increase in us true religion,
nourish us with all goodness,
and of your great mercy keep us in the same;
through Jesus Christ your Son our Lord,
who is alive and reigns with you,
in the unity of the Holy Spirit,
one God, now and for ever.

| *Reflection by* **Helen Orchard**

Psalms 27, 150
Ecclesiasticus 48.1-10
or 1 Kings 19.1-16
1 John 3.1-3

Tuesday 6 August
Transfiguration of our Lord

1 Kings 19.1-16
'... the Lord is about to pass by' (v.11)

High on the mountain, Elijah hears the voice of God as he passes by. It is not what he expects and, overawed, he covers his face with his cloak.

High on the mountain, Peter hears the voice of God as Christ is transfigured before him. It is not what he expects and, overawed, he offers a pragmatic suggestion to try and contain the situation.

Oftentimes, when we want guidance or support, we wish that the Lord would 'pass by', revealing something to us, or speaking words of direction and guidance. But the longer we have been Christians, the more we come to realize that the God who goes before and after us rarely communicates with us in the way we expect. In fact, the more we try to make God 'happen', the more elusive he may seem. Our God cannot be conscribed or contained within a shelter made by human hands.

God does not appear to Elijah in the demonstrations of power that he might have expected: wind, earthquake and fire. Instead, something more profound is given, something that can barely be described by the text: the 'still, small voice', or the 'sound of sheer silence', depending on the translation. By watching and waiting, Elijah has allowed himself to be found by God who, passing by, provides that which he really needs.

Reflection by **Helen Orchard**   221

Wednesday 7 August

Psalm 119.1-32
Jeremiah 29.1-14
2 Corinthians 12

Jeremiah 29.1-14

'... seek the welfare of the city where I have sent you into exile'
(v.7)

Jeremiah's letter to the exiles in Babylon reveals what a controversial, but also pastoral, prophet he is. While the prophets in Babylon are still encouraging the exiles to think they will be home in two years, Jeremiah prepares them for the long haul. His advice is a sound strategy for survival in a foreign land: settle down and make the best of it. Build, plant, eat, marry and multiply so that you may be in a good position to start again when you do return.

He goes a step further than practical instruction, however, by also issuing a revolutionary spiritual imperative: 'Seek the welfare (*shalom*) of the city ... and pray to the Lord on its behalf'. Is this just a recommendation based on political expediency? After all, things will go better for the exiles if they accommodate their imperial oppressors and contribute to peace and prosperity in Babylon. Or is there more to it than that? It places a responsibility on the exilic community to look beyond itself and its woes. Put into the language of Jesus, it also sounds rather like a command to love your enemies and pray for your persecutors.

When prompted to pray 'forgive us our trespasses', Judah refused. Now the exiles are given an even harder prayer to pray, 'forgive those who trespass against us'. Which is the more pressing for you today?

COLLECT

Lord of all power and might,
the author and giver of all good things:
graft in our hearts the love of your name,
increase in us true religion,
nourish us with all goodness,
and of your great mercy keep us in the same;
through Jesus Christ your Son our Lord,
who is alive and reigns with you,
in the unity of the Holy Spirit,
one God, now and for ever.

| *Reflection by* **Helen Orchard**

Thursday 8 August

Jeremiah 30.1-11

'Ask now, and see, can a man bear a child?' (v.6)

Chapters 30 to 33 of Jeremiah are often referred to as the 'Book of Comfort', containing the reassurance that God will bring his people back to their own land, giving the exiles hope.

It begins with an arresting metaphor: that of men acting as though they were in labour. It is a ludicrous and mocking (as well as sexist) image: those brave soldiers, now pale and clutching their stomachs in fear and panic as though they were women in distress. Jeremiah uses the childbirth metaphor more than any other prophet. But it is the pain of labour without the subsequent joy of bringing new life into the world. Thus the metaphor conveys a suffering that is unproductive and points to death, rather than life, through panic, terror, distress and 'no peace'.

Whether or not we have borne children, we may have experienced the physical pain caused by overwhelming fear and panic, or been with someone to whom that has happened. The physical response can seem to take us over and it is impossible to think clearly or act rationally. It is worth remembering in those moments the One whose labour pains have been worthwhile, bringing life to those who walk in the valley of the shadow of death and soothing children in distress. Have no fear – I am with you to save you; you will have quiet and ease, says the Lord, comforting as a mother comforts her child (Isaiah 66.13).

> Generous God,
> you give us gifts and make them grow:
> though our faith is small as mustard seed,
> make it grow to your glory
> and the flourishing of your kingdom;
> through Jesus Christ our Lord.

COLLECT

Friday 9 August

Jeremiah 30.12-22

'I will restore health to you, and your wounds I will heal' (v.17)

Today's metaphor for the exile involves sickness and healing, but the prophet employs extreme language to show how poor is the prognosis. The sickness is incurable: there is no medicine for such grievous wounds and God's people are pronounced terminally ill.

We expect that the 'therefore' of verse 16 will announce the death knell, but instead there is a surprise *volte-face*: the devourers will be devoured, foes made captive, plunderers plundered and predators become prey. Even more miraculous, God will restore health and heal wounds. The impossible will be possible because God will bring about a great reversal.

What has prompted this? Is it perhaps the taunt of the nations: 'It is Zion; no one cares for her!'? That statement is a lie that seems to demand a response. After all, it is one thing for God to punish his people. It is quite another for the nations to say that God's people have been cast out because they are unloved. As we will see tomorrow, God's love for Zion is everlasting, and it is this love that enables the wounds that were incurable to be healed. Indeed, love is the cause of all divine reversals and the reason why nothing is impossible for God. The defeat of death itself is wrought by the one who, though rich, became poor; though equal with God, he emptied himself and took the form of a slave that he might lift up the lowly.

COLLECT

Lord of all power and might,
the author and giver of all good things:
graft in our hearts the love of your name,
increase in us true religion,
nourish us with all goodness,
and of your great mercy keep us in the same;
through Jesus Christ your Son our Lord,
who is alive and reigns with you,
in the unity of the Holy Spirit,
one God, now and for ever.

| *Reflection by* **Helen Orchard**

Psalms 20, 21, **23**
Jeremiah 31.1-22
James 1.12-end

Saturday 10 August

Jeremiah 31.1-22

'I have loved you with an everlasting love.' (v.3)

The language of everlasting love is something we may more easily associate with pop songs and rom-coms than religion. It evokes scenes of misty-eyed swooning passion and rash declarations in the early stages of a love affair. However, the everlasting love that Yahweh declares for Israel is of a much more gritty nature, though it is no less passionate. It is a love that does not burn down to embers over the course of time, but always blazes brightly. The purging that is punishment from God is simply one way in which the flame of his love radiates.

The real test of everlasting love is shown through a faithfulness that, following such purging, enables the relationship to start anew. It is the pattern of death and resurrection that is hard-wired into Christian life. We see this in the threefold promise of verses 4-5, each couplet of which begins with 'Again'. Urban, social and rural life will be restored and, in verse 6, so will the spiritual centre when sentinels call 'Come, let us go up to Zion' in an allusion to temple worship.

Starting afresh requires letting go of what has gone before in a kind of holy forgetting of what was there before the cleansing fire. It is only in this way that Israel who 'played the whore' (Jeremiah 3.1) can be like a virgin again. What is it that we need to forget in order for love to begin again?

Reflection by **Helen Orchard** | 225

Monday 12 August

Jeremiah 31.23-25, 27-37

'I will put my law within them, and I will write it on their hearts'
(v.33)

Jeremiah contains quite a few references to the human heart, most of them unfavourable. Specifically, 'the heart is devious above all else; it is perverse – who can understand it?' (Jeremiah 17.9). In biblical thought, the heart was not simply the seat of emotion but also of volition: it knows and wills as well as feels. When we learn that 'The sin of Judah is written with an iron pen; with a diamond point it is engraved on the tablet of their hearts' (Jeremiah 17.1), we realize that a significant cardiac intervention will be required for health to be restored.

In today's passage we learn of the treatment plan: it is nothing less than a new covenant. Instead of a law chipped out on tablets of stone, a more delicate keyhole procedure is proposed. The law will be skilfully inscribed on the heart of each of God's people. As a result they will all 'know' God, a word that indicates the intimate personal knowledge shared by two parties who are committed wholly to one another in relationship.

How is your heart bearing up this morning: robust or fragile; tender or sclerotic? Sometimes it can be difficult to remember that God has written his law of love on our own hearts, but just remembering that can help to soften it. In Book IV of *Against Heresies*, the early Church Father St Irenaeus advises, 'Offer to him your heart in a soft and tractable state ... lest you lose the impression of his fingers'.

COLLECT

Almighty Lord and everlasting God,
we beseech you to direct, sanctify and govern
    both our hearts and bodies
in the ways of your laws
    and the works of your commandments;
that through your most mighty protection, both here and ever,
we may be preserved in body and soul;
through our Lord and Saviour Jesus Christ,
who is alive and reigns with you,
in the unity of the Holy Spirit,
one God, now and for ever.

| *Reflection by* **Helen Orchard**

Tuesday 13 August

Jeremiah 32.1-15

'Houses and fields and vineyards shall again be bought in this land'
(v.15)

Context is everything. There is nothing unusual about Jeremiah buying a piece of land from his cousin Hanamel to keep it in the family. The noteworthy fact is that the field is in the middle of a war zone and, given that the Babylonians have only temporarily withdrawn from besieging Jerusalem and will certainly be back, purchasing land is not necessarily a wise move. However, discerning that it is 'of the Lord', Jeremiah accedes, and the details of the transaction are carefully recorded for posterity in the presence of witnesses.

It is theology rather than economics that is needed to interpret this act. In the midst of losing the entire land to the Babylonians, and the crisis of the people being deported, there remains one field on which Jeremiah has staked a claim. It is a symbol of hope in the midst of a hopeless situation. Though the purchase deeds are put in a jar for long-term storage, one day trading will resume. Judah will suffer judgement, Jerusalem will be destroyed, but Jeremiah makes a practical investment in God's promise of future restoration, whenever that might be.

It is the spiritual equivalent of speculating to accumulate. Taking a risk of faith to enact a divine directive will yield unimagined blessings, however foolhardy others consider the action to be at the time.

Lord God,
your Son left the riches of heaven
and became poor for our sake:
when we prosper save us from pride,
when we are needy save us from despair,
that we may trust in you alone;
through Jesus Christ our Lord.

COLLECT

Wednesday 14 August

Psalm **34**
Jeremiah 33.1-13
James 3

Jeremiah 33.1-13

'Call to me and I will answer you' (v.3)

God's servant Jeremiah may be under arrest, but there is no confinement on earth that can prevent God from revealing his vision for the future freedom of Judah. This chapter contains seven promises, three of which we learn of today. Where there is death, dearth and sin, there will be healing, prosperity and cleansing. Where towns are at present desolate, there will be singing and laughing and thanksgiving. Where there is uninhabited wasteland, shepherds will pasture their flocks.

There is only one prerequisite to enable this vision to become reality. 'Call to me', says the Lord. 'Call to me and I will answer you, and will tell you great and hidden things that you have not known.' It is an invitation rather than a diktat: an invitation from the all-powerful God who established the earth to the powerless, landless Israel. The God who seemed to be out of reach invites the people to turn to their maker in their hour of distress. If they do, they will receive the promise of a future they could not have imagined.

Often, the most difficult step in the midst of a trouble of our own making is the heartfelt plea for help. Whether prompted by fear or sorrow, it requires the humility to accept that we are not master of our own destiny, but need one who is both powerful and merciful, to come to our aid.

COLLECT

Almighty Lord and everlasting God,
we beseech you to direct, sanctify and govern
    both our hearts and bodies
in the ways of your laws
    and the works of your commandments;
that through your most mighty protection, both here and ever,
we may be preserved in body and soul;
through our Lord and Saviour Jesus Christ,
who is alive and reigns with you,
in the unity of the Holy Spirit,
one God, now and for ever.

| *Reflection by* **Helen Orchard**

Psalms 98, 138, 147.1-12
Isaiah 7.10-15
Luke 11.27-28

Thursday 15 August
The Blessed Virgin Mary

Isaiah 7.10-15
'Ask a sign of the Lord your God ...' (v.11)

The promise that a young woman will bear a child and call him Immanuel takes our minds to Gospel accounts of the nativity. But these words don't only refer to a distant future; they are first a prophetic message to King Ahaz and the people of Judah.

Judah is besieged by its northern neighbours, Israel ('Ephraim' in preceding verses) and Syria ('Aram' or 'Damascus'). Ahaz' solution is to seek help from Assyria, hoping his enemies' enemy might become his friend. However, Assyria will turn out to be even worse. So, although the two neighbours will withdraw by the time the promised child is responsible for his actions (around 12 or 13 years old), leaving the land sufficiently at peace to enjoy 'curds and honey', later verses warn that Assyria's more terrible arrival will soon follow.

The prophet has already told Ahaz that trusting in God, not Assyria, is the only option. It's true that Deuteronomy 6.16 warns against 'putting God to the test' through disobedience, but other passages recount how 'by signs and wonders' God readily demonstrates that his people may rely upon him (Deuteronomy 4.32-40). Here, it is Ahaz, and his faith, that is really put to the test.

Since God always invites us to put our trust in him, can we see this as an invitation to ask him to open our eyes to see more clearly the fingerprints of his presence in our world?

COLLECT

Almighty God,
who looked upon the lowliness of the Blessed Virgin Mary
and chose her to be the mother of your only Son:
grant that we who are redeemed by his blood
may share with her in the glory of your eternal kingdom;
through Jesus Christ your Son our Lord,
who is alive and reigns with you,
in the unity of the Holy Spirit,
one God, now and for ever.

Reflection by **Sarah Rowland Jones** |

Friday 16 August

Jeremiah 35

'I have spoken to them and they have not listened' (v.17)

Jeremiah sets the example of the Rechabites before the citizens of Jerusalem to make a point. Instructed by their ancestor to live according to specific countercultural precepts, the Rechabites have exercised obedience for centuries and cannot be swayed by Jeremiah's test to drink wine. The key to their success is their willingness to listen. The word 'obey' translates the Hebrew verb *shama`* in many Bibles, but it literally means to hear or listen. It is the most important word in this passage, appearing eight times. On three occasions the Rechabites are commended for listening to their ancestor. Five times the Jerusalemites are castigated for not listening to their God. Listening is the first step of obedience, but the people of Judah will not incline their ear to Yahweh.

Listening to God is so important that it is the pre-eminent prayer of the Jewish faith. Derived from Deuteronomy 6.4-9, the *Shema*, which begins 'Hear, O Israel, the Lord our God, the Lord is one', is the prayer said daily by faithful Jews. For us, too, listening is foundational. Mark's Gospel tells of a scribe who came to Jesus and asked him which is the first of all the commandments. Jesus' answer is: 'The first is, "Hear, O Israel: the Lord our God ... is one; you shall love the Lord your God with all your heart, and with all your soul, and with all your mind, and with all your strength."' (Mark 12.29-30)

COLLECT

Almighty Lord and everlasting God,
we beseech you to direct, sanctify and govern
    both our hearts and bodies
in the ways of your laws
    and the works of your commandments;
that through your most mighty protection, both here and ever,
we may be preserved in body and soul;
through our Lord and Saviour Jesus Christ,
who is alive and reigns with you,
in the unity of the Holy Spirit,
one God, now and for ever.

| *Reflection by* **Helen Orchard**

Saturday 17 August

Jeremiah 36.1-18

'It may be ... that all of them will turn from their evil ways' (vv.3,7)

Even to the last, with the Babylonians banging on the door, there is hope that Judah will repent. 'It may be that they will turn', says Yahweh, and Jeremiah echoes this hope to Baruch. We do not know the contents of the scroll, but we know it comes from God and has one purpose: to prompt repentance, enabling salvation. Baruch is mandated to read the scroll in the temple on a fast day when, perhaps, it may have more impact: fasts were normally called in time of emergency. We don't learn of the people's response, but the scroll quickly comes to the attention of temple officials who request a second reading. So politically inflammatory are its contents that the reading causes consternation: it must go straight to King Jehoiakim, but not via Baruch who, with Jeremiah, must now go into hiding.

That hope of God, of Jeremiah, may resonate with us if we have had the experience of being continually let down by another. We hope that this time there may be, just perhaps, a different outcome. It can be a heart-breaking position to be in, especially when a loved one has set a course that is ultimately self-destructive.

At such times it is comforting to remember that God stands with us as one who knows how to be faithful to the faithless; whose love 'bears all things, believes all things, hopes all things, endures all things' (1 Corinthians 13.7).

Lord God,
your Son left the riches of heaven
and became poor for our sake:
when we prosper save us from pride,
when we are needy save us from despair,
that we may trust in you alone;
through Jesus Christ our Lord.

COLLECT

Monday 19 August

Psalm **44**
Jeremiah 36.19-end
Mark 1.1-13

Jeremiah 36.19-end

'Take another scroll and write ...' (v.28)

In the fourth year of King Jehoiakim of Judah, the word of the Lord came to Jeremiah. He dictated a scroll to the scribe Baruch, calling the house of Judah to turn from evil, and so find forgiveness and avoid disaster. Baruch then read it to officials and people in the temple, where Jeremiah was forbidden to go. Baruch is then called to read it to the palace officials, who warn Baruch and Jeremiah to hide, before taking it to the king and his inner circle. To the alarm of the palace officials, they treat it with utter contempt.

Speaking truth to power is rarely welcome, as it so often challenges not only policies, but also the very basis of authority – which, as Paul points out, is ultimately only found in God (Romans 13.1). But it takes more than refusing to hear, and burning the written word, to silence the truth.

And so Jeremiah and Baruch are called upon to write again – and to write more, spelling out the consequences that follow from failing to heed the life-giving words of truth. The Lord hides them while they do it – it's not a guarantee they'll avoid persecution for all time, but the call to write once more comes with the opportunity to do so.

Where are we given opportunities to keep on speaking up for truth, for voicing God's loving and redemptive perspectives on the issues of the day?

COLLECT

Almighty God,
who sent your Holy Spirit
to be the life and light of your Church:
open our hearts to the riches of your grace,
that we may bring forth the fruit of the Spirit
in love and joy and peace;
through Jesus Christ your Son our Lord,
who is alive and reigns with you,
in the unity of the Holy Spirit,
one God, now and for ever.

| *Reflection by* **Sarah Rowland Jones**

Psalms **48**, 52
Jeremiah 37
Mark 1.14-20

Tuesday 20 August

Jeremiah 37

'Now Jeremiah was still going in and out ...' (v.4)

Zedekiah is now the king of Judah, courtesy of the ruthless Chaldeans, who control Babylon. Against them are pitched their rivals, the other regional power, Egypt. Jerusalem is caught between the two, both geographically and politically.

Swayed by factions favouring the Egyptians, Zedekiah and the city now resist the Chaldeans. On the face of it, this might seem to make sense, as the Chaldeans withdraw from Jerusalem when the Egyptian army marches out, appearing to come to Judah's aid.

But this is blind short-termism, to which a weak king such as Zedekiah is susceptible, being swayed by the latest events or the latest opinions around him. While he wants to hear Jeremiah's views – perhaps half-daring to believe he is a prophet – he's only prepared to see him secretly.

Jeremiah, in contrast, seeks a life of constancy, both in persistently speaking whatever words the Lord gives him, and in trusting his life to this bigger perspective and message. So now we hear of him attempting to visit his property, perhaps the same land that he bought earlier (Jeremiah 32), believing that God's promises provided a context for long-term investment.

What are the long-term plans that God has placed in your heart? What does it mean to remain faithful to them in face of the short-term ups and downs of life?

Gracious Father,
revive your Church in our day,
and make her holy, strong and faithful,
for your glory's sake
in Jesus Christ our Lord.

COLLECT

Wednesday 21 August

Psalm 119.57-80
Jeremiah 38.1-13
Mark 1.21-28

Jeremiah 38.1-13

'... pull the prophet up ... before he dies' (v.10)

It isn't easy to accept that God may want to teach and shape us using people we don't like and events we don't welcome – though, with hindsight, we may recognize how he did 'work ... for good' (Romans 8.28) through them, despite our resistance!

Zedekiah doesn't know whether to recognize and value Jeremiah as a true prophet or not. Now that Jeremiah's message is so unwelcome to those around the king, he wavers, and lets them act against Jeremiah. Zedekiah is altogether a weak character.

That said, Jeremiah's message is undoubtedly a hard one: that God intends to work through the Chaldeans' victory, and therefore the people of Jerusalem should surrender to them. The city's nobles see this as treachery and threaten Jeremiah's life. The spineless king just lets them imprison him without food or water.

But someone is braver – a foreigner, a eunuch, and so doubly despised. Yet he has access to the king, and dares challenge him over Jeremiah's fate. Away from the nobles, the king has sufficient courage to send Ebed-melech to rescue Jeremiah from likely death.

God's capacity to use failures and outcasts, and work through unwelcome circumstances isn't always what we expect or want. Let's pray that even in our weakest moments, we may have eyes to see, ears to hear, and determination to respond.

COLLECT

Almighty God,
who sent your Holy Spirit
to be the life and light of your Church:
open our hearts to the riches of your grace,
that we may bring forth the fruit of the Spirit
in love and joy and peace;
through Jesus Christ your Son our Lord,
who is alive and reigns with you,
in the unity of the Holy Spirit,
one God, now and for ever.

Psalms 56, **57** (63*)
Jeremiah 38.14-end
Mark 1.29-end

Thursday 22 August

Jeremiah 38.14-end

'I am afraid ...' (v.19)

Poor Zedekiah, he does make life difficult for himself! He's afraid of the city officials who had imprisoned Jeremiah for saying the people should surrender to the Chaldeans. And he's afraid of the people who have already gone over to the Chaldeans. He's even afraid of being discovered talking with Jeremiah, while simultaneously being desperate to know what Jeremiah has to say. And yet he is the king.

Power does not always lie where we expect it. Some people ostensibly with high positions may have very little freedom of action in practice. Perhaps, like Zedekiah, they cannot see any way forward that they know themselves capable of taking.

Jeremiah, however, sees with the clarity of God's viewpoint. His is a very measured judgement of political reality, through which theological discernment speaks. The choice is clear, 'if ... then ... if ... then ...'. Jeremiah also knows that the king technically has the power to put him to death, and that he probably won't heed his advice. Yet he has a freedom and even power that the king lacks. And so he doesn't paint the king into a corner, but, by agreeing to hide the truth from the officials, gives him time and space to continue pondering God's message.

When we find ourselves in positions of weakness, may we nonetheless hold on to the freedom that God's perspective provides, and act with strength and generosity.

Gracious Father,
revive your Church in our day,
and make her holy, strong and faithful,
for your glory's sake
in Jesus Christ our Lord.

COLLECT

Reflection by **Sarah Rowland Jones** | 235

Friday 23 August

Jeremiah 39

'The word of the Lord came ...' (v.15)

Zedekiah could not bring himself to trust God's word, and the nobles refused to listen. As Jeremiah foretold, the city falls. Still the king will not surrender, but flees, leaving his people in the lurch. He is captured, and taken before Nebuchadrezzar, whom he (as vassal king) has betrayed, and he, his sons and nobles suffer horrifying consequences. Having refused to submit to Babylon willingly, now he is taken there in chains. Zedekiah has drawn upon himself the terrible consequence of his choices, and through them, God's purpose has worked itself out – but more through death than through the life that was offered, if he had only taken God's path.

The people of the city, whether or not they had previously surrendered to the Chaldeans, are taken to Babylon, already promised as a place of refining and blessing, where they can prosper, and from which they as a people will return (Jeremiah 29.1-17).

Jeremiah's reputation is known to the Chaldeans. He stays in Jerusalem. The word of the Lord comes again, but not for the king or nation, but for a specific individual: a word of reassurance for Ebed-melech, who trusted God and took risks.

In all sorts of ways, God works in, through, with, despite, notwithstanding, and at every level of, current affairs. It may not always be clear to us, but we can be sure that he is never absent. He's always present and active.

COLLECT | Almighty God,
who sent your Holy Spirit
to be the life and light of your Church:
open our hearts to the riches of your grace,
that we may bring forth the fruit of the Spirit
in love and joy and peace;
through Jesus Christ your Son our Lord,
who is alive and reigns with you,
in the unity of the Holy Spirit,
one God, now and for ever.

| *Reflection by* **Sarah Rowland Jones**

Psalms 86, 117
Genesis 28.10-17
John 1.43-end

Saturday 24 August
Bartholomew the Apostle

Genesis 28.10-17

'Surely the Lord is in this place' (v.16)

'Here is truly an Israelite in whom there is no deceit!' says Jesus of the approaching Nathanael, who is generally identified with the Apostle Bartholomew (John 1.43-51). This is in stark contrast to the ultimate Israelite, Israel himself, this being the name given to Jacob after he wrestles with the God-figure at the Jabbok river (Genesis 32.24-32). For Jacob was known for his deceit (Genesis 27.35).

The Greek translation of the Old Testament, current in Jesus' time, uses exactly the same word for Jacob's duplicity as does John's Gospel for Nathanael's guilelessness. Jesus further links the deceit-free Nathanael to the deceitful Jacob as he quotes this passage, telling Nathanael he will 'see heaven opened and the angels of God ascending and descending upon the Son of Man'.

Wherever we are on the spectrum of guile – from Jacob's near-inability to handle anything with straightforward honesty, through to the sincerity of Nathanael-Bartholomew – God extends to us a ladder, a bridge, on which his angels, his messengers, travel back and forth between earth and heaven. More than this, Jesus Christ, fully human and fully God, is that two-way conduit: praying for us at the Father's right hand (Romans 8.34) and himself the fulfilment of God's promises (2 Corinthians 1.20).

'I am with you' says the Lord to Jacob. 'I am with you' says Jesus to his followers. Wherever we are, heaven's communications channel is always open. What do you have to say today?

COLLECT

Almighty and everlasting God,
who gave to your apostle Bartholomew grace
truly to believe and to preach your word:
grant that your Church
may love that word which he believed
and may faithfully preach and receive the same;
through Jesus Christ your Son our Lord,
who is alive and reigns with you,
in the unity of the Holy Spirit,
one God, now and for ever.

Reflection by **Sarah Rowland Jones** | 237

Monday 26 August

Psalm 71
Jeremiah 41
Mark 2.23 – 3.6

Jeremiah 41

'Then Ishmael took captive all the rest of the people' (v.10)

Now everything goes from bad to worse. Gedaliah and those around him are killed by Ishmael, who is a member of the royal family and so, we assume, hostile to Babylon (as well as being, as we read on Saturday, in league with Judah's longstanding rivals the Ammonites, whose kingdom is over the Jordan near contemporary Amman). Not only does Ishmael abuse Gedaliah's hospitality before he kills him, he also murders pilgrims on the way to Jerusalem – sparing only those who promise financial gain. Then he takes the local population hostage and heads towards the Jordan. The tenor of this account shows Ishmael is clearly viewed as a bad piece of work.

Gedaliah's supporter, Johanan, rescues the hostages. But they nonetheless fear that the Chaldeans will take revenge on them as Judeans, since Ishmael, himself a Judean, was responsible for Gedaliah's murder. It seems the only option will be to flee to Egypt ... but that's something Jeremiah has already warned against (Jeremiah 24.8).

Human minds are made for storytelling. We try to make sense of personal and corporate events, past and present, by weaving a narrative through them, and strive to find plot and meaning and purpose to give shape to it all. But sometimes we aren't given that perspective. Sometimes, the best we can do is to pray for those who are caught up in circumstances that are beyond their control and understanding.

COLLECT

Let your merciful ears, O Lord,
be open to the prayers of your humble servants;
and that they may obtain their petitions
make them to ask such things as shall please you;
through Jesus Christ your Son our Lord,
who is alive and reigns with you,
in the unity of the Holy Spirit,
one God, now and for ever.

| *Reflection by* **Sarah Rowland Jones**

Psalm **73**
Jeremiah 42
Mark 3.7-19*a*

Tuesday 27 August

Jeremiah 42

'...we will obey the voice of the Lord our God' (v.6)

What do we make of the Bible when it says both that God's purposes are unchanging (Hebrews 6.17), and that God delights to 'do a new thing' (Isaiah 43.19)? It rather depends on how we look at events.

Johanan and the people now call on Jeremiah to seek a word from the Lord 'your God'. Jeremiah reminds them the Lord is actually *their* God too! And so they promise to 'obey the voice of the Lord our God', no matter what they are asked.

At the end of ten days (do we have that sort of patience nowadays?), a word comes from the Lord. Once again it is in an 'if ... then ... if ... then ...' form of invitation and warning. Jeremiah delivers the message with much cynicism that his listeners, who have never heeded God's word before, will do so now.

At first glance the invitation and warning seem to be the opposite of the earlier word, which was an instruction to leave the city and surrender to the Chaldeans. Now it is a call to stay put. Yet this is what it means to be subject to God's working through the Chaldeans in the new circumstances of Jerusalem's fall – it is the same objective, taking new shape in a changed context.

Perhaps our expectations in discerning God's presence and leading need to be more dynamic and imaginative than we realize.

Lord of heaven and earth,
as Jesus taught his disciples to be persistent in prayer,
give us patience and courage never to lose hope,
but always to bring our prayers before you;
through Jesus Christ our Lord.

COLLECT

Reflection by **Sarah Rowland Jones** | 239

Wednesday 28 August

Psalm **77**
Jeremiah 43
Mark 3.19*b*-end

Jeremiah 43

'… also the prophet Jeremiah and Baruch son of Neriah' (v.6)

In Jeremiah 39 we read how Jeremiah and Ebed-melech were spared from the general exile to Babylon. But there are no guarantees that any of us will receive special treatment, as a general rule. Being faithful doesn't provide an all-purpose 'get out of jail free' card.

Jeremiah has made it abundantly clear that the people are not to flee to Egypt. But, despite promising they will heed whatever word from the Lord Jeremiah brings them, this is what they decide to do. It seems that the devil they know – the risks of Egypt – is easier to contemplate than the counterintuitive promise of God's blessing under ruthless pagan Chaldean rule. So, excusing themselves with the claim that Baruch is treacherously biased and has distorted Jeremiah's ability to proclaim the Lord's word truly, they set off for Tahpanhes.

Jeremiah and Baruch have no option but to go too. Though they have spoken out repeatedly, they nonetheless remain intrinsically bound to the community to which they belong. And now they must share that community's fate. It's a sobering thought. And yet, even in Egypt, far from Jerusalem, the word of the Lord continues to come to Jeremiah. It is a consistent message of condemnation for those who do not submit to the Chaldeans, God's instrument of refining. And Jeremiah, prevented from responding in obedience to God's word, nonetheless keeps on speaking judgement, which is now upon himself too. That's true faithfulness.

COLLECT

Let your merciful ears, O Lord,
be open to the prayers of your humble servants;
and that they may obtain their petitions
make them to ask such things as shall please you;
through Jesus Christ your Son our Lord,
who is alive and reigns with you,
in the unity of the Holy Spirit,
one God, now and for ever.

| *Reflection by* **Sarah Rowland Jones**

Psalm **78.1-39***
Jeremiah 44.1-14
Mark 4.1-20

Thursday 29 August

Jeremiah 44.1-14

'Why are you doing such great harm to yourselves ...?' (v.7)

God never gives up on his people – even though they have done what he told them not to do, and have gone where he told them not to go. So now the Judeans are in Egypt, settled in various places around the Nile delta. And still the word of the Lord comes to them, through Jeremiah.

At first reading, it seems an outpouring of wrath: 'Why do you provoke me to anger ...?' But the root of God's message does not lie in punitive rage. Rather, it flows from God's response to the capacity of the Judeans deliberately to put themselves in harm's way. The disaster that lies in store for them is what they have drawn upon themselves as the consequences of their choices to do things their own, destructive, way.

Humanity has such a propensity for living with our finger on the self-destruct button. Even St Paul bewails the conundrum that so often, despite knowing what we ought to do, and even desiring to do it, we nonetheless do the opposite (Romans 7.15).

When I was a teenager, my parents were never more angry with me than when they thought I'd put my safety and wellbeing at risk. They were incensed, not because they didn't love me, but because they did, and feared for me. God's anger is the same, flowing out of his heartbreak that his people have chosen to do such harm to themselves.

Lord of heaven and earth,
as Jesus taught his disciples to be persistent in prayer,
give us patience and courage never to lose hope,
but always to bring our prayers before you;
through Jesus Christ our Lord.

COLLECT

Friday 30 August

Psalm **55***
Jeremiah 44.15-end
Mark 4.21-34

Jeremiah 44.15-end

'... we are not going to listen' (v.16)

What makes a deity worth worshipping? The Judeans in Egypt think they know. It is the one who brings food, prosperity, good fortune. This is what they experienced when they followed 'the queen of heaven', whereas want, violence and death came on them when they stopped honouring her. Therefore, they think they can see where their best interests lie, and it is not with Jeremiah and his Lord.

They have a point to which Scripture does not give easy answers. Sometimes prosperity does come to 'the wicked'. There is no simple correlation between apparent blessing and faithfulness.

We see from Jeremiah's perspective, and know they've got it wrong. In believing they have autonomy to choose their god for themselves, turning their backs on the Lord, and returning to Egypt, they have literally taken themselves back into bondage, enslaving themselves to ignorance, and the death it will bring.

But they've not asked the right question. It isn't as though the Lord has failed them. For, in refusing to heed Jeremiah, as they have consistently done, they have never actually trusted the Lord and so never discovered the truth of his promises. As G. K. Chesterton put it for our own times: 'Christianity has not been tried and found wanting, it has been found difficult and not tried.' Oh that people would dare to 'taste and see that the Lord is good' (Psalm 34.8).

COLLECT

Let your merciful ears, O Lord,
be open to the prayers of your humble servants;
and that they may obtain their petitions
make them to ask such things as shall please you;
through Jesus Christ your Son our Lord,
who is alive and reigns with you,
in the unity of the Holy Spirit,
one God, now and for ever.

| *Reflection by* **Sarah Rowland Jones**

Psalms **76**, 79
Jeremiah 45
Mark 4.35-end

Saturday 31 August

Jeremiah 45

'I will give you your life ...' (v.5)

Baruch's life has been tough. At great personal risk, he has not only been Jeremiah's scribe, but also his public mouthpiece, conveying his words to hostile authorities when Jeremiah was prevented from doing so himself. For supporting Jeremiah and his message that God's purposes would be served through submitting to the Chaldeans, he has received threats to his life and been denounced when people held back from criticizing Jeremiah directly.

Today's passage refers back to Chapter 36, when Baruch wrote the first scroll. It seems Baruch was already fearful of the consequences of being allied with Jeremiah. But God's assurance came to him then, that his life would be saved, no matter where the future took him. We read these words with the hindsight of knowing Baruch did not go to Babylon, but, with Jeremiah, was swept off to Egypt, where the Lord explicitly said they should not go. Now, despite being where he should not be, he is reminded the Lord will nonetheless preserve his life.

It may seem a meagre hope, especially when coupled with the warning not to seek great things for himself. Yet St Paul also reminds us not to think too highly of ourselves (Romans 12.3). In the grander scheme of things, worldly success counts for little alongside bearing fruit that lasts (John 15.16), as Baruch's writings have. And each new day of life is an opportunity for each of us to bear such fruit.

Lord of heaven and earth,
as Jesus taught his disciples to be persistent in prayer,
give us patience and courage never to lose hope,
but always to bring our prayers before you;
through Jesus Christ our Lord.

COLLECT

Reflection by **Sarah Rowland Jones** | 243

Monday 2 September

Psalms **80**, 82
Micah 1.1-9
Mark 5.1-20

Micah 1.1-9

'... the Lord is coming out of his place' (v.3)

The book of Micah, attributed to a Judean prophet born in the eighth-century BC, is rich in how it presents God's variety of ways of relating to humanity. God is compassionate and merciful, but at the same time angry and destructive. Micah does not allow us to sidestep the much-avoided issue of the anger of God. Yet he articulates an honest and realistic message of hope to the troubled and crushed.

Micah begins with God's case against the very people he is in a covenant relationship with (Chapters 1–3). However, Micah does not call Israel and Judah only, but all the peoples and the earth to listen. The Lord is not a local deity, but the Lord over all the peoples and the earth. Israel has failed, and God is bringing judgement upon her. And all nations are called to listen, because even in her failure, Israel remains a witness to the nations. Israel's punishment is a witness to God's justice and fairness.

Micah portrays God as both transcendent and immanent; he is far but comes near. Micah speaks about 'the Lord from his holy temple' and the Lord who is 'coming out of his place'. God's appearance has awesome and frightening effects on the natural world, but it seems that the people, especially the chosen people of God, are slow to perceive his manifestation. God's people seem to take God for granted and might become unable to see God acting in their history.

COLLECT

O God, you declare your almighty power
most chiefly in showing mercy and pity:
mercifully grant to us such a measure of your grace,
that we, running the way of your commandments,
may receive your gracious promises,
and be made partakers of your heavenly treasure;
through Jesus Christ your Son our Lord,
who is alive and reigns with you,
in the unity of the Holy Spirit,
one God, now and for ever.

Reflection by **John Perumbalath**

Psalms 87, **89.1-18**
Micah 2
Mark 5.21-34

Tuesday 3 September

Micah 2

'... the Lord alters the inheritance of my people' (v.4)

In the previous chapter, Micah rebuked people for their sins against the Lord. Here he is concerned about their sins against each other. He speaks against land grabbing in particular. The land was given to families as a sacred trust; God had given everyone the right to enjoy it. What does this say about a world where the majority of the material resources, including the land, belongs to the minority of the population? And what does it say about our desire to have more, while many have nothing?

This greedy and covetous people believed they were favoured by God. They had a particular understanding of God – a God of long-suffering and patience who defends his people with mighty acts. They felt protected and believed that God would not interfere in their lives, as taught by their favourite preachers. They thought their inheritance was safe. No wonder that they opposed Micah's preaching about a God who was going to judge them. Micah points out that this understanding of God that knows only of blessing, protection and success is inadequate and flawed. God cares how we live in relationship with him, with other human beings and with the whole of creation. God is angry and hurt when we hurt each other.

Micah's words place a particular responsibility on those who have been given much. Even those people who are close to God are liable to sin and will need to face the consequences of their actions.

God of glory,
the end of our searching,
help us to lay aside
all that prevents us from seeking your kingdom,
and to give all that we have
to gain the pearl beyond all price,
through our Saviour Jesus Christ.

COLLECT

Wednesday 4 September

Psalm 119.105-128
Micah 3
Mark 5.35-end

Micah 3

'But as for me, I am filled with power ...' (v.8)

Micah now turns to the rulers and the prophets who abuse their power and position. Rulers, prophets and priests have sold out their integrity for money. The rulers have become oppressors. The religious leaders have become greedy rather than godly. The prophets do not convey a message from the Lord; rather they say messages to please people who pay them money.

These prophets are going to be judged. They will face darkness – they will not be given a vision or revelation from God. They will be disgraced and shamed because they will not have any answers from God. God will judge those who have corrupted their prophetic office for personal gain.

When Micah offers the message of God, he is risking his own life. He tells the uncomfortable truth in spite of the opposition from the people he is speaking to. He does not fall for the easy route of pleasing people with what they want to hear, but speaks what they *need* to hear from God. He is not going to be paid by his people for this job, but he is filled with power and the spirit of the Lord.

The temptation to please those who meet the costs of ministry is real for many ministers of the gospel. Congregations might expect to be uplifted and comforted, not to be scolded by their ministers. How might we preach and hear the 'offensive' side of the gospel in faithfulness to God?

COLLECT

O God, you declare your almighty power
most chiefly in showing mercy and pity:
mercifully grant to us such a measure of your grace,
that we, running the way of your commandments,
may receive your gracious promises,
and be made partakers of your heavenly treasure;
through Jesus Christ your Son our Lord,
who is alive and reigns with you,
in the unity of the Holy Spirit,
one God, now and for ever.

| *Reflection by* **John Perumbalath**

Psalms 90, **92**
Micah 4.1 – 5.1
Mark 6.1-13

Thursday 5 September

Micah 4.1 – 5.1

'... out of Zion shall go forth instruction' (4.2)

The passage consists of a stark contrast between the grand vision of the future glory of God and the deep humiliation experienced by God's people. There is both an assurance and a challenge here.

The assurance is that God hasn't given up on his people. But there is no promise of a short cut to heavenly bliss. Micah does not play down the reality of suffering, nor does he promise a way to bypass the pain to be endured. Any message of hope in the context of suffering has to take the pain of the people seriously.

The challenge is about obedience to the missional purposes of God. Walking the talk is essential as well as recognizing God's intentions for the world. God's future is not limited to his favourites. God's chosen people will need to act as an agent of God so that other nations will also be restored to God. Micah invites us to work towards God's vision of unity and peace in this world.

The nations assemble together to watch the fall of God's people – but God has other intentions. God uses human decisions, good and bad, to work out his own purpose for the world. Human sinfulness contradicts God's will, but God is able to use our sinful decisions towards his goals of peace and justice.

COLLECT

God of glory,
the end of our searching,
help us to lay aside
all that prevents us from seeking your kingdom,
and to give all that we have
to gain the pearl beyond all price,
through our Saviour Jesus Christ.

Friday 6 September

Psalms **88** (95)
Micah 5.2-end
Mark 6.14-29

Micah 5.2-end

'And they shall live secure ...' (v.4)

Security is the exciting substance of the hope that Micah talks about. In an insecure world of poverty, conflicts and calamities, God gives us an assurance that we cannot find elsewhere. As Christians we find God's provision for us in Christ who will 'feed his flock' and 'shall be the one of peace' and 'shall be great to the ends of the earth'.

In order to receive this security that God offers, however, the people of God must stop relying on their current sources of support in which they put their trust. They surely trust in their own military resources, 'horses' and 'chariots'. God will cut them off from these sources of support. Their defence systems include walled 'cities' and 'strongholds'. God will throw them down.

Instead of seeking God's word, the people seek 'sorceries' and 'soothsayers' who offer false confidence and hope. They also bow down to the work of their own hands – images and pillars – in which idolatry becomes self-worship. They need to stop relying on these false sources of support.

Modern human beings also put their trust in military devices and defence systems and, to a great extent, indulge in self-worship by depending on their own capabilities. We cannot find ourselves secure in God while we remain self-reliant or dependent on other external sources that make us feel safe.

COLLECT

O God, you declare your almighty power
most chiefly in showing mercy and pity:
mercifully grant to us such a measure of your grace,
that we, running the way of your commandments,
may receive your gracious promises,
and be made partakers of your heavenly treasure;
through Jesus Christ your Son our Lord,
who is alive and reigns with you,
in the unity of the Holy Spirit,
one God, now and for ever.

| *Reflection by* **John Perumbalath**

Psalms 96, **97**, 100
Micah 6
Mark 6.30-44

Saturday 7 September

Micah 6

'... what does the Lord require of you?' (v.8)

In this chapter we find a God who interrogates his people, asking a series of questions. God expects his people to question themselves and reflect on what they do and believe rather than leading an unexamined life.

The questions show that the people of God haven't got it right about their relationship with God. Israel imagines its relationship with God in terms of commodities, in the way that neighbouring peoples do. God, however, understands his relationship with his people in terms of a *covenant*. And a covenant places responsibilities on both the parties. God calls out to his people with his compassion, mercy, grace and redemption before he expects anything of them.

Micah summarizes how God expects his people to live: doing, loving and walking. Justice is something that we do, establishing equity for all, particularly for the powerless. It is a positive action, not passive wishing. We are to 'love kindness'. The word used here implies a strong element of loyalty, for example, between a husband and wife. It calls for right relationships with our fellow humans. 'Walk humbly' here is not much about having humility but being careful and wise. 'Walk' refers to the whole orientation of one's life (Micah 4.2,5), one of living in the reality of God's grace.

God is more concerned about how we live our everyday life than how we perform our religious rites.

God of glory,
the end of our searching,
help us to lay aside
all that prevents us from seeking your kingdom,
and to give all that we have
to gain the pearl beyond all price,
through our Saviour Jesus Christ.

COLLECT

Monday 9 September

Psalms **98**, 99, 101
Micah 7.1-7
Mark 6.45-end

Micah 7.1-7

'I will look to the Lord ...' (v.7)

In this poignant lament, we are given an intimate portrayal of the prophet's inner life. His hearers must have felt that he had a hard interior, but here he weeps over his nation's state of affairs. As a true prophet, Micah loves his people and is pained by the message he holds and delivers. He does not feel at home with the people with whom he lives. No one listens to him. And there is no decent person around. No one can be trusted.

In a corrupt society, people lose confidence in others. Disobedience to God's work and neglect of ethical values result in chaos and anarchy in the society. Micah painfully watches how sin has destroyed the most basic of human relations.

What should we do when our society is disintegrating around us? Micah knows that God will hear and redeem his people. He does not give up when his society looks to be beyond redemption. He continues to speak out for those on the margins and waits for God his Saviour.

Words 'wait for' and 'look to' come across as passive verbs in English. But the Hebrew words suggest *active* participation through faith, prayer and hope. So while the whole society was crumbling, there was one man and the Lord staying put and firm. Who do we wait for or look to when our world is plunged into chaos?

COLLECT

Almighty and everlasting God,
you are always more ready to hear than we to pray
and to give more than either we desire or deserve:
pour down upon us the abundance of your mercy,
forgiving us those things of which our conscience is afraid
and giving us those good things which we are not worthy to ask
but through the merits and mediation
of Jesus Christ your Son our Lord,
who is alive and reigns with you,
in the unity of the Holy Spirit,
one God, now and for ever.

| *Reflection by* **John Perumbalath**

Psalm **106*** *(or* 103)
Micah 7.8-end
Mark 7.1-13

Tuesday 10 September

Micah 7.8-end

'Who is a God like you ...?' (v.18)

All our reflection on God and our inquiry into how he relates to the world should naturally end in worship. The book of Micah, after all its discussions on judgement and hope, ends with a closing liturgy.

It is normal that God is mocked when things go wrong in the world as if God were non-existent, weak or indifferent. The liturgy starts with a sarcastic question, 'Where is the Lord your God?'. It then celebrates a God who is active and present, pardoning, forgiving, forgetting and delivering, and a shepherd who defends and cares for his people.

The tension between justice and mercy runs throughout the book and is present in the closing liturgy too. While holding on to his own standards of justice, God is pulled towards mercy and forgiveness. We need to hold this tension in our understanding and proclamation of the gospel. We often try to resolve the tension by emphasizing only one side of the message.

There is no God like the Lord. The conclusion of the book describes God using words such as faithfulness, compassion, loyalty, love, forgiveness and mercy. This vision of God should be proclaimed loudly in a world where most people may have heard of only a punishing and avenging God. It is also necessary to have that proclamation made in order to put the hard words present in the book in a proper perspective.

God of constant mercy,
who sent your Son to save us:
remind us of your goodness,
increase your grace within us,
that our thankfulness may grow,
through Jesus Christ our Lord.

COLLECT

Wednesday 11 September

Habakkuk 1.1-11

'... how long shall I cry for help?' (v.2)

Habakkuk is a book about the realization of God's purposes and will for his world. Set in the context of the rise of Chaldeans (Babylonians) as the new world power in the late seventh century BC, the prophet first questions God's inactivity but then moves towards the recognition of God's purposes and worship.

Where is God when the world is in trouble? Habakkuk asks this question not as someone sceptical about God but as a person of deep faith, constant prayer and intimate communion with God. We *can* have honest conversations with God! Indeed, Scripture has a long tradition of people arguing with God, including the Psalmists, Jeremiah and Moses.

The prophet is frustrated over the loss of law and justice, and over his own helplessness in the situation. He can't see God doing anything either. But God *is* at work. When we think that God is indifferent, he might actually be involved in a way we don't recognize. In this case, God uses unlikely instruments – Babylonians. God does direct human initiatives toward his ends.

Habakkuk defends the cause of the victims of injustice, even to the point of questioning the way God handles their case. God's response does not always satisfy the prophet. But the debate in the book underlines the ability of the believers to complain to God about the pain and distress of their world and to petition God to act.

COLLECT

Almighty and everlasting God,
you are always more ready to hear than we to pray
and to give more than either we desire or deserve:
pour down upon us the abundance of your mercy,
forgiving us those things of which our conscience is afraid
and giving us those good things which we are not worthy to ask
but through the merits and mediation
of Jesus Christ your Son our Lord,
who is alive and reigns with you,
in the unity of the Holy Spirit,
one God, now and for ever.

Reflection by **John Perumbalath**

Psalms 113, 115
Habakkuk 1.12 – 2.5
Mark 7.24-30

Thursday 12 September

Habakkuk 1.12 – 2.5

'I will stand at my watch-post ...' (2.1)

Habakkuk is not only willing to argue with God but is also persistent in getting the answer. He will watch from his tower on the city wall. Answers for complex questions in life do not appear overnight.

The prophet now affirms that God rules history. He moves on from his initial accusation that God is indifferent but still cannot understand why God uses the wicked Babylonians to punish his own people. He finds it contrary to God's name and God's nature and justice. God's answer is brief and cryptic. He just assures Habakkuk that his waiting will not be futile. Wait he must, if the vision seems to tarry.

In his description of Babylonians, Habakkuk attacks the imperialistic practices then and now – expansion of control over other countries, exploiting their resources and destroying them. For Western readers, Habakkuk is an encouragement to look at international politics from the other side.

Habakkuk does not propose a simple solution to the problem of injustice, but the 'righteous' become part of the solution. They will long and work for justice and righteousness. They 'live by their faith', which means that they will have the strength to go on through their faithfulness and vision. They will place trust in the vision they received from God rather than in the brute facts of existence.

God of constant mercy,
who sent your Son to save us:
remind us of your goodness,
increase your grace within us,
that our thankfulness may grow,
through Jesus Christ our Lord.

COLLECT

Friday 13 September

Psalm 139
Habakkuk 2.6-end
Mark 7.31-end

Habakkuk 2.6-end

'... let all the earth keep silence before him!' (v.20)

Habakkuk touches here on two resources for coping with the problem of injustice. The first we read about yesterday: the prophetic vision of the reliability of God's rule. The Lord in his holy temple is in control. He rules every age, and evil receives its just due. This assurance instils in us hope and confidence as we struggle with injustice and wickedness.

The second is the lesson from history itself that these forms of injustice, depicted here in terms of imperial power, do not endure. There is a principle of justice operating in the world by which tyrannical powers and pretensions will be destroyed. The wisdom of these sayings can be observed in the modern era, for example in those forces that have undermined colonialism during the latter half of the twentieth century.

Application of this wisdom is not limited to international politics but extends to an individual level as well. The main pursuits described here – wealth, security, fame – are elemental drives of much human endeavour. Habakkuk reminds us that these 'prizes' cannot be ensured. As these goals are normally gained at the expense of others, they carry with them the seeds of their own ruin.

Habakkuk introduces these profound lessons by the use of some mocking riddles but the rude mockery is brought to an end with the call to silence, reminding the readers who is in control.

COLLECT

Almighty and everlasting God,
you are always more ready to hear than we to pray
and to give more than either we desire or deserve:
pour down upon us the abundance of your mercy,
forgiving us those things of which our conscience is afraid
and giving us those good things which we are not worthy to ask
but through the merits and mediation
of Jesus Christ your Son our Lord,
who is alive and reigns with you,
in the unity of the Holy Spirit,
one God, now and for ever.

| *Reflection by* **John Perumbalath**

Psalms 2, 8, 146
Genesis 3.1-15
John 12.27-36a

Saturday 14 September
Holy Cross Day

Genesis 3.1-15

'Have you eaten from the tree ...?' (v.11)

Holy Cross Day commemorates the story of Helena, Mother of the Emperor Constantine, who is said to have discovered a cross while exploring ruins in the city of Jerusalem. The cross has become the universally recognized symbol of the Christian faith. The symbol of the cross is prefigured in the story of the Garden of Eden. Two trees are set in the garden: the tree of life and the tree of the knowledge of good and evil (Genesis 2.9). In eating the forbidden fruit from the second tree, Adam and Eve overreach themselves, and God drives them out of Paradise. This ensures that the tree of life is saved from the destructive impulses of human beings.

At the heart of the Christian faith is the gospel account of the historic crucifixion of Jesus. The cross came to be seen as answer to Adam and Eve's sin, enabling reconciliation between humanity and God. The cross of Jesus is the tree of life manifested in human history.

So we should be thankful for the cross and reflect on its life-giving mystery, not only because Jesus suffered for our sins, but because it has produced new life, bearing fruit in the forgiveness of sins and in holy lives.

As the carol puts it: 'The tree of life my soul has seen, laden with fruit and always green'.

Almighty God,
who in the passion of your blessed Son
made an instrument of painful death
to be for us the means of life and peace:
grant us so to glory in the cross of Christ
that we may gladly suffer for his sake;
who is alive and reigns with you,
in the unity of the Holy Spirit,
one God, now and for ever.

COLLECT

Monday 16 September

Psalms 123, 124, 125, **126**
Haggai 1.1-11
Mark 8.11-21

Haggai 1.1-11

'... my house lies in ruins' (v.9)

The short book of Haggai begins with a prophetic trumpet blast addressed to the two most powerful figures of the Jewish community, the governor of the Persian province of Judah and the high priest. It is an immediate call to action. The signs of social disintegration are obvious: poor harvests, gross inequality of income, rampant inflation. All this is the result of wrong priorities. The exiles have returned to their land, but the temple, the seat of God's name, lies in ruins. Until it is rebuilt and worship is restored, nature will remain on strike and human society continue to deteriorate.

In our society, where worship is increasingly seen as a leisure activity for individuals who find it beneficial, it may be hard to receive the urgency of the message. Yet we should bear in mind that while the Christian call is not necessarily to restore sacred buildings, we are meant as a Christian community to *be* the temple, the royal priesthood that offers worship on behalf of all. When we see disturbing signs of social disharmony, we should perhaps consider the quality of our worship.

If we are not putting God first in our lives, we can hardly expect others to do so for us. We may have a prophetic message for society as a whole, but unless it is rooted in true worship, it is unlikely to bear fruit.

COLLECT

Almighty God,
who called your Church to bear witness
that you were in Christ reconciling the world to yourself:
help us to proclaim the good news of your love,
that all who hear it may be drawn to you;
through him who was lifted up on the cross,
and reigns with you in the unity of the Holy Spirit,
one God, now and for ever.

| *Reflection by* **Angela Tilby**

Psalms **132**, 133
Haggai 1.12 – 2.9
Mark 8.22-26

Tuesday 17 September

Haggai 1.12 – 2.9

'I am with you, says the Lord' (1.13)

The response to Haggai's audacious message is immediate. Governor, high priest and community recognize that God is challenging them. God is among them ready to act, stirring them up from within. As they internalize the summons, God provides the energy and the vision to begin the work of restoration.

The community makes a start on the huge task, and the date of commencement is noted for posterity. But it is only a beginning, and at first there is little to show for their efforts. After a month of labour, people are perhaps beginning to be discouraged, and it is at this point that they receive a fresh vision. The temple they are building will be even more glorious than the temple that was destroyed. This time 'the treasure of all nations' will come to it.

No doubt these prophetic words were originally taken to indicate a comeuppance for Israel's enemies. The deprivation the nations inflicted on Israel will be reversed as the same nations contribute to Israel's restoration. The prophecy looks forward to Israel's vocation to be a 'light to the nations' (Isaiah 49.6). The restoration of the temple is central to the mission of God. We forget the centrality of worship at our peril.

Almighty God,
you search us and know us:
may we rely on you in strength
and rest on you in weakness,
now and in all our days;
through Jesus Christ our Lord.

COLLECT

Wednesday 18 September

Haggai 2.10-end

'From this day on I will bless you' (v.19)

God's promise of blessing begins to be realized as work on the temple proceeds. One immediate sign of the revival of the nation is a new concern for the meaning of holiness. The people need to rediscover the law and its application to daily life. There is a necessary reawakening of priestly learning and discernment. The ritual laws determining what is clean and unclean need to be rediscovered and reintroduced. These are not petty or arbitrary rules. They are the gift of a God who invites us to distinguish between sacred and profane, good and evil. There is no opposition between ritual law and social righteousness; they go together, and when they go together, they bring about a recovery of the natural world. Where there has been dearth, there will be blessing.

The architects of restoration are Zerubbabel, the governor, and Joshua, the high priest. Zerubbabel was a descendent of David, and his appointment represents the lifting of the curse that was put on David's descendants when Judah was defeated. Zerubbabel will be as close to God as a signet ring on God's finger.

As we attempt to live holy lives in the world, we should be reassured that God gives us specific challenges in order to bless us and bring us into an intimate relationship with him. He wants to make us his own.

COLLECT

Almighty God,
who called your Church to bear witness
that you were in Christ reconciling the world to yourself:
help us to proclaim the good news of your love,
that all who hear it may be drawn to you;
through him who was lifted up on the cross,
and reigns with you in the unity of the Holy Spirit,
one God, now and for ever.

| *Reflection by* **Angela Tilby**

Psalms 143, 146
Zechariah 1.1-17
Mark 9.2-13

Thursday 19 September

Zechariah 1.1-17

'Return to me, says the Lord of hosts, and I will return to you' (v.3)

The prophecies gathered together in the book of Zechariah are difficult to place historically, and their detail is often obscure. It is also not easy to chart exactly how these prophecies fit with the accounts given in the books of Ezra and Nehemiah. What does seem clear is that the accession of Darius as King of Persia opened up new possibilities for the returned exiles. The prophet's message is focused on spiritual revival and national restoration. The vision of the horsemen patrolling the earth may be derived from the prophet's experience of seeing Persian mounted militia guarding the borders of Darius' empire.

The new ruler has brought an end to upheaval and uncertainty, and the heavenly horsemen have been sent out to declare peace. This is the cue for the interceding angel to plead with God for the restoration of Jerusalem after the prophesied 70 years of exile. In response to the angel's request, the Lord sends a message of comfort and reassurance.

We should note here that God's justice is always restorative. Discipline and even punishment play a part in God's providence, but the point is always to bring us back to him, no matter what we have done. In this sense, the suffering of God's people can rightly be seen as sacramental; it brings healing and new hope.

Almighty God,
you search us and know us:
may we rely on you in strength
and rest on you in weakness,
now and in all our days;
through Jesus Christ our Lord.

COLLECT

Friday 20 September

Psalms 142, **144**
Zechariah 1.18 – end of 2
Mark 9.14-29

Zechariah 1.18 – end of 2

'I will come and dwell in your midst, says the Lord' (2.10)

God is bringing judgement on the 'horns' of the aggressive powers that have led to Judah's downfall and exile. God's people will return from exile to form a purified community in the holy land. This is a new beginning beyond the dreams of the former exiles. The population will grow without limit; settlements will spread without the need for walls, because God will protect them. The wall of divine fire is mirrored by the glory within. Of course the imagery of restoration was not fulfilled in every detail; the process took much longer than might have been expected and was full of setbacks and disappointments.

From New Testament times, this prophecy acquired a new relevance. The promise of God's return to Zion came to have a Messianic flavour. Verse 10 of chapter 2 is still quoted in the liturgy on Palm Sunday, and verse 13 comes into liturgical texts at Christmas and at the Eucharist. The promise here is fulfilled many times in the life of Israel, in the experience of the Church and in the hopes of all Christian people. The heart of the promise for Christians is Jesus Christ, Emmanuel, 'God with us'.

Our response to this is not only joy, but also the sheer silence of wonder and contemplation.

COLLECT

Almighty God,
who called your Church to bear witness
that you were in Christ reconciling the world to yourself:
help us to proclaim the good news of your love,
that all who hear it may be drawn to you;
through him who was lifted up on the cross,
and reigns with you in the unity of the Holy Spirit,
one God, now and for ever.

Psalms 49, 117
1 Kings 19.15-end
2 Timothy 3.14-end

Saturday 21 September
Matthew, Apostle and Evangelist

2 Timothy 3.14-end

'... continue in what you have learned and firmly believed' (v.14).

The choice of reading for St Matthew's day focuses on Matthew as an inspired composer of scripture, one of the four evangelists.

Tradition identifies Matthew with the tax collector (called Levi in Mark's and Luke's Gospels) whose story is told in Matthew 9.9. Matthew's Gospel is extraordinarily rich in the teachings of the Lord, set out in such a way as to be memorized, internalized and handed on. Matthew's Gospel is a manual of Christian belief and behaviour, a model for teachers and catechists. This is why it comes first in the New Testament, although most think it was written after Mark.

The early Christians inherited from the Jews a sense that God was a communicator who addressed them through Scripture. Timothy is therefore encouraged to remember the Scripture teaching he has received and to continue to respond to it. He has been taught it from childhood, and so Scripture has accompanied him throughout his life. It helps to think of the Scriptures as being alive in the sense that they generate life, faith and obedience.

Verse 16 is often used as a proof text for the theory of verbal inspiration. But the point being made here is more that Scripture is formative for Christians; it sustains and nourishes faith, which is why a daily encounter with Scripture is so much to be treasured.

O Almighty God,
whose blessed Son called Matthew the tax collector
to be an apostle and evangelist:
give us grace to forsake the selfish pursuit of gain
and the possessive love of riches
that we may follow in the way of your Son Jesus Christ,
who is alive and reigns with you,
in the unity of the Holy Spirit,
one God, now and for ever.

COLLECT

Monday 23 September

Zechariah 4

'Not by might, nor by power, but by my Spirit,
says the Lord of hosts' (v.6)

The imagery of the olive trees endlessly supplying the olive lamps affirms that God will indeed be present in the restored temple; the oil that keeps the sanctuary alight comes from living trees and cannot run out. The foundation of the temple has been laid, but the work is not complete. Zerubbabel the governor is charged with finishing the work, 'not by might, not by power, but by my spirit'. He and Joshua are the earthly agents represented by the 'anointed ones'. Restoration cannot be achieved merely by political means. Without a spiritual foundation there can be no authentic hope, and hope for God's people cannot be detached from God's providence over the whole earth. God's 'eyes' range everywhere.

In our own context, we need to recover the assurance that God has a purpose for us, while recognizing that there is much more going on than we can understand or even be aware of. Aligning ourselves to God's will demands continual spiritual honesty and commitment. We cannot see the outcome of our daily work and service, but we can pray that it will prove fruitful. The 'anointed ones' – the branches that convey the oil to the lamps – are also 'anointers', and we should remember that we too are anointed for God's work, sealed by the Spirit through our baptism.

COLLECT

Almighty God,
whose only Son has opened for us
a new and living way into your presence:
give us pure hearts and steadfast wills
to worship you in spirit and in truth;
through Jesus Christ your Son our Lord,
who is alive and reigns with you,
in the unity of the Holy Spirit,
one God, now and for ever.

Psalms **5**, 6 (8)
Zechariah 6.9-end
Mark 10.1-16

Tuesday 24 September

Zechariah 6.9-end

'... he shall build the temple of the Lord' (v.12)

The restoration of temple and nation comes nearer with the symbolic crowning of Joshua. A group of returning exiles provide precious gold and silver, and Joshua is dignified with the royal diadem. But he is not to rule alone. The 'Branch' is the one who will bring the temple to completion, and this refers to Zerubbabel the governor. Priest and governor will rule together as earthly counterparts of the heavenly 'anointed ones' of yesterday's reading. The crown is to be kept in the temple under the care of the returning exiles, and also as an encouragement for others to come 'from afar' and help in the building project.

It is difficult to reconstruct the exact political circumstances in which the new temple was begun. But it was a project of immense importance in the history of God's people. It represented the return of God himself to the Promised Land and was a sign of his eternal commitment to his people.

We are sometimes discouraged from putting too much store by our sacred buildings, but we should remember that many were constructed for the future, as a sign of God's blessing to generations not yet born. We should not be content with a throwaway world or a throwaway Church, but build for tomorrow with our hearts set on eternity.

> Merciful God,
> your Son came to save us
> and bore our sins on the cross:
> may we trust in your mercy
> and know your love,
> rejoicing in the righteousness
> that is ours through Jesus Christ our Lord.

COLLECT

Reflection by **Angela Tilby**   263

Wednesday 25 September

Zechariah 7

'Render true judgements; show kindness and mercy to one another' (v.9)

The role of the temple in teaching and maintaining the faith is expressed in the question that comes about ritual mourning. This was instituted after the destruction of the earlier temple, and the question focuses on whether ritual mourning is appropriate now the restoration is underway. The answer leads back to earlier prophetic utterances about the relationship between worship and obedience. The people are slow to learn the lessons of prosperity. When times are good, it is right to respond with gratitude to God and with generosity to the poor.

This theme is expanded by verses that echo the teaching of the former prophets and by Deuteronomy: the genuineness of obedience to God is measured by the level of social justice. Long ingrained habits of oppression and dishonesty have reaped a harvest of wrath. The exile and devastation of the once-pleasant land must be interpreted as divine punishment for disobedience. The new community of returned exiles, along with the survivors who stayed on in the land after Judah's defeat, must now take to heart the lessons that their forebears failed to learn.

Christian faith inherits this prophetic standpoint. Our obedience to God is shown not only in our readiness to worship, but also in our readiness to create a genuinely inclusive society where the needs of the vulnerable come first.

COLLECT

Almighty God,
whose only Son has opened for us
a new and living way into your presence:
give us pure hearts and steadfast wills
to worship you in spirit and in truth;
through Jesus Christ your Son our Lord,
who is alive and reigns with you,
in the unity of the Holy Spirit,
one God, now and for ever.

| *Reflection by* **Angela Tilby**

Thursday 26 September

Zechariah 8.1-8

'... should it also seem impossible for me, says the Lord of hosts?'
(v.6)

This oracle comes with a beautiful description of the restored Jerusalem, now a faithful city, secure in the blessing of the Lord. Both external and internal threats have been overcome. The streets are safe, and it is easy to imagine the contented elderly sitting outside in the evening sun as the children play unafraid in the streets. It is an image of peace, prosperity and flourishing.

The prophet knows how unlikely the fulfilment of this prophecy must seem to his contemporaries, who are just clinging on to the survival of their hopes. The response that Zechariah mediates from God is not a rebuke but a call to faith. What is impossible for the survivors to imagine is not impossible for God, because God is the source of all possibilities. He envisages a good future even when this seems unthinkable.

Jesus perhaps had this text in mind when he spoke of salvation to those who feared they were outside the community of the faithful (Mark 10.27). The image of the peaceful city could help our prayers today as we think of those cities of today where there is terror and violence, and where children are in constant danger. Within God's imagination, these places of desolation can be restored to peace. But it requires, on the human side, faith, vision and persistence.

Merciful God,
your Son came to save us
and bore our sins on the cross:
may we trust in your mercy
and know your love,
rejoicing in the righteousness
that is ours through Jesus Christ our Lord.

COLLECT

Friday 27 September

Zechariah 8.9-end

'Do not be afraid, but let your hands be strong' (v.13)

The beginnings of a return from exile have come with many problems, both for those trying to pick up their families' former lives and for those who have remained in the ruined land. There is social upheaval, violence and insecurity. But a new era is beginning; a new Jerusalem is rising from the ashes of the past, and what is needed now is faith and commitment. The peace that God is bringing will affect the natural world as well as the human world. There will be plenty for all, and hope and flourishing. The fasts, which were the subject of inquiry in the previous chapter, are to become festivals. Jerusalem will be a sanctuary not only for the Jewish people, but for the nations.

The final image of ten men taking hold of the robe of a Jew and asking for guidance to Jerusalem points to the mission of Israel to be a light to the nations. It is not clear here whether those seeking God are seeking to be guided by the moral precepts of the Jewish faith or whether they are to become Jews. That debate, and that dilemma, will have to wait until New Testament times. God invites us today to keep faith. We should strive to turn away from bitter memories of disaster and to anticipate the blessing God has in store for us.

COLLECT

Almighty God,
whose only Son has opened for us
a new and living way into your presence:
give us pure hearts and steadfast wills
to worship you in spirit and in truth;
through Jesus Christ your Son our Lord,
who is alive and reigns with you,
in the unity of the Holy Spirit,
one God, now and for ever.

| *Reflection by* **Angela Tilby**

Psalms 20, 21, **23**
Zechariah 9.1-12
Mark 10.46-end

Saturday 28 September

Zechariah 9.1-12

'Lo, your king comes to you; triumphant and victorious is he' (v.9)

For Christians, the centre of today's passage is the prophecy of the victorious king coming into the holy city. This passage has coloured the Gospel accounts of Palm Sunday when Jesus entered Jerusalem on a donkey before his passion. The 'colt, the foal of a donkey' is not a second beast as Matthew's Gospel seems to understand it (Matthew 21.7) but a poetic phrase which could be rendered as: 'He's on a donkey, yes the foal of a donkey!'.

This victorious king is reminiscent of royal figures in the Psalms, godly rulers who emerge after trials and defeat to rule God's people in humility (Psalms 2.6-7; 110). The humiliation of the Son of God occurs after his victorious entry, not before, but it leads to the final victory of life over death. In its context, the prophet promises that God's appointed ruler will be the bringer of peace, not only to Israel but also to the nations that have oppressed and made war against her.

The hint in both the original prophecy and the Christian interpretation of it is that God's greatest victory is not vengeance, but mercy. He comes to us as he came to the newly restored Jerusalem in the humility that rebukes our pride and sin. The challenge to us is to be humble enough to join him on the road to peace.

COLLECT

Merciful God,
your Son came to save us
and bore our sins on the cross:
may we trust in your mercy
and know your love,
rejoicing in the righteousness
that is ours through Jesus Christ our Lord.

Monday 30 September

Zechariah 10

'Ask rain from the Lord ...' (v.1)

Throughout the books of the psalms and the prophets, the parched ground is a vivid image of the human soul and human life without God. This chapter of Zechariah is best read as a collection of shorter oracles on different themes. It is introduced by this powerful cry for each person to seek spiritual renewal directly from the Lord. Where intermediaries and institutions have failed, it remains possible to cry out directly to God and for God's refreshing rains to fall.

The image of the desert thirsting for rain remains powerful in our contemporary world, particularly in a time when the climate is changing and the deserts are expanding. Pope Benedict said at his inauguration in 2005: 'The external deserts in the world are growing because the internal deserts have become so vast.'

Most of us will experience life as a desert in some season of our lives. Benedict speaks in the same homily of the deserts of poverty, of abandonment, of destroyed love, of emptiness. Our lives need the gentle rain of God's Spirit and God's life in order to be watered, to be refreshed, to become fruitful again.

Ask rain from the Lord today ...

COLLECT

God, who in generous mercy sent the Holy Spirit
    upon your Church in the burning fire of your love:
grant that your people may be fervent
in the fellowship of the gospel
that, always abiding in you,
they may be found steadfast in faith and active in service;
through Jesus Christ your Son our Lord,
who is alive and reigns with you,
in the unity of the Holy Spirit,
one God, now and for ever.

Zechariah 11.4-end

'I tended the sheep' (v.7)

For Zechariah, the image of shepherding is an image of leadership. Short oracles about shepherds are scattered through chapters 9 to 14. They are mainly oracles of judgement for those who have failed in their critical task of leading the nation in a time of great peril in the period after the exile (v.17).

Verses 4 to 15 are slightly different, but focus on a similar theme. Here the prophet is asked to undertake powerful symbolic actions, like the prophets who have gone before him. In this case he is asked to become a shepherd, symbolizing the role of leadership or kingship, but the prophet is asked to shepherd a flock being made ready for slaughter.

This oracle is not about the responsibility of leaders but of those being led. The people stand under God's judgement but cannot see the danger they are in. The prophet's terrible breaking of the staff of Favour and the staff of Unity symbolizes a deep change in God's relationship with his people.

The passage as a whole inspires us to reflect on leadership and communities. We reflect first on the qualities required in a good shepherd, the opposite of the worthless shepherd described here. These qualities are modelled by the Lord Jesus Christ, the Good Shepherd. Second, we reflect on the qualities required in a community, which must receive and respond to the care and leadership that is offered. Leadership is a relationship not simply a function.

Lord God,
defend your Church from all false teaching
and give to your people knowledge of your truth,
that we may enjoy eternal life
in Jesus Christ our Lord.

COLLECT

Reflection by **Steven Croft**   269

Wednesday 2 October

Zechariah 12.1-10

'... when they look on the one whom they have pierced' (v.10)

Zechariah's perspective now shifts to the distant future, to the last days, as the prophet seeks to nurture hope in the fragile remnant of the nation. The time will come when Jerusalem and Judah are restored to the centre of God's purpose for the world. In that time, God will graciously pour out his Spirit, a spirit of compassion and supplication. Renewal will begin with God's actions and God's grace.

In reponse to this grace and in this season, God's people will look on the one whom they have pierced and mourn. It is not clear what this verse means in its original context. Some think the verse refers to Israel's treatment of kings and rulers and compare it with Isaiah 53. Others believe it refers to Israel's treatment of God himself. The nation has rejected God's grace and love.

John's Gospel places this prophecy from Zechariah at the very end of his description of the crucifixion (John 19.37). In doing so, John picks up both of these meanings in the text (as well as a more literal prophecy about the piercing of Christ's side with a spear).

We reflect on this verse today in the light of John's Gospel. Let us open ourselves afresh to God's Spirit of compassion and supplication and to a still deeper understanding of the cost of our salvation.

COLLECT

God, who in generous mercy sent the Holy Spirit
    upon your Church in the burning fire of your love:
grant that your people may be fervent
in the fellowship of the gospel
that, always abiding in you,
they may be found steadfast in faith and active in service;
through Jesus Christ your Son our Lord,
who is alive and reigns with you,
in the unity of the Holy Spirit,
one God, now and for ever.

| *Reflection by* **Steven Croft**

Psalm **37***
Zechariah 13
Mark 12.1-12

Thursday 3 October

Zechariah 13

'On that day a fountain shall be opened ...' (v.1)

Zechariah 13 contains a further oracle on shepherds and leadership (vv.7-9) – this time ending on a note of hope and restoration. There is another oracle on the end of prophecy: the institution has lost its credit with the nation (vv.2-6). These verses yield fascinating insights into the craft of the prophets and their role in the life of the nation.

Yet the opening verse holds our attention as it continues the theme of yesterday's reading. God has stirred the community to repentance through the gift of the Spirit. Through the eyes of faith, we see God's Son, the one who was pierced, and see how much Christ suffered for our sins. But we do not simply mourn his death.

We see in his sacrifice, with Zechariah, a fountain to cleanse from sin and impurity: a place to be washed, to be made new, to be forgiven, to be restored. We see here the meaning of this death: the one, perfect and sufficient sacrifice, oblation and satisfaction for the sins of the whole world.

We look back down 2,000 years and see clearly in history what Zechariah only saw darkly through a glass: generations of people from every nation who have found – and still find – forgiveness and a new beginning in the death of Jesus Christ. A fountain has indeed been opened. Hallelujah.

Lord God,
defend your Church from all false teaching
and give to your people knowledge of your truth,
that we may enjoy eternal life
in Jesus Christ our Lord.

COLLECT

Friday 4 October

Zechariah 14.1-11

'On that day his feet will stand on the Mount of Olives' (v.4)

Zechariah looks forward in his vision and sees the intermingling of two themes. The first is judgement and the continued suffering of his city and people: warfare and battle and pain. The second is grace and the redeeming of the city and the establishing of God's reign.

For all his prophetic gifts, Zechariah cannot yet see how all of this will come about. The feet of God will indeed stand on the Mount of Olives: but God will come in human flesh and blood, as a gentle carpenter, healer and teacher. Jesus will kneel in agony in the garden seeking strength and courage for the great act of redemption. Jesus will bear in his own death the suffering of the world. The victory will not be over human armies through conquest but over sin and death, for all time, through sacrifice.

Our vision, like Zechariah's, is incomplete. There are many things we do not understand. There is still terrible violence, theft, rape and exile. But we are not left like Zechariah to gaze forward in confusion. We are called continually to look back – to re-member his death and resurrection especially in the Eucharist.

As we look back, our vision of the present and the future is renewed. We find fresh hope and strength and purpose for our lives and for the world.

COLLECT

God, who in generous mercy sent the Holy Spirit
    upon your Church in the burning fire of your love:
grant that your people may be fervent
in the fellowship of the gospel
that, always abiding in you,
they may be found steadfast in faith and active in service;
through Jesus Christ your Son our Lord,
who is alive and reigns with you,
in the unity of the Holy Spirit,
one God, now and for ever.

| *Reflection by* **Steven Croft**

Psalms 41, **42**, 43
Zechariah 14.12-end
Mark 12.18-27

Saturday 5 October

Zechariah 14.12-end

'Holy to the Lord' (v.20)

Zechariah's final vision is of the final days, the end of time, cast in the language of the apocalyptic, nurturing hope for the community of exiles gathered around the reconstructed temple built in the ruins of Jerusalem. God's purposes will yet be fulfilled in this city, and they are purposes for the whole earth and for all the nations.

The prophet draws on the images of his fellow prophets and psalmists to describe that great day: light and not darkness; warmth and not frost; living waters; the whole earth united with the Lord as king (Zechariah 14.6-9). The pictures he connects and recasts will be used in the New Testament to paint a picture of God's kingdom and God's reign. There will be judgement and destruction throughout the earth. However, the end of the story will be a world united in the worship of the King, the Lord of hosts, in the great autumn festival of Israel, the festival of booths, when the whole earth seeks renewal for the land and spiritual renewal and unites in the glory and worship of God.

The final images are both homely and powerful. It is the whole city now that is consecrated to God and made holy: every bell on the horse's bridle, every cooking pot. The invitation to all of us is to holiness: to consecrate each moment of our lives to God as we wait for the coming of his kingdom.

Lord God,
defend your Church from all false teaching
and give to your people knowledge of your truth,
that we may enjoy eternal life
in Jesus Christ our Lord.

COLLECT

Monday 7 October

Psalm **44**
Ecclesiasticus 1.1-10
or Ezekiel 1.1-14
Mark 12.28-34

Mark 12.28-34

'Which commandment is the first of all?' (v.28)

The testing questions continue. The scribe is not mean-minded or hostile. He is really interested in what Jesus might say, but he is the kind of person who wants to spend too long with the footnotes. He lives for the debate. The question, 'Which commandment is the first of all?', is often asked; it is a 'big question'. It is another way of challenging someone to name the real priority: what matters most of all?

The answer to that question is supposed to be unambiguous: it is *this*; it is not *that*. Jesus says something startling: 'Love God; love your neighbour'. There is not one priority; there are two – it is this *and* that. You cannot love God if you do not love your neighbour. The scribe's first assumption was mistaken; faith is not an idea, something you debate. Faith is a way of life; it is an attitude.

Interestingly, our scribe is quick to applaud what Jesus says, 'You are right, Teacher'. Still, however, he is interested in priorities and shifts the discussion slightly. Yes, he argues, love in action matters more than what you do at the temple. He is still debating the point. He is no better than 'not far' from the kingdom.

While we discuss the details, the love of God and neighbour grows cold. Faith is like swimming. You have to commit not debate. First you get in; then you work out how it is done.

COLLECT

O Lord, we beseech you mercifully to hear the prayers
    of your people who call upon you;
and grant that they may both perceive and know
    what things they ought to do,
and also may have grace and power faithfully to fulfil them;
through Jesus Christ your Son our Lord,
who is alive and reigns with you,
in the unity of the Holy Spirit,
one God, now and for ever.

Psalms **48**, 52
Ecclesiasticus 1.11-end
or Ezekiel 1.15 – 2.2
Mark 12.35-end

Tuesday 8 October

Mark 12.35-end

'Beware of the scribes' (v.38)

Another edgy encounter in the Temple. This time, Jesus demonstrates that he too can ask hard questions: 'Is the Messiah the son of David?' It is a question that Mark believes to be crucial. Matthew and Luke tell us that Jesus was indeed the 'son of David'. Mark does not. The title is only given to Jesus by the cheering crowd, in Jerusalem, waving their palm branches. They knew exactly what it meant. They were looking for a leader who would restore David's kingdom. That was not what Jesus ever intended. He rejects the title and all that political ambition and hankering for the past.

That done, he then attacks another assumption. We are used to thinking of the little story of the widow's mite as a moving example of selfless devotion: a woman giving her last coins. That is not what Jesus sees. He knows that she has just beggared herself, given 'all she had to live on'. The temple is imposing a crushing burden. There are terrible expectations in this passage, expectations urged on the faithful in the name of God.

Faith is at its most seductive when it wants us to make a grand gesture, but too often it imposes itself on those who need helping up, not putting down. Those of us who have faith can expect too much, impose too many rules. Beware of the scribe within!

COLLECT

Lord of creation,
whose glory is around and within us:
open our eyes to your wonders,
that we may serve you with reverence
and know your peace at our lives' end,
through Jesus Christ our Lord.

Wednesday 9 October

Psalm **119.57-80**
Ecclesiasticus 2
or Ezekiel 2.3 – 3.11
Mark 13.1-13

Mark 13.1-13

'Look, Teacher, what large stones ...!' (v.1)

The temple was built to impress, and the disciples were duly astounded. This was Herod's temple, built out of limestone; it shone in the sun. The stones were indeed big. In the tunnels by Temple Mount, you can find one that is 44 feet long and 11 feet high (13.4 by 3.4 metres). Already though, we are falling into the trap that had gripped the excited disciple: 'Look, Teacher, what large stones!' It is too easy to concentrate on the stones. For faithful Jews, the temple was the place where heaven touched earth. It was the place to feel and know the presence of the living God. The trouble is, religious architecture can be distracting. 'Look, Teacher, what large stones!'

Jesus' reply takes us by surprise. He says things that we have not heard him say. He talks about destruction and war. Bad as that sounds, it is just 'the beginning of the birth pangs'. Commentaries on Mark's Gospel give these verses special treatment because the imagery is so powerful. Just possibly, however, we ought not to be too surprised at what Jesus says. After all, his ministry began with an equally powerful note of proclamation: 'The time is fulfilled, and the kingdom of God has come near' (Mark 1.15). That was always the gospel. The hope was always that the world would become a royal highway to the kingdom. Jesus always looked for a change of direction.

Disciples can too easily get distracted; the architecture gets in the way.

COLLECT

O Lord, we beseech you mercifully to hear the prayers
of your people who call upon you;
and grant that they may both perceive and know
what things they ought to do,
and also may have grace and power faithfully to fulfil them;
through Jesus Christ your Son our Lord,
who is alive and reigns with you,
in the unity of the Holy Spirit,
one God, now and for ever.

| *Reflection by* **David Hoyle**

Thursday 10 October

Mark 13.14-23

'... signs and omens, to lead astray' (v.22)

This crisis will be terrible, 'suffering, such as has not been from the beginning of the creation'. Our only hope lies in the fact that God has 'cut short those days'. This is shattering drama, and we are supposed to notice. We are imagining the loss of everything that faithful Jews would depend upon. If Jerusalem and the temple are lost, the centre can no longer hold; everything falls apart. The size and scale of this crisis is what matters, the fact that it beggars the imagination.

It is no surprise, however, that most readers want to get quickly into the detail. Just *exactly* what will happen, and when? That strange phrase 'desolating sacrilege' harks back to the Book of Daniel and to the desecration of the temple in 167 BC. Is Mark asking us to imagine it will happen again? Is Jesus announcing a prophecy that will be fulfilled when Titus lays siege to Jerusalem in AD 70?

It is all very interesting, but we must resist the temptations to debate the outcome. We will not have time for details; there is no pausing to get a coat. Christ warns us that false Messiahs will flourish signs and omens and must be ignored. We must not be caught looking backwards into history nor deep into a crystal ball. Christ wants us to be alert, attentive to what we have been told. Something new is beginning, and it will demand our best efforts and our absolute attention.

Lord of creation,
whose glory is around and within us:
open our eyes to your wonders,
that we may serve you with reverence
and know your peace at our lives' end,
through Jesus Christ our Lord.

COLLECT

Reflection by **David Hoyle**   277

Friday 11 October

Mark.13.24-31

'From the fig tree learn its lesson' (v.28)

The mood of crisis is sustained. The sun and moon will go dark. At this defining moment, we are to look for a vision foretold long ago, 'the Son of Man coming in clouds'. It is a promise from the book of Daniel (7.13). The language is striking: a scene from the end of days. Notice though, that in all the high drama, it is an ordinary *human* figure that we will see. He will bring rescue and redemption. In the midst of terrible loss and carnage, all will be gathered in. Angels will range to the very ends of heaven. They will lose nothing.

Then, abruptly, the mood and the language change. We have been battered with apocalyptic imagery, a glimpse of the end times. Now, we must think of a fig tree. We have met a fig tree before, (Mark 11.13-14, 20-21). That fig tree was withered; this fig tree is bursting into leaf. What was dead is suddenly alive.

This is a rollercoaster, vivid and disturbing ideas, and then a lesson from nature. This is meant to unsettle us; it is intended to give us a sense of urgency. As we acknowledge that all creation is in God's hands, we must not miss the hints that salvation lies in simple things: knowing the Son of God; knowing the difference between life and death.

COLLECT

O Lord, we beseech you mercifully to hear the prayers
    of your people who call upon you;
and grant that they may both perceive and know
    what things they ought to do,
and also may have grace and power faithfully to fulfil them;
through Jesus Christ your Son our Lord,
who is alive and reigns with you,
in the unity of the Holy Spirit,
one God, now and for ever.

| *Reflection by* **David Hoyle**

Psalm **68**
Ecclesiasticus 4.29 – 6.1
or Ezekiel 9
Mark 13.32-end

Saturday 12 October

Mark 13.32-end

'Keep awake' (vv.35, 37)

At the end of all those startling visions of the end of time, Jesus offers us a little parable. Unusually, this teaching is addressed specifically to disciples. The message is simple enough, 'keep awake'. In the short parable, though, there is a telling bit of detail. The master might return 'in the evening, or at midnight, or at cockcrow, or at dawn'. In the 1950s, a commentator called R. H. Lightfoot noticed that these four 'watches' of the Roman night were also significant moments in the passion narrative. The Last Supper took place in the evening. Jesus was held by the High Priest at midnight. At cockcrow, Peter denied him, and, in the morning, Jesus was handed over to the Romans. So, our attention is directed to the story that is about to unfold. That helps us hear the bitter irony in that injunction to 'keep awake', knowing, as we do, that the disciples will fall asleep in Gethsemane.

We are disciples too. This message, 'keep awake', is for us. The urgent command to all disciples is to keep our eyes open. The kingdom is near; critical decisions are at hand. Are we paying attention? Do we realize the significance of what is before us? The journalist and writer Philip Toynbee observed: 'The basic command of religion is not "do this" or "do not do that!" but, simply, "look".'

Reflection by **David Hoyle** | 279

Monday 14 October

Mark 14.1-11

'She has done what she could' (v.8)

This story, of the woman and the jar of ointment, is told in all four Gospels, but it is told with different emphasis. In Luke, for example, the woman is a notorious sinner. Mark implies that she is actually a person of status; it is costly ointment she brings. He also has rather more to say about her and her actions, 'She has done what she could'. It would not have been unusual for a guest to have oil poured on his head at a dinner. That was a mark of hospitality. We should notice that it is a *woman* who performs the action. As at the resurrection, it is a woman who grasps the significance of the moment. Anointing like this, on the head, is a mark of kingship and later arguments will rage around whether or not Jesus is a king. The silent woman is in no doubt.

The central significance of what she does, however, lies elsewhere. She has anointed Jesus for burial. She knows that his death is fundamental to his vocation. Peter objected when Jesus told him he must die. This woman understands that death is not the end of what Jesus does, but *part* of what he does.

Buried hastily, Jesus was not anointed at his death and those who came to put that right were interrupted by his resurrection. This woman has seized the opportunity others miss. She has acknowledged Christ and proclaimed the good news of life triumphant over death.

COLLECT

Almighty God,
you have made us for yourself,
and our hearts are restless till they find their rest in you:
pour your love into our hearts and draw us to yourself,
and so bring us at last to your heavenly city
where we shall see you face to face;
through Jesus Christ your Son our Lord,
who is alive and reigns with you,
in the unity of the Holy Spirit,
one God, now and for ever.

| *Reflection by* **David Hoyle**

Psalm **73**
Ecclesiasticus 7.27-end
or Ezekiel 11.14-end
Mark 14.12-25

Tuesday 15 October

Mark 14.12-25

'... one of you will betray me' (v.18)

'On the night before he died he had supper with his friends.' So says the eucharistic prayer. The truth is, of course, that when Jesus sat down to supper, not everyone at the table was a friend. Mark keeps reminding us of the danger, the anger and hostility. Jesus has already been anointed for burial. We have started to think about his death. The careful preparations for keeping the Passover alert us to the fact that Jesus and his followers knew they were being watched. The business of following the man with the water jar is a strategy for finding your way to a safe house.

Then, at the table, we hear the prophecy of the betrayal, it is 'one who is eating with me'. We must pick up the signals that Mark sends, telling us that Jesus is opposed, hated and betrayed. He began the Gospel telling us, in the first verse, that this is the Christ, the Son of God. Now we learn that, when God lives among us, we are unable to bear his presence and we kill him. Even our communion service, when we share in this supper and celebrate our unity with Christ and one another, should remind us of the danger of betrayal and tell us that this body was broken, this blood spilt. This supper is where communion begins. All our unity starts here. We need to remember that unity has to be wrestled out of betrayal, hatred and violence. Communion is not won lightly.

Gracious God,
you call us to fullness of life:
deliver us from unbelief
and banish our anxieties
with the liberating love of Jesus Christ our Lord.

COLLECT

Reflection by **David Hoyle**

Wednesday 16 October

Psalm **77**
Ecclesiasticus 10.6-8, 12-24
or Ezekiel 12.1-16
Mark 14.26-42

Mark 14.26-42

'... not what I want, but what you want' (v.36)

Jesus and the disciples sing a hymn at the end of supper. The hymn was the 'Egyptian Hallel' (Psalms 114 and 115). It was a Passover song of praise for the God who delivers his people. So, the decisive night begins with an announcement that God is sovereign. As Psalm 115 puts it, 'Our God is in the heavens; he does whatever he pleases' (Psalm 115.3). What follows is what the Father *wants*. Jesus understands that; he has predicted his own betrayal and his coming death. Now, he tells his disciples that they will desert him. He recalls a prophecy of Zechariah, 'Strike the shepherd, that the sheep may be scattered' (Zechariah 13.7).

Mark has quoted Zechariah once before, where Jesus remarks that the crowd is like 'sheep without a shepherd' (Mark 6.34). Jesus steps into the role Zechariah anticipated as God's promises are worked out. The covenant with God has been broken, but it will be restored. The sheep will be scattered, but Jesus, the shepherd, will go before them (to Galilee) and they will be gathered again.

Peter refuses to accept it. He will never deny Christ. He fails almost immediately, and we begin to notice how isolated Jesus has become, set apart and awake in Gethsemane. A deep mystery is now worked out, under God's direction. Jesus in solitary anguish binds himself to what his Father wills. Jesus' vocation is indistinguishable from the life and love of his Father.

COLLECT

Almighty God,
you have made us for yourself,
and our hearts are restless till they find their rest in you:
pour your love into our hearts and draw us to yourself,
and so bring us at last to your heavenly city
where we shall see you face to face;
through Jesus Christ your Son our Lord,
who is alive and reigns with you,
in the unity of the Holy Spirit,
one God, now and for ever.

Thursday 17 October

Mark 14.43-52

'... he left the linen cloth and ran off naked' (v.51)

The pace quickens; Judas arrives '*Immediately*, while he was still speaking'. Mark uses that word 'immediately' a good deal; the whole gospel is urgent, and it looks for an urgent response. Yet, for all that haste, the gospel happens in God's time, there is nothing accidental or careless. The purposes of God drive the narrative. We are reminded of that when Jesus explains that the scriptures must 'be fulfilled'. Even Judas is an agent of God's purpose, but that does not alter his guilt. There is no getting away from the fact that he chooses a travesty of love to condemn Christ. Judas is 'the betrayer' and uses a kiss to identify Jesus. Then, the simmering violence that has surrounded Jesus explodes for a moment. Jesus himself is not seduced by the violence; he points out it was never necessary.

The young man who runs away is the really interesting detail. He is found only in Mark. Remember, nothing happens by accident in this story. There are two distinctive words that are used, words to identify both the 'young man' and the 'cloth'. We will hear those Greek words just once more. The same words describe the cloth that will cover the dead Christ (Mark 15.46) and the young man (now fully clothed in white), who announces that Jesus has been 'raised' (Mark 16.5)?. As Zechariah foretold, the disciples are scattered, but what was scattered will be gathered and what was lost will be regained.

Gracious God,
you call us to fullness of life:
deliver us from unbelief
and banish our anxieties
with the liberating love of Jesus Christ our Lord.

COLLECT

Friday 18 October
Luke the Evangelist

Psalms 145, 146
Isaiah 55
Luke 1.1-4

Luke 1.1-4

'... an orderly account of the events' (v.1)

Luke wants us to know that he is a historian: 'This is what actually happened.' He wants us to know that the story of Jesus, Peter, Andrew and Judas is not a fiction. What we deal in, Luke tells us, is not mystery, but history. His introduction, that dedication to Theophilus, is just the way contemporary historians wrote. St Luke, the historian, insists on an orderly account, lists of events and eyewitnesses. Luke sets out his stall. 'In the days of King Herod of Judea' (Luke 1.5), he begins. He does it again, famously, in a passage we hear each Christmas: 'In those days a decree went out from Emperor Augustus that all the world should be registered' (Luke 2.1).

Luke wants to tell us *when* these things happened. This is not a 'Once upon a time' sort of story; it is not myth, nor make-believe. It is history. That is what Christianity is, the record of what was and is. Let's be clear about this. When everyone is asking us to debate the propositions that there probably is (or probably isn't) a God, this is one answer. Christianity does not ask us to speculate and imagine; it asks us to weigh evidence. It happened, says Luke, in the days of the Emperor Octavian, named 'Augustus' by the Senate in AD 27.

We deal in history not mystery. That is why every time we say the creed, we speak of Jesus Christ who was crucified under Pontius Pilate. History not mystery.

COLLECT

Almighty God,
you called Luke the physician,
whose praise is in the gospel,
to be an evangelist and physician of the soul:
by the grace of the Spirit
and through the wholesome medicine of the gospel,
give your Church the same love and power to heal;
through Jesus Christ your Son our Lord,
who is alive and reigns with you,
in the unity of the Holy Spirit,
one God, now and for ever.

| *Reflection by* **David Hoyle**

Saturday 19 October

Mark 14.66-end

'I do not know this man' (v.71)

Peter has been clear. In fact, he has been *vehement*: 'Even though I must die with you, I will not deny you' (Mark 14.31). All that resolve evaporates in an instant. Jesus was clear-eyed about the horror that lay ahead. In Gethsemane, Jesus came to terms with the commitment he had to make, aligning his will to the will of the Father. Peter, by contrast, made promises he had never really understood. He could not match intention and action.

Peter denies Christ, but he does not betray him. Judas turned on Christ and twisted love into hatred. Even as he reaches the point of crisis, Peter's love for Christ reduces him to tears. He speaks a greater truth than he understands. He genuinely does not *know* this man.

The whole gospel begs the question, 'Who is Jesus?' Jesus himself asks the question 'Who do you say that I am?' (Mark 8.29). Demons acknowledge Jesus as the Christ, and a Gentile centurion, at the foot of the cross, will identify him. Peter, though, has still not truly seen, or known, Christ. Rowan Williams has written: 'I shall never know him. There is always more than I can say or think and when I believe I have understood him, he will turn and look out of such silence that I'll know I have still known nothing'.

COLLECT

Almighty God,
you have made us for yourself,
and our hearts are restless till they find their rest in you:
pour your love into our hearts and draw us to yourself,
and so bring us at last to your heavenly city
where we shall see you face to face;
through Jesus Christ your Son our Lord,
who is alive and reigns with you,
in the unity of the Holy Spirit,
one God, now and for ever.

Reflection by **David Hoyle** | 285

Monday 21 October

Mark 15.1-15

'Are you the King of the Jews?' (v.2)

The act that won Pilate his place in history must have seemed fairly insignificant to him. Luke tells us that the chief priests did their utmost to make sure Pilate couldn't brush the charges aside. They accused Jesus of perverting the Jewish nation, encouraging people to evade tax, and claiming to be the Messiah (Luke 23.2). But Pilate realized that accusations that Jesus was a criminal stemmed from jealously. He made his decision to sentence Jesus to death on the basis of what was most likely to win him approval at a time of political tension. It was easy for him in the end. Little did he know!

Jesus, in contrast, understood precisely what the trial was about. It wasn't about whether he was a criminal; it was about his identity. That was the only question to which he responded with anything but silence.

In the early years of the Christian Church, martyrs dragged before the court would sometimes reply to their accusers again and again with the single phrase: *'Christianus sum'* ('I am a Christian'). They too knew that no matter what charges they faced, it was their identity that was on trial. All of us, in time or in eternity, will have to answer questions such as those flung at Jesus in these verses. I pray that at that point I will have the courage to own Jesus as my Lord and make clear my true identity: *'Christianus sum.'*

COLLECT

Almighty and everlasting God,
increase in us your gift of faith
that, forsaking what lies behind
and reaching out to that which is before,
we may run the way of your commandments
and win the crown of everlasting joy;
through Jesus Christ your Son our Lord,
who is alive and reigns with you,
in the unity of the Holy Spirit,
one God, now and for ever.

| *Reflection by* **Peter Graystone**

Psalms 87, **89.1-18**
Ecclesiasticus 17.1-24
or Ezekiel 18.1-20
Mark 15.16-32

Tuesday 22 October

Mark 15.16-32
'... that we may see and believe' (v.32)

The most notable feature of the way Mark describes the crucifixion of Jesus is its restraint. We don't hear the screams or smell the stench. As John Calvin commented: 'These matters call for secret meditation, rather than for ornament of words.'

People have always been capable of doing together what they would never dream of doing on their own. So the soldiers vented all their anti-Jewish feelings on Jesus.

People find themselves caught up in desperate situations quite by accident. So, against his will, Simon finds himself caught up in the tragedy. No one knows what impact it had on him, but because his children are named and known, it is possible that they may have become followers of Jesus (Romans 16.13).

Dreadful ironies overcome people in times of tragedy. James and John, watching at a distance, must have seen the bandits mock Jesus from left and right and realized that they were occupying the very places they had asked to take in happier times (Mark 10.37,38).

And through it all we see the exhausted isolation of Jesus – his title ridiculed, his words distorted, his helplessness mocked and the worship that should rightfully be his parodied.

My God, this was a terrible way to die. My God, I thank you that you endured it because of your love for me.

God, our judge and saviour,
teach us to be open to your truth
and to trust in your love,
that we may live each day
with confidence in the salvation which is given
through Jesus Christ our Lord.

COLLECT

Wednesday 23 October

Psalm **119.105-128**
Ecclesiasticus 18.1-14
or Ezekiel 18.21-32
Mark 15.33-41

Mark 15.33-41

'My God, my God, why have you forsaken me?' (v.34)

During the twenty-four hours that lead to his death, Jesus seems totally alone. The leaders of God's people, who had so longed for their Messiah, had not recognized him and instead handed him over to their enemies. It was as if the totally just, totally powerful God was suddenly unjust or powerless. Jesus' deep knowledge of Scripture prompts him to bring to mind Psalm 22 and its desolate opening words: 'My God, my God, why have you forsaken me?' ('*Eloi, Eloi, lema sabacthani.*') One onlooker misunderstands and another has a surprising revelation.

The person who gets it wrong hears Jesus' cry and mistakes *Eloi* for Elijah. In the circumstances it was an understandable mistake. But all it leads to is Jesus' agony being prolonged as the bystanders force drink upon him to see whether he might be rescued through a spectacular miracle.

The person with a revelation was a Roman soldier. Although we probably shouldn't read into his recognition of a son of God all that we would like to from a Christian perspective, it was nevertheless a godly and unexpected response. ('A son of God' could also have meant 'a fine fellow', v.39.)

Which one would I have been: the one who gets it wrong or the one who has a revelation? Probably neither. When I picture the scene I am among those who watch from a distance, terrified and heartbroken. I hope I would have had the courage to stay to the end.

COLLECT

Almighty and everlasting God,
increase in us your gift of faith
that, forsaking what lies behind
and reaching out to that which is before,
we may run the way of your commandments
and win the crown of everlasting joy;
through Jesus Christ your Son our Lord,
who is alive and reigns with you,
in the unity of the Holy Spirit,
one God, now and for ever.

Psalms 90, **92**
Ecclesiasticus 19.4-17
or Ezekiel 20.1-20
Mark 15.42-end

Thursday 24 October

Mark 15.42-end

'... waiting expectantly for the kingdom of God' (v.43)

The figure of Joseph of Arimathea has fascinated people, particularly in Britain where legends about him persist. Perhaps it's because he appears so late in the story of Jesus' life, and people like to invent what they cannot know. However, there are three things that we do know about him.

His actions were courageous. He was a member of the Jewish Council before whom Jesus had been dragged. Longing for the kingdom of God to come, Luke tells us he knew that their decision to send Jesus to Pilate was wrong (Luke 23.51). He certainly risked his credibility by going to Pilate to ask for the body to be released, and then giving Jesus a tomb. After hours of the darkness of Calvary, he offers the first pinprick of light.

He must have known his actions were useless. He suddenly felt he needed to commit himself, even though it was too late to save Jesus. As far as he knew, Jesus was past the need for the care that was being given to him. But he realized that the Jewish laws required him to act speedily because the Sabbath was approaching (see also Deuteronomy 21.22,23).

Nevertheless, his actions were beautiful. They were a gesture of love without any expectation of reward. So is every trip to put fresh flowers on an old grave. Without any way of realizing it, Joseph was preparing Jesus for resurrection.

God, our judge and saviour,
teach us to be open to your truth
and to trust in your love,
that we may live each day
with confidence in the salvation which is given
through Jesus Christ our Lord.

COLLECT

Friday 25 October

Psalms **88** (95)
Ecclesiasticus 19.20-end
or Ezekiel 20.21-38
Mark 16.1-8

Mark 16.1-8

'He has been raised; he is not here' (v.6)

This was the original ending of Mark's Gospel. It seems abrupt and almost unsatisfactory. We want the story to end in an emotional reunion, not in fear and confusion.

But there is something we tend to forget. There were no witnesses to Jesus' resurrection. There were, of course, witnesses to the wonderful appearances of Jesus in the weeks that followed. There was rejoicing, there was teaching, and there was preparation for the future. But about the event that changed the course of history and eternity we know nothing at all.

Like a thriller writer, Mark lays out the evidence for what had taken place. The stone had been rolled back. A young man had news that seemed unbelievable. It was without doubt the tomb in which Joseph and the women had laid Jesus. And now it was empty. Unlike a thriller writer, however, this is not the evidence surrounding a sudden death, but a sudden life. Mark's startling ending does not leave us asking, 'Who on earth did it?' but, 'Who on earth is it?'

So what do we conclude? In the dark of the night, in the silence of a grave, without an announcement of any kind, without anyone watching, and needing help from nobody, Jesus had quietly got on with what God alone can do. He had risen from the dead.

COLLECT

Almighty and everlasting God,
increase in us your gift of faith
that, forsaking what lies behind
and reaching out to that which is before,
we may run the way of your commandments
and win the crown of everlasting joy;
through Jesus Christ your Son our Lord,
who is alive and reigns with you,
in the unity of the Holy Spirit,
one God, now and for ever.

| *Reflection by* **Peter Graystone**

Psalms 96, **97**, 100
Ecclesiasticus 21.1-17
or Ezekiel 24.15-end
Mark 16.9-end

Saturday 26 October

Mark 16.9-end

'... the Lord worked with them and confirmed the message' (v.20)

Yesterday's reflection, ending with frightened women yet to meet the risen Jesus, is the original ending to Mark's Gospel and makes it feel unfinished. Maybe something unexpected prevented Mark from completing it. Maybe a column of a scroll was destroyed. However, the appendix that we read today, added some time later, is unfinished in a different sense. The final verse sees the work of the resurrected Jesus continuing. But now it is not taking place *for* his disciples, but *with* them.

All four Gospels end with a challenge to the first followers of Jesus that is ongoing for those who love him today. In Matthew, Jesus' unfinished commission is, 'Go therefore and make disciples ... I am with you' (28.19,20). In Luke, 'You are witnesses ... stay here in the city until you have been clothed with power from on high' (24.48,49). In John it is repeatedly, 'Follow me' (21.22). In each case, the followers of Jesus are not left alone, but there is work to be done. As a result of the resurrection, we are now partners worldwide in his purposes.

Wherever the good news is being proclaimed, Jesus and his followers are collaborating. Through the miraculous (usually less perplexing than those in verse 17), through healing, through signs of hope brought to the poor, the downtrodden, the broken hearted, Jesus and his followers are collaborating. The gospel has barely begun.

God, our judge and saviour,
teach us to be open to your truth
and to trust in your love,
that we may live each day
with confidence in the salvation which is given
through Jesus Christ our Lord.

COLLECT

Reflection by **Peter Graystone** | 291

Monday 28 October
Simon and Jude, Apostles

Psalms 116, 117
Wisdom 5.1-16
or Isaiah 45.18-end
Luke 6.12-16

Luke 6.12-16

'... he called his disciples and chose twelve of them' (v.13)

I've tried to imagine this scene, but it's difficult. There were more than twelve people accompanying Jesus, and presumably they included women. So how did he announce that twelve of them were going to have a special role? Did he call a dozen men by name and have them step forward from the crowd, like children picking members of a sports team? Did he move through the group, quietly sitting beside individuals and explaining that he had a leadership plan for them? Was the atmosphere tense? Was there disappointment among those who were not chosen?

Jesus chose two sets of brothers – James and John, Andrew and Simon – but only one received a new name. He also chose Thomas, whom we learn was a twin (John 20.24), but not his brother or sister. Riskily he chose Simon, who with a nickname 'the Zealot' must have wanted to seize the country back from the Romans by any means, violent or peaceful.

Some of the twelve became footnotes of history. Some who were not chosen, including many women, became vital to Jesus' ministry and the founding of the Church. Judas became a traitor.

We are all becoming something as we walk alongside Jesus. In our diversity, Jesus does not smooth out differences. Instead, he opens opportunities to serve him. Our willingness to do so, in ways that are eye-catching or hidden, is the answer to his prayer.

COLLECT

Almighty God,
who built your Church upon the foundation
 of the apostles and prophets,
with Jesus Christ himself as the chief cornerstone:
so join us together in unity of spirit by their doctrine,
that we may be made a holy temple acceptable to you;
through Jesus Christ your Son our Lord,
who is alive and reigns with you,
in the unity of the Holy Spirit,
one God, now and for ever.

| *Reflection by* **Peter Graystone**

Psalm **106*** (*or* 103)
Ecclesiasticus 22.27 – 23.15
or Ezekiel 33.1-20
John 13.12-20

Tuesday 29 October

John 13.12-20

'I have set you an example' (v.15)

Humility was despised as a sign of weakness in the ancient world. But the kingdom of God has different values altogether. In the kingdom, the way to show leadership is to stoop down in service.

At the point we join this story, Jesus has stripped off his robe and done what a servant was expected to do – washed feet. He has shown what authentic Christian action looks like. It looks like menial service. It is even more telling that this did not come at a moment of triumph, when charity is relatively easy, but at a low point when Jesus knew his betrayal was close.

There was gracious love involved in Jesus' actions that night, but there was also challenge. He had demonstrated what it means to be a servant because he expected his followers to do the same. Of those who have received his grace, much is expected. We too need to strip off any 'robe' that gives us the appearance of superiority if we are to be useful in Jesus' service. To humble yourself involves removing anything that distances you from fellow human beings when you seek to serve them – whether it is the need to be appreciated, or to control the outcome, or to have your status recognized. We are not employees with rights; we are servants with obligations. We need both Jesus' example and his challenge because humility is harder than it seems.

Blessed Lord,
who caused all holy Scriptures to be written for our learning:
help us so to hear them,
to read, mark, learn and inwardly digest them
that, through patience, and the comfort of your holy word,
we may embrace and for ever hold fast
the hope of everlasting life,
which you have given us in our Saviour Jesus Christ,
who is alive and reigns with you,
in the unity of the Holy Spirit,
one God, now and for ever.

COLLECT

Reflection by **Peter Graystone**

293

Wednesday 30 October

John 13.21-30

'And it was night' (v.30)

The dark of Judas' treachery was not forgotten by the first churches, even in the light of the resurrection. Peter made reference repeatedly to the fact that Jesus was betrayed (Acts 1.16, 2:23) and so did Paul (1 Corinthians 11.23). Everything we read here suggests that Judas' actions took Jesus' followers by surprise. They assumed he left the meal to prepare for the next day to be business as usual.

On that Passover night, only Jesus seems to have known what lay ahead for both him and Judas. For the host of the meal to offer someone a piece of dipped bread as he did was an honour. Was it a final attempt to make Judas change his mind? Or was it (and this is a disturbing thought) a way of Jesus participating in Judas' actions? Was his sin completely beyond redemption? Or is it possible that the forgiveness that swept from the cross through all times and places was sufficient to go with Judas to his suicidal end and offer him a way back to God?

What was in Judas' heart when he stepped from that room into the night? There are many inventive theories about why he did what he did to his friend but, actually, nobody knows. It leaves me thinking about friends I have betrayed, mainly in small ways. Why did I do those things? Oh why? Do you find yourself thinking the same?

COLLECT

Blessed Lord,
who caused all holy Scriptures to be written for our learning:
help us so to hear them,
to read, mark, learn and inwardly digest them
that, through patience, and the comfort of your holy word,
we may embrace and for ever hold fast
   the hope of everlasting life,
which you have given us in our Saviour Jesus Christ,
who is alive and reigns with you,
in the unity of the Holy Spirit,
one God, now and for ever.

Thursday 31 October

John 13.31-end

'... as I have loved you, you also should love one another' (v.34)

The words 'commandment' and 'love' sit uneasily in the same sentence. Love is not something you can force yourself to have. You can say that you love someone. Or pretend. You can perform loving actions to help someone. But deep down in your heart you know whether or not you genuinely love somebody, and you can't control it.

However, there is something new about Jesus' order that his followers should love each other. The context for it is that we have been loved by Jesus with an extraordinary, sacrificial, unending love. When we surrender to being loved so perfectly, loving others is an inevitable consequence. By getting to know God, we get to know love (1 John 4.7). By opening ourselves to the Holy Spirit, we are filled with God's love for us (Romans 5.5). If you cannot bring yourself to love a fellow Christian, change will come only by realizing anew what it means to be loved by Christ.

In the context of these words, Peter blundered into a promise to be faithful to Jesus that he broke within hours. Asked on three occasions whether he knew Jesus, he pretended he did not. It's not surprising, then, that when he met with Jesus after the resurrection and had a chance to be reconciled, Jesus did not ask him, 'Do you regret denying me?' Instead he asked, 'Do you love me?' (John 21.15-17).

Merciful God,
teach us to be faithful in change and uncertainty,
that trusting in your word
and obeying your will
we may enter the unfailing joy of Jesus Christ our Lord.

COLLECT

Friday 1 November
All Saints' Day

Psalms 15, 84, 149
Isaiah 35.1-9
Luke 9.18-27

Luke 9.18-27
'... follow me' (v.23)

When Jesus said that men and women who want to follow him must 'deny themselves and take up their cross', a shudder must have passed through everyone who heard. A person who took up a cross was on the way to his execution. He wasn't coming back. The chilling phrase comes several times in the Gospels, but Luke adds an even more sobering word: 'daily'. Making a decision to follow Jesus no matter what it costs is not a once-in-a-lifetime resolution, but one that needs to be renewed again and again and again.

What does it mean in practice? According to Jesus, three things. First, the inclination to put yourself first needs to die. To deny yourself means to decide consciously that personal decisions will be made on the basis of what builds the kingdom of God and fulfils the purposes of Jesus in the world.

Second, the longing to own possessions needs to die. We need food and shelter obviously, but it's impossible to put both things and Jesus at the centre of our life's ambition.

Third, the desire to admired by people needs to die. Jesus knew that if he was to be despised and rejected, his followers would also find themselves ridiculed and constrained. We have no right to expect anything other.

Don't take the question, 'Who do you say I am?' lightly. Jesus is not looking for an intelligent answer, but a lifetime's commitment.

COLLECT

Almighty God,
you have knit together your elect
in one communion and fellowship
    in the mystical body of your Son Christ our Lord:
grant us grace so to follow your blessed saints
in all virtuous and godly living
that we may come to those inexpressible joys
that you have prepared for those who truly love you;
through Jesus Christ your Son our Lord,
who is alive and reigns with you,
in the unity of the Holy Spirit,
one God, now and for ever.

| *Reflection by* **Peter Graystone**

Psalms 120, **121**, 122
Ecclesiasticus 28.14-end
or Ezekiel 36.16-36
John 14.15-end

Saturday 2 November

John 14.15-end
'Do not let your hearts be troubled' (v.27)

'Don't be afraid,' was God's message to those who came immediately before Jesus, and the reason there was no need for fear was that the Holy Spirit was in action (Luke 1.30, 35). 'Don't be afraid,' was Jesus' message to those who would come after him, and the reason there was no need for fear was that the Holy Spirit was in action.

Who is this Spirit who can drive out human fear? One who stands alongside us with help. That's the meaning of the word 'Paraclete', which translators struggle with, often settling on 'Advocate' or 'Counsellor'. Where once Jesus stood by his disciples, strong and enlightening, the Spirit will now be present.

The Spirit is one who dwells within Christian people – one who is and always has been at work in the whole world. The Spirit is the very image of God that makes humans human. But there is something unique about the way the Spirit is revealed to Jesus' followers which feels like setting up home together.

The Spirit is one who will ensure that Jesus is never forgotten. Both for those discovering Jesus for the first time, and for those remembering everything the Saviour said and did, the Spirit is the source of knowledge.

Who is this Spirit? In every way God himself, come to us to be all that Jesus was to his disciples. So don't be afraid.

COLLECT

Blessed Lord,
who caused all holy Scriptures to be written for our learning:
help us so to hear them,
to read, mark, learn and inwardly digest them
that, through patience, and the comfort of your holy word,
we may embrace and for ever hold fast
the hope of everlasting life,
which you have given us in our Saviour Jesus Christ,
who is alive and reigns with you,
in the unity of the Holy Spirit,
one God, now and for ever.

Reflection by **Peter Graystone**

Monday 4 November

Psalms **2**, 146 *or* 123, 124, 125, **126**
Isaiah 1.1-20
Matthew 1.18-end

Isaiah 1.1-20

'... though your sins are like scarlet' (v.18)

'Out, damned spot, out, I say!' Shakespeare's Lady Macbeth is overheard muttering as she sleepwalks and tries to rub off the blood she sees on her hands. In doing so, she reveals her part in murder. The guilt she has suppressed in order to make and keep her husband king has become too strong for her increasingly fragile mind. She may have become queen, but she has lost her sense of who she is and her guilt destroys her.

For those of us in the UK, our attention is drawn, this week, to the colour red. Red poppies are a reminder of the blood of violent death, but much more, of the heroism and patriotism of those who gave their lives in war. To wear a poppy expresses gratitude to those who died in order that the country could come through war with its national identity intact and its way of life preserved and passed on.

Isaiah calls the people of Jerusalem back to themselves as God's people. Their 'hands are full of blood' and they no longer know where their loyalties lie. God longs for this people to come to him, for the scarlet sins can only lead to destruction. God longs for the children whom he has reared to learn to do good. Their sins are red as crimson, but they can be covered as with snow, become clean like wool.

We find our identity in Christ, as a new creation. The old has gone and the new has come.

COLLECT

Almighty and eternal God,
you have kindled the flame of love in the hearts of the saints:
grant to us the same faith and power of love,
that, as we rejoice in their triumphs,
we may be sustained by their example and fellowship;
through Jesus Christ your Son our Lord,
who is alive and reigns with you,
in the unity of the Holy Spirit,
one God, now and for ever.

| *Reflection by* **Justine Allain Chapman**

Psalms **5**, 147.1-12 *or* **132**, 133
Isaiah 1.21-end
Matthew 2.1-15

Tuesday 5 November

Isaiah 1.21-end

'Afterwards you shall be called the city of righteousness' (v.26)

'Doom and more doom' seems to be the refrain of much Old Testament prophecy. We can feel bemused, as Christians, by a picture of a wrathful and punishing God who delights in destruction. Isaiah is compelled to speak to the people of Jerusalem in the eighth century BC at a time of uncertainty. The Northern Kingdom of Israel had fallen; Judah too was under threat from the Assyrian army and Isaiah looked for meaning.

When things go wrong in human life, it is natural to ask why God has allowed them to happen. Any crisis, national or personal brings with it the need for change. A crisis is an invitation to change, to reassess our priorities. The call to repent is not a sentence but an invitation. There will be an 'afterwards', a time when the crisis is over.

Isaiah urges the wealthy, the exploitative and the complacent to repent. Perhaps if we think of ourselves as having much, we hear his words as God wanting to condemn. If we have known poverty and injustice, it may be that we simply hear the truth that justice in a society is the outworking of fair treatment for all citizens.

In Christ we know that the truth will set us free, however hard it may be to hear. Death and destruction are never the end of the story. There is an afterwards, newness of life, whatever crisis befalls us.

God of glory,
touch our lips with the fire of your Spirit,
that we with all creation
may rejoice to sing your praise;
through Jesus Christ our Lord.

COLLECT

Wednesday 6 November

Psalms **9**, 147.13-end
or **119.153-end**
Isaiah 2.1-11
Matthew 2.16-end

Isaiah 2.1-11

'... they shall beat their swords into ploughshares' (v.4)

Farmers plough the fields in the autumn after harvesting old crops and before planting seeds. Turning over the earth exposes weeds that would otherwise take root. The furrows created by the plough provide the place for the seeds to have the best chance of growth.

You can make a weapon from the cutting edge of the plough, the ploughshare, and use it in war. In peace, swords can be forged into ploughshares. To do this means not only turning tools from one mode of being to another, but also attitudes. Significant calculations are needed. How much energy and resources are to be put into defence and how much into the ploughing? The wrong balance will make people vulnerable to death either from attack or by starvation.

In the parable of the sower (Mark 4.1-20), Jesus tells us that God sows the seed. To be fruitful, our hearts need to be ready to receive the seed. We might ask God to unearth what holds us back from making peace or being at peace. For our own tools, of time, money and talents, to be invested in peace making, we will need to spend less on defending ourselves. We can find ourselves needlessly poised to react defensively in the face of sharp words.

As we take time in this season to consider our calling in the service of the Prince of Peace, we can expect to find ourselves blessed as children of God.

COLLECT

Almighty and eternal God,
you have kindled the flame of love in the hearts of the saints:
grant to us the same faith and power of love,
that, as we rejoice in their triumphs,
we may be sustained by their example and fellowship;
through Jesus Christ your Son our Lord,
who is alive and reigns with you,
in the unity of the Holy Spirit,
one God, now and for ever.

| *Reflection by* **Justine Allain Chapman**

Thursday 7 November

Isaiah 2.12-end

'For the Lord of hosts has a day' (v.12)

We all have days, anniversaries, when we celebrate and remember. We look back and we look forward with joy and with sorrow. This season is full of those days and some touch us personally.

Isaiah looks forward to a day when 'the pride of everyone shall be brought low', for only then will God be exalted. Many people look back on the day when they were brought low, but are grateful for the way in which they have grown personally and spiritually. In his book *Falling Upward*, the spiritual writer Richard Rohr talks of two halves of life. In the first half we build up our identity and seek success. The second and deeper half comes through an experience of being brought low. We need not fall down, however, when we are brought low; we can fall upward.

Pride comes before a fall. Pride is a deadly sin that particularly affects religious people. It expresses itself in self-sufficiency, in superiority and in being judgemental. A humble person, by contrast, knows their need of God and their worth in God's sight. Being secure, they recognize their need of other people and the gifts and talents of others.

As Mary sang the Magnificat (Luke 1.46-55), she looked forward, as Isaiah did, to a day when the proud would be scattered and the humble lifted high. She would ponder that day when an angel announced her part in bringing Christ into the world, Immanuel, God with us.

God of glory,
touch our lips with the fire of your Spirit,
that we with all creation
may rejoice to sing your praise;
through Jesus Christ our Lord.

COLLECT

Friday 8 November

Psalms **16**, 149 *or* 142, **144**
Isaiah 3.1-15
Matthew 4.1-11

Isaiah 3.1-15

'And I will make boys their princes' (v.4)

Isaiah prophesies the prospect of anarchy. Judah is under threat from an expansionist Assyria, which on conquering a nation not only took tribute but deported the leading elements of the population to other parts of the empire in order to prevent revolt. This created a vacuum of power, skills and experience.

Such a vacuum can be also found in modern societies where respect and celebrity status come from making money and being famous rather than for public service. It can be difficult to find good leaders for local government and the charity sector, for example, so that the people who fill these leadership roles may be less well suited to them. Edmund Burke, the eighteenth-century Irish statesman, is often quoted as saying that 'the only thing necessary for the triumph of evil is for good men to do nothing'.

Living with weak or failing leadership in the workplace, church or family is difficult. It demands care in discerning what agency we have to resist evil and promote good. Offering gratitude, a listening ear or advice might be a way forward. It might be a time to dig up a talent we have buried and offer it.

When the disciples were fretting because of the crowds, it was a boy who offered his loaves and fishes to Jesus to feed the five thousand. God uses those who listen and respond, and the choice often surprises the old and wise. What surprises may also delight and open our way to something new.

COLLECT
| Almighty and eternal God,
you have kindled the flame of love in the hearts of the saints:
grant to us the same faith and power of love,
that, as we rejoice in their triumphs,
we may be sustained by their example and fellowship;
through Jesus Christ your Son our Lord,
who is alive and reigns with you,
in the unity of the Holy Spirit,
one God, now and for ever.

| *Reflection by* **Justine Allain Chapman**

Saturday 9 November

Isaiah 4.2 – 5.7

'... there will be a canopy ... a refuge and a shelter' (4.5-6)

At a Jewish wedding, the couple stands underneath a canopy or *chuppah*. This covering symbolizes the new home created by the marriage and points to the public nature of a new household. The canopy calls to mind the beloved in the Song of Songs, brought into the banqueting house, remembering that his 'banner over me was love' (Song of Songs 2.4, KJV).

In Isaiah's famous parable of the vineyard, God is disappointed with the lack of good grapes on the vines and so lays the vineyard to waste, untended and exposed to the elements. This is what will happen to the nation, Isaiah prophesies, but there will be survivors, who will be saved in order to be fruitful. Just as God saved the nation at the exodus, he will save them again; they will know his presence in the cloud and flame as they did in the wilderness, long ago. The canopy will show where God is and will protect them from heat, storm and rain.

Public organizations, including churches, have not always safeguarded or protected the vulnerable. In our day, much abuse has been uncovered, and concerted efforts have been made to have better practices put in place. Churches have, over the ages, been involved in providing shelter and rescuing victims so that they might flourish as survivors.

Jesus, the true vine, invites us to abide in him, to bear the pruning in order to be fruitful.

God of glory,
touch our lips with the fire of your Spirit,
that we with all creation
may rejoice to sing your praise;
through Jesus Christ our Lord.

COLLECT

Reflection by **Justine Allain Chapman** | 303

Monday 11 November

Isaiah 5.8-24

'Surely many houses shall be desolate' (v.9)

It is always twilight and raining in the dismal town where new residents quarrel with their neighbour within a day of arriving. They have moved from that street in a week, to repeat the pattern, and they can do so because just by thinking of a house, a new one is built. So the town grows, empty and mean. In his book *The Great Divorce*, C. S. Lewis paints a picture of hell or purgatory as empty, desolate and expanding by the inability of the residents to live in peace. It is Sheol, which 'has enlarged its appetite'.

Isaiah berates the nobles of Jerusalem for building up property and wealth so there is no room for anyone else, and thus no justice for the poor. He predicts that military defeat and exile will leave the houses desolate.

Today, we remember the cost of war and the task of rebuilding once there is peace. Peace is built not by investment in property, but by connections with people. Jesus told his disciples that there are many dwelling places in his father's house (John 14.2). Christians have an important role to play in welcoming the stranger and those who have been displaced, by personal hospitality, almsgiving and working for the structures of society to enable flourishing for all.

We pledge ourselves as children of God to be peacemakers, remembering Christ's words: 'I will come again and take you to myself, so that where I am, there you may be also' (John 14.3).

COLLECT

Almighty Father,
whose will is to restore all things
in your beloved Son, the King of all:
govern the hearts and minds of those in authority,
and bring the families of the nations,
divided and torn apart by the ravages of sin,
to be subject to his just and gentle rule;
who is alive and reigns with you,
in the unity of the Holy Spirit,
one God, now and for ever.

304 | *Reflection by* **Justine Allain Chapman**

Psalms **21**, 24 *or* **5**, 6 (8)
Isaiah 5.25-end
Matthew 5.13-20

Tuesday 12 November

Isaiah 5.25-end

'He will raise a signal for a nation far away' (v.26)

We do not think of God as playing toy soldiers with the nations of the world, but here Isaiah depicts God whistling for the finely tuned Assyrian army who recognize the signal and will march to bring defeat and destruction. Isaiah knows that God is the God of Israel, in a special relationship forged during the history of the nation, but he also glimpses God as the ruler of all nations. We glimpse this too and are more likely to pray for peace when war looms, and even when enemies and allies are identified; we do not just pray that our side wins.

Prophets read the signs of the times and in them where God is at work. With the benefit of a hindsight that the Old Testament prophets did not have, we can see that God is creator, at work in nature, history, humanity, in the Church and also beyond it. Like the prophets, we are often very aware of the impact of sin, and we can wonder where God is.

The twentieth-century British theologian and missionary, Lesslie Newbigin spoke of mission as finding out what God is doing and joining in. There are signs of the kingdom of God in each person, religion and locality. We can be surprised, sometimes shamed, to see compassionate action, courage or forgiveness shown by a group other than our own. We might rejoice that God's whistle is heard far away, and with others we can join in making peace for all nations.

God, our refuge and strength,
bring near the day when wars shall cease
and poverty and pain shall end,
that earth may know the peace of heaven
through Jesus Christ our Lord.

COLLECT

Wednesday 13 November

Psalms **23**, 25 *or* **119.1-32**
Isaiah 6
Matthew 5.21-37

Isaiah 6

'Here am I' (v.8)

In our great churches and cathedrals, pilgrims and tourists visit to light candles as symbols of their prayers – that whatever darkness is upon them, they might find light. These holy buildings are steeped in human history, often partly ruined and with a mismatch of styles. Their walls have soaked up the joys and sorrows of prayer and so are shaped by heaven.

Isaiah, living in dark times, knew all too well both the internal moral degeneracy of his city and the external threat to it, so he went to the temple to pray. Like a sacred building, he identified with his earthly setting, as a man of unclean lips, and with God, able to see his glory filling the whole world.

Just as a holy building does not have to be perfect to be a place of encounter with God, neither does Isaiah have to be holy to see God. Isaiah had to be 'here', in the right place, in the present moment and with the right openness of heart, to become a messenger of God in his city.

Accepting we are here, both where we are and where we come from, can help us to see with clarity God's holiness, love for those we live among and desire to free us from sin. Perhaps you can light a candle for those in darkness. You might pray that God will fan into flame the gift that is within so that you might endure and be sent (2 Timothy 1.6).

COLLECT

Almighty Father,
whose will is to restore all things
in your beloved Son, the King of all:
govern the hearts and minds of those in authority,
and bring the families of the nations,
divided and torn apart by the ravages of sin,
to be subject to his just and gentle rule;
who is alive and reigns with you,
in the unity of the Holy Spirit,
one God, now and for ever.

| *Reflection by* **Justine Allain Chapman**

Psalms **26**, 27 *or* 14, **15**, 16
Isaiah 7.1-17
Matthew 5.38-end

Thursday 14 November

Isaiah 7.1-17

'Take heed, be quiet, do not fear' (v.4)

The Northern kingdom of Israel had fallen to the Assyrians, and fortified cities in Judah were being destroyed. Jerusalem had resisted an attack, but the king and the people were terrified. It was only a matter of time, after all, before Jerusalem would succumb to her enemies.

Fear is an appropriate response to a dangerous situation, but after the immediate danger has passed, it paralyses us. The habits that were once essential, like keeping watch hourly, on a person, for example, now simply exhaust you. A period of remission might only be for a short while, more like sheltering under some trees from the rain, but it gives relief in which to grasp life.

Isaiah recommended that the king be calm and take advice. Quietened, the king might be open to seeing that peace would last for some time, the number of years it takes a baby to become a child. Ahaz might have been fed up with advisors saying everything was going to be all right, when how could they know? He seems not to dare to trust that there would be peace for a time, or perhaps the prospect of war hanging over him was intolerable.

Are there habits and fears that you hold onto, but are not necessary for the time being, at least, and you could put them down? King Ahaz wasn't able to relax and trust God when Isaiah went to see him. Later, in naming the child Immanuel, he came recognize that God was with them.

> God, our refuge and strength,
> bring near the day when wars shall cease
> and poverty and pain shall end,
> that earth may know the peace of heaven
> through Jesus Christ our Lord.

COLLECT

Reflection by **Justine Allain Chapman** | 307

Friday 15 November

Psalms 28, **32** *or* 17, **19**
Isaiah 8.1-15
Matthew 6.1-18

Isaiah 8.1-15

'He will become a sanctuary' (v.14)

In the year King Uzziah died, Isaiah saw the Lord, but he didn't know then how long he would have to prophesy to people who wouldn't listen. In the year his second son, Maher-shalal-hash-baz, was born, Isaiah knew there was nothing that could be done to prevent foreign invasion, not banding together or taking counsel with other nations. He did have a timescale now: the time it would take for his son to speak was the length of time before disaster would come.

Disaster would come not just on the nation who had sinned, but on the prophet's family too, with two children to protect and keep from starvation. This child wasn't called Immanuel, but 'the spoil speeds, the prey hastes'. This child was born to parents who knew God. That didn't bring immunity from difficulty, but the burden of knowing what was inevitable. Isaiah felt the pull of the fear of enemy attack, but the stronger pressure of the hand of God to fear him as the holy one.

The reassurance for Isaiah and his family was that God would become a sanctuary. Quite what form of protection, safety or refuge God would provide, like the exact timescale, was unknown, but it would come.

Many refugee families today, like Mary, Joseph and Jesus before them, seek sanctuary from hardship and starvation. Many seek it in God and from those of us who live in safety committed to serving the holy one.

COLLECT

Almighty Father,
whose will is to restore all things
in your beloved Son, the King of all:
govern the hearts and minds of those in authority,
and bring the families of the nations,
divided and torn apart by the ravages of sin,
to be subject to his just and gentle rule;
who is alive and reigns with you,
in the unity of the Holy Spirit,
one God, now and for ever.

| *Reflection by* **Justine Allain Chapman**

Psalms **33** *or* 20, 21, **23**   ## Saturday 16 November
Isaiah 8.16 – 9.7
Matthew 6.19-end

Isaiah 8.16 – 9.7

'Prince of Peace' (9.6)

In the midst of chaos, war or busyness, we long for a peace that marks an end and, after a pause for rest, heralds a new beginning.

Isaiah depicts the reign of the Prince of Peace as bringing an end to oppression. He frees humanity by breaking the burdensome yokes, which he depicts as bars heavy across the shoulders of the oppressed. The Prince of Peace, unlike Atlas, the Titan, who was condemned to hold up the sky with his shoulders, carries the authority for governing the world easily. The authority rests upon his shoulders and as Wonderful Counsellor he can fulfil the responsibilities of governing not only to end war and injustice, but also to establish peace. This is because the peace of God grows from the inside out.

We often imagine ourselves with the cares of the world on our shoulders and can find it difficult to lay them down. Jesus called those who felt burdened or heavy laden to go to him. He promised rest, an easy yoke and a light burden (Matthew 11.30). When we can pause and rest, we can more easily glimpse God, and see light in darkness. This emerging hope enables a new beginning in us and for our world. Christ's peace grows within us and becomes established as we grow in love. This peace is a gift given to be shared.

God, our refuge and strength,
bring near the day when wars shall cease
and poverty and pain shall end,
that earth may know the peace of heaven
through Jesus Christ our Lord.

COLLECT

Reflection by **Justine Allain Chapman** | 309

Monday 18 November

Psalms 46, **47** or 27, **30**
Isaiah 9.8 – 10.4
Matthew 7.1-12

Isaiah 9.8 – 10.4

'... his hand is stretched out still' (9.12, 17, 21; 10.4)

Isaiah is scathing about the apostasy of the people of Israel. 'Everyone was godless and an evildoer.' It's one of the bleakest of all biblical passages. Not even a single faithful person is to be found. That's why God's hand is stretched out in judgement against his people. '... his anger has not turned away; his hand is stretched out still' is repeated four times.

Human hands can be threatening when clenched in a fist, raised in a frightening salute or holding a gun. But hands can also calm the troubled child. Couples in love or taking vows hold hands. Hands can be the agent of healing, whether sacramentally or in an operating theatre. Little wonder that the imagery of the hand of God is so powerful.

Christians cannot read this passage, though, without thinking of other outstretched hands – the hands of Jesus nailed to the cross. His hands were stretched out not in condemnation but compassion. The hands of Jesus also touched lepers and embraced children. They were laid on the sick, the blind, the deaf and the lame. We cannot see the hand of the Lord 'stretched out still' without recognizing the reconciling work of the hands of Jesus Christ in our world. A prayer frequently misattributed to St Teresa of Avila says that Christ now has no hands on earth but ours. To whom will we stretch out our hands today?

COLLECT

Heavenly Father,
whose blessed Son was revealed
    to destroy the works of the devil
and to make us the children of God and heirs of eternal life:
grant that we, having this hope,
may purify ourselves even as he is pure;
that when he shall appear in power and great glory
we may be made like him in his eternal and glorious kingdom;
where he is alive and reigns with you,
in the unity of the Holy Spirit,
one God, now and for ever.

| *Reflection by* **Graham James**

Psalms 48, **52** *or* 32, **36**
Isaiah 10.5-19
Matthew 7.13-end

Tuesday 19 November

Isaiah 10.5-19

'Shall the axe vaunt itself over the one who wields it?' (v.15)

God uses the Assyrians to punish the unfaithful people of Israel. The King of Assyria thinks it's his strength and wisdom that have made him so powerful. He boasts of his wisdom and understanding. When referring to his victories he claims 'by the strength of my hand I have done it'. The God of Israel finds this blasphemy more than he can tolerate. So a wasting sickness is visited upon Assyria's stout warriors. The destruction of Israel eventually destroys Assyria as well.

The arrogance of the powerful that lies at the heart of this passage has not vanished from the face of the earth. Those who win wars can delude themselves over their capabilities, power and leadership. Such hubris can backfire.

The warning in this passage may not be directed only towards the politically or economically powerful, however. Many of us may be inordinately proud of our own small achievements. The danger is that we do not give God (or anyone else) credit for the talents with which we've been endowed or the advantages we may have received. We can be more like the King of Assyria than we realize. It's those *without* arrogance who always give others the credit, who are both the most humble but also the most appealing people. They are also, as Jesus teaches us in the Sermon on the Mount, those who will eventually inherit the earth.

Heavenly Lord,
you long for the world's salvation:
stir us from apathy,
restrain us from excess
and revive in us new hope
that all creation will one day be healed
in Jesus Christ our Lord.

COLLECT

Wednesday 20 November

Psalms **56**, 57 *or* **34**
Isaiah 10.20-32
Matthew 8.1-13

Isaiah 10.20-32

'... a remnant will return' (v.22)

A remnant is a small piece of material left over when most of a roll of cloth has been sold. Remnants are usually to be obtained quite cheaply. A 'remnant sale' offers a bargain or two. A remnant is not usually well regarded. But when God sees a small number of his people who have kept faithful while the rest have given themselves to the pleasures and vices of the world, he gives this remnant his blessing and a new significance. No one can claim remnant status for themselves, however. That would be blasphemous and boastful. God decides who forms a true remnant.

So it's odd that some religious people choose to designate themselves as 'the remnant', and even use that language. *The Remnant* is a traditionalist Catholic newspaper established 50 years ago to oppose what its contributors believed to be the heretical teaching of the Second Vatican Council. By contrast, the 'Remnant of Israel Ministry' proclaims that only the Aryan race fulfils every detail of biblical prophecy.

We should take warning. There is something comforting about considering ourselves as part of a righteous minority. It's very easy to think we are the faithful ones when others have gone astray. The faithful remnant is a recurring theme in Scripture. But the spiritual vanity in declaring ourselves as such is a present danger. It isn't the spiritually conceited upon whom God looks with favour. Are we sure we've resisted this temptation?

C O L L E C T	Heavenly Father,
	whose blessed Son was revealed
	to destroy the works of the devil
	and to make us the children of God and heirs of eternal life:
	grant that we, having this hope,
	may purify ourselves even as he is pure;
	that when he shall appear in power and great glory
	we may be made like him in his eternal and glorious kingdom;
	where he is alive and reigns with you,
	in the unity of the Holy Spirit,
	one God, now and for ever.

| *Reflection by* **Graham James**

Psalms 61, **62** *or* **37***
Isaiah 10.33 – 11.9
Matthew 8.14-22

Thursday 21 November

Isaiah 10.33 – 11.9
'The wolf shall live with the lamb ...' (11.6)

The image of a lion lying down with a lamb is a commonplace one in the Christian imagination. It presents a picture of the messianic age when predators and prey will live in harmony and 'the earth will be full of the knowledge of the Lord'.

But it's a mistaken image. The biblical text doesn't mention the lion alongside the lamb. It's the calf and the fatling that accompany the king of the jungle. In any case, this isn't a prediction of a complete vegetarian takeover of the animal kingdom. That's not what animates these images. It's the nations antagonistic to Israel that are given the names of hunting animals devouring their prey. Assyria, Philistia and Manasseh are all included.

This passage anticipates a new age when all these nations will live at peace with Israel and honour the God of Israel too. In that era 'a little child shall lead them'. The Christian instinct is to think of this as a messianic prophecy in relation to Jesus Christ. But Christ has come, and predatory nations still devour the earth. Lions and wolves do not live at peace. There is still much peacemaking to be done before any little child is safe from the harm that warlike and devouring nations inflict upon our world. It's why so many Christians work for peace. Christ invites us to join him in peacemaking.

Heavenly Lord,
you long for the world's salvation:
stir us from apathy,
restrain us from excess
and revive in us new hope
that all creation will one day be healed
in Jesus Christ our Lord.

COLLECT

Friday 22 November

Psalms **63**, 65 *or* 31
Isaiah 11.10 – end of 12
Matthew 8.23-end

Isaiah 11.10 – end of 12

'... with joy you will draw water from the wells of salvation' (12.3)

Chapter 12 of the long book of the prophet Isaiah has only six verses, but it packs a punch. It is a glorious vision of Israel's restoration, remaking and renewal. At the heart of it is an image of drawing water.

We are mostly constituted of water. We can go without food for a long time, but deprived of water for just a couple of days, we become desperate, soon reaching the point of death. Give us too much water and we will drown. Water gives life but can also take it away.

Perhaps this is why Jesus promises not just water but 'living water' twice in John's Gospel. He does so first to the Samaritan woman at Jacob's well (John 4.10), a sign that the living water he offers is for everyone, not just his own people. At the feast in Jerusalem Jesus says: 'Let anyone who is thirsty come to me and drink ... out of the believer's heart shall flow rivers of living water' (John 7.37-38).

It's no surprise that water baptism so quickly became the mark of being a Christian. It builds on the image of living water drawn from the wells of salvation in Isaiah and exemplified in Christ's ministry. It is not simply the washing away of sin that animates our understanding of baptism, but a much deeper and richer biblical inheritance. Do we honour the gift of water, the source of all life, sufficiently in the light of all this?

COLLECT

Heavenly Father,
whose blessed Son was revealed
    to destroy the works of the devil
and to make us the children of God and heirs of eternal life:
grant that we, having this hope,
may purify ourselves even as he is pure;
that when he shall appear in power and great glory
we may be made like him in his eternal and glorious kingdom;
where he is alive and reigns with you,
in the unity of the Holy Spirit,
one God, now and for ever.

| *Reflection by* **Graham James**

Psalms **78.1-39** *or* 41, **42**, 43
Isaiah 13.1-13
Matthew 9.1-17

Saturday 23 November

Isaiah 13.1-13

'The oracle concerning Babylon ...' (v.1)

In the ancient world, an oracle was a word (from the Latin *orare*, to speak) that came from the gods through a priest or priestess. As time went on, the priest or priestess uttering the prediction became the oracle themselves. Oracles were portals through which the gods spoke directly to people. In our own day, we may speak of someone as 'an oracle' if we think they are full of wisdom, though it's a term now most frequently used ironically.

Isaiah claimed nothing for himself. He was simply the chosen vessel through whom the God of Israel spoke directly to his people. These oracles against foreign nations are not uttered to give the people of Israel a sense of their own superiority. Rather they show that God's sovereignty is over the whole earth. Human pride and arrogance, wherever it is found, will fall under God's judgement. Israel's God isn't better than other gods. He is simply the Lord of all the earth.

Such a belief offers liberation from the need to seek revenge or to bring down the haughty and the proud. In his own good time, God will do this. And if we anticipate his judgement, we risk being condemned ourselves. Jesus makes this explicit when he tells us 'do not judge, so that you may not be judged' (Matthew 7.1). It is one of the hardest of the teachings of Jesus for sinful humanity to obey. For it isn't wise judgement we should avoid, it's easy condemnation.

Heavenly Lord,
you long for the world's salvation:
stir us from apathy,
restrain us from excess
and revive in us new hope
that all creation will one day be healed
in Jesus Christ our Lord.

COLLECT

Monday 25 November

Psalms 92, **96** *or* 44
Isaiah 14.3-20
Matthew 9.18-34

Isaiah 14.3-20

'You have become like us!' (v.10)

Isaiah 14 is described as a taunt against Babylon. This powerful imperial power that held the people of Israel as captives is receiving its comeuppance. Babylon claimed the sort of ascendency on earth that gave it presumptions of divine authority. Its rulers thought of themselves as gods. But now they are 'brought down to Sheol' and lie in the ground with maggots for company 'and worms [for] covering'.

There's an unmistakable gleefulness in these taunts. We like to see the mighty cast down. It appeals to our basest instincts even when justice merits it, as it appears to do in the case of Babylon. The historical experience of Israel and the nations surrounding Babylon regarded that country's assault on common humanity, disregard of the poor and desire to rule the world at any cost, as things that deserved to be destroyed.

The strangest taunt, though, is the one 'You have become like us!' In other words, Babylon is now as weak as the rest of humanity, enfeebled 'like us'. Babylon is reduced to our level. There would come a time, however, when God himself 'becomes like us'. No longer is it a taunt against the powerful. In the weakness of the Christ-child, humanity is given a new dignity. When God becomes like us, we do not sneer but are more likely to be struck dumb in amazement.

COLLECT

Eternal Father,
whose Son Jesus Christ ascended to the throne of heaven
    that he might rule over all things as Lord and King:
keep the Church in the unity of the Spirit
and in the bond of peace,
and bring the whole created order to worship at his feet;
who is alive and reigns with you,
in the unity of the Holy Spirit,
one God, now and for ever.

| *Reflection by* **Graham James**

Tuesday 26 November

Isaiah 17
'Damascus will cease to be a city ...' (v.1)

Within recent memory, relationships between Christians, Muslims and other faith traditions were more harmonious in Syria than almost anywhere else in the Middle East. That's gone (and the ancient Christian communities in Syria decimated), and Damascus itself, once recognized as a beautiful city, has experienced terrible destruction. However, it's unlikely it will 'cease to be a city' any time soon. This has not prevented some searchers of Old Testament prophecies from claiming that Isaiah 17 is coming to fulfilment now. As it is, Isaiah was much more concerned with his own generation than with events nearly 3,000 years later.

The destruction of both Damascus and also the northern kingdom of Israel (Ephraim) are linked in this prophecy. Damascus was captured by the Assyrians in 732 BC and the northern kingdom fell ten years later, in 722 BC.

Even so, we cannot read this passage without thinking of Damascus in our own age. Some time ago, I heard a young Christian in the city rejoicing that he and his wife had been blessed by the birth of their first child. They were staying, whatever the circumstances, he said, for their child was a sign of hope for their country and of their faith in Jesus Christ. Such trust in a positive outcome for Damascus offers the most inspiring prophetic witness in our own age. It should not surprise us that the birth of a child in an occupied land should be so significant.

God the Father,
help us to hear the call of Christ the King
and to follow in his service,
whose kingdom has no end;
for he reigns with you and the Holy Spirit,
one God, one glory.

COLLECT

Wednesday 27 November

Psalms 110, 111, **112**
or **119.57-80**
Isaiah 19
Matthew 10.16-33

Isaiah 19

'Blessed be Egypt my people ...' (v.25)

After Moses led the Israelites from captivity to the Promised Land there continued to be connections between Israel and Egypt. Solomon married the daughter of an Egyptian king, the customary way to seek an alliance (1 Kings 3.1). Israel also asked for Egyptian help in their fight against Assyria (2 Kings 18.21). But relationships were not always harmonious. An Egyptian Pharaoh killed Josiah, king of Judah (2 Kings 23). The ally in one age became the enemy in the next. Here Isaiah proclaims an oracle against Egypt. His prophecy of destruction was total. Nothing would be spared. The Nile would dry up and Egyptian cities would be flattened by the hand of God.

Yet from verse 16 onwards, there's a radical change of tone. Isaiah says that Egypt and Assyria are both to be accepted into the people of God on equal terms. Those who live in certain Egyptian cities will even speak Hebrew, a metaphor not simply for Egypt being an ally of Israel but a people adopting Israel's faith in the one Lord God of all the earth. God becomes Egypt's redeemer. None of this is a reward for good behaviour. It simply happens because God wills it. It's free and undeserved grace. It's a glimpse of what will be the gospel.

As we observe the relationship between Israel and Egypt today, Isaiah's prophecy has lost none of its hope or relevance.

COLLECT

Eternal Father,
whose Son Jesus Christ ascended to the throne of heaven
    that he might rule over all things as Lord and King:
keep the Church in the unity of the Spirit
and in the bond of peace,
and bring the whole created order to worship at his feet;
who is alive and reigns with you,
in the unity of the Holy Spirit,
one God, now and for ever.

| *Reflection by* **Graham James**

Psalms **125**, 126, 127, 128
or 56, **57** (63*)
Isaiah 21.1-12
Matthew 10.34 – 11.1

Thursday 28 November

Isaiah 21.1-12

'Fallen, fallen is Babylon ...' (v.9)

The ancient city of Babylon is situated in modern Iraq, about 50 miles south of Baghdad. Surprisingly little of it has ever been excavated. Babylon was once the most populous city in the ancient world, perhaps reaching 200,000 people in the 6th and 7th centuries BC. Its population grew through the practice of removing people from conquered territories to the capital city as a means of consolidating power.

Their exile in Babylon was a collective trauma for the people of Israel. 'By the rivers of Babylon – there we sat down and there wept when we remembered Zion', they lamented (Psalm 137.1).

Isaiah has a vision of the fall of Babylon. You'd think he'd rejoice but instead he says 'my loins are filled with anguish' and 'my mind reels, horror has appalled me'. There is no cheering when Babylon, the persecutor of Israel, is destroyed. Babylon's downfall reveals how nations that abuse their power are eventually led to their destruction. It's a sign of the world under judgement.

Perhaps it's no surprise that Saddam Hussein sought to rebuild old Babylon and also styled himself 'son of Nebuchadnezzar', the Babylonian king of the time of the Jewish captivity. In recent times, there has been renewed destruction of the ancient land of Babylon. But Isaiah's parable holds true. The twenty-first century fall of Iraq has seen no victors. Isaiah's words of grief are echoed in our own age.

God the Father,
help us to hear the call of Christ the King
and to follow in his service,
whose kingdom has no end;
for he reigns with you and the Holy Spirit,
one God, one glory.

COLLECT

Reflection by **Graham James** | 319

Friday 29 November

Isaiah 22.1-14

'Let us eat and drink for tomorrow we die' (v.13)

Herodotus, the Greek historian, describes an Egyptian custom where at grand banquets a servant would bring in a coffin containing the wooden carving of a corpse painted to look like a dead person as clearly as possible. It would be shown to each guest as a reminder of their mortality. They would also be told 'gaze here, drink and be merry, for when you die, such shall you be'. The finality of death becomes a call to live for pleasure, an invitation to indulgence.

Isaiah weeps bitter tears for his own people when they exhibit a similar attitude by living only for the moment. The likely setting for this oracle is the remarkable deliverance of Jerusalem, 'tumultuous city', from an Assyrian attack under Sennacherib in 701 BC. Instead of weeping and mourning when under siege, the people of Jerusalem feasted saying 'Let us eat and drink for tomorrow we die'. When delivered, they rejoiced again but gave no credit to God. The implication is that their heedlessness of the Lord meant that the demands of justice and mercy meant nothing to them.

Living for today and today alone is sometimes regarded as sage advice. But when Jesus said 'do not worry about tomorrow' (Matthew 6.34), it was an invitation to trust in God for the future, and not to live only for the present moment.

COLLECT

Eternal Father,
whose Son Jesus Christ ascended to the throne of heaven
    that he might rule over all things as Lord and King:
keep the Church in the unity of the Spirit
and in the bond of peace,
and bring the whole created order to worship at his feet;
who is alive and reigns with you,
in the unity of the Holy Spirit,
one God, now and for ever.

Psalms 47, 147.1-12
Ezekiel 47.1-12
or Ecclesiasticus 14.20-end
John 12.20-32

Saturday 30 November
Andrew the Apostle

Ezekiel 47.1-12
'... it will be a place for the spreading of nets' (v.10)

Ezekiel's vision of swift-flowing water emerging from the temple in Jerusalem promises new life for the whole of creation. Trees will bear constant fruit. Rivers will be full of fish. It's not hard to see why this passage is chosen for the feast of St Andrew, one of the fishermen who followed Jesus.

In John's Gospel, Andrew is the first disciple to follow Jesus. The Greek Orthodox Church refers to Andrew as *Protokletos*, 'the first called'. When Andrew rates a mention in the Gospels, he is often bringing people to Jesus, whether it's his brother Simon, the boy with the loaves and fish at the feeding of the five thousand, or the Greeks who first approached Philip with their request, 'Sir, we want to see Jesus'.

Although Andrew is the first disciple to be called and a key part of some Gospel narratives, it is Peter, James and John who are at the heart of the apostolic band. Andrew is not included, for example, on the Mount of Transfiguration. He exemplifies a disciple who is always introducing others to Christ but then content to fade into the background. That may be why his subsequent history is so disputed. His net did spread wide. All who claim the name of Christian may owe more to Andrew than we ever know – and perhaps to other similar self-effacing evangelists as well.

Almighty God,
who gave such grace to your apostle Saint Andrew
that he readily obeyed the call of your Son Jesus Christ
and brought his brother with him:
call us by your holy word,
and give us grace to follow you without delay
and to tell the good news of your kingdom;
through Jesus Christ your Son our Lord,
who is alive and reigns with you,
in the unity of the Holy Spirit,
one God, now and for ever.

COLLECT

Reflection by **Graham James** | 321

Seasonal Prayers of Thanksgiving

Advent

Blessed are you, Sovereign God of all,
to you be praise and glory for ever.
In your tender compassion
the dawn from on high is breaking upon us
to dispel the lingering shadows of night.
As we look for your coming among us this day,
open our eyes to behold your presence
and strengthen our hands to do your will,
that the world may rejoice and give you praise.
Blessed be God, Father, Son and Holy Spirit.
Blessed be God for ever.

Christmas Season

Blessed are you, Sovereign God,
creator of heaven and earth,
to you be praise and glory for ever.
As your living Word, eternal in heaven,
assumed the frailty of our mortal flesh,
may the light of your love be born in us
to fill our hearts with joy as we sing:
Blessed be God, Father, Son and Holy Spirit.
Blessed be God for ever.

Epiphany

Blessed are you, Sovereign God,
king of the nations,
to you be praise and glory for ever.
From the rising of the sun to its setting
your name is proclaimed in all the world.
As the Sun of Righteousness dawns in our hearts
anoint our lips with the seal of your Spirit
that we may witness to your gospel
and sing your praise in all the earth.
Blessed be God, Father, Son and Holy Spirit.
Blessed be God for ever.

Blessed are you, Lord God of our salvation,
to you be glory and praise for ever.
In the darkness of our sin you have shone in our hearts
to give the light of the knowledge of the glory of God
in the face of Jesus Christ.
Open our eyes to acknowledge your presence,
that freed from the misery of sin and shame
we may grow into your likeness from glory to glory.
Blessed be God, Father, Son and Holy Spirit.
Blessed be God for ever.

Blessed are you, Lord God of our salvation,
to you be praise and glory for ever.
As a man of sorrows and acquainted with grief
your only Son was lifted up
that he might draw the whole world to himself.
May we walk this day in the way of the cross
and always be ready to share its weight,
declaring your love for all the world.
Blessed be God, Father, Son and Holy Spirit.
Blessed be God for ever.

Blessed are you, Sovereign Lord,
the God and Father of our Lord Jesus Christ,
to you be glory and praise for ever.
From the deep waters of death
you brought your people to new birth
by raising your Son to life in triumph.
Through him dark death has been destroyed
and radiant life is everywhere restored.
As you call us out of darkness into his marvellous light
may our lives reflect his glory
and our lips repeat the endless song.
Blessed be God, Father, Son and Holy Spirit.
Blessed be God for ever.

Blessed are you, Lord of heaven and earth,
to you be glory and praise for ever.
From the darkness of death you have raised your Christ
to the right hand of your majesty on high.
The pioneer of our faith, his passion accomplished,
has opened for us the way to heaven
and sends on us the promised Spirit.
May we be ready to follow the Way
and so be brought to the glory of his presence
where songs of triumph for ever sound:
Blessed be God, Father, Son and Holy Spirit.
Blessed be God for ever.

Blessed are you, creator God,
to you be praise and glory for ever.
As your Spirit moved over the face of the waters
bringing light and life to your creation,
pour out your Spirit on us today
that we may walk as children of light
and by your grace reveal your presence.
Blessed be God, Father, Son and Holy Spirit.
Blessed be God for ever.

Blessed are you, Sovereign God,
ruler and judge of all,
to you be praise and glory for ever.
In the darkness of this age that is passing away
may the light of your presence which the saints enjoy
surround our steps as we journey on.
May we reflect your glory this day
and so be made ready to see your face
in the heavenly city where night shall be no more.
Blessed be God, Father, Son and Holy Spirit.
Blessed be God for ever.

The Lord's Prayer and The Grace

Our Father in heaven,
hallowed be your name,
your kingdom come,
your will be done,
on earth as in heaven.
Give us today our daily bread.
Forgive us our sins
as we forgive those who sin against us.
Lead us not into temptation
but deliver us from evil.
For the kingdom, the power,
and the glory are yours
now and for ever.
Amen.

(or)

Our Father, who art in heaven,
hallowed be thy name;
thy kingdom come;
thy will be done;
on earth as it is in heaven.
Give us this day our daily bread.
And forgive us our trespasses,
as we forgive those who trespass against us.
And lead us not into temptation;
but deliver us from evil.
For thine is the kingdom,
the power and the glory,
for ever and ever.
Amen.

The grace of our Lord Jesus Christ,
and the love of God,
and the fellowship of the Holy Spirit,
be with us all evermore.
Amen.

An Order for Night Prayer (Compline)

The Lord almighty grant us a quiet night and a perfect end.
Amen.

Our help is in the name of the Lord
who made heaven and earth.

A period of silence for reflection on the past day may follow.

The following or other suitable words of penitence may be used

**Most merciful God,
we confess to you,
before the whole company of heaven and one another,
that we have sinned in thought, word and deed
and in what we have failed to do.
Forgive us our sins,
heal us by your Spirit
and raise us to new life in Christ. Amen.**

O God, make speed to save us.
O Lord, make haste to help us.

**Glory to the Father and to the Son
and to the Holy Spirit;
as it was in the beginning is now
and shall be for ever. Amen.
Alleluia.**

The following or another suitable hymn may be sung

Before the ending of the day,
Creator of the world, we pray
That you, with steadfast love, would keep
Your watch around us while we sleep.

From evil dreams defend our sight,
From fears and terrors of the night;
Tread underfoot our deadly foe
That we no sinful thought may know.

O Father, that we ask be done
Through Jesus Christ, your only Son;
And Holy Spirit, by whose breath
Our souls are raised to life from death.

The Word of God

Psalmody

One or more of Psalms 4, 91 or 134 may be used.

Psalm 134

1   Come, bless the Lord, all you servants of the Lord, ♦
    you that by night stand in the house of the Lord.

2   Lift up your hands towards the sanctuary ♦
    and bless the Lord.

3   The Lord who made heaven and earth ♦
    give you blessing out of Zion.

**Glory to the Father and to the Son
and to the Holy Spirit;
as it was in the beginning is now
and shall be for ever. Amen.**

Scripture Reading

*One of the following short lessons or another suitable
passage is read*

You, O Lord, are in the midst of us and we are called by
your name; leave us not, O Lord our God.

Jeremiah 14.9

(or)

Be sober, be vigilant, because your adversary the devil is
prowling round like a roaring lion, seeking for someone
to devour. Resist him, strong in the faith.

1 Peter 5.8,9

(or)

The servants of the Lamb shall see the face of God, whose
name will be on their foreheads. There will be no more night:
they will not need the light of a lamp or the light of the sun,
for God will be their light, and they will reign for ever and
ever.

Revelation 22.4,5

The following responsory may be said

Into your hands, O Lord, I commend my spirit.
Into your hands, O Lord, I commend my spirit.
For you have redeemed me, Lord God of truth.
I commend my spirit.
Glory to the Father and to the Son
and to the Holy Spirit.
Into your hands, O Lord, I commend my spirit.

Or, in Easter

Into your hands, O Lord, I commend my spirit.
   Alleluia, alleluia.
Into your hands, O Lord, I commend my spirit.
   Alleluia, alleluia.
For you have redeemed me, Lord God of truth.
Alleluia, alleluia.
Glory to the Father and to the Son
and to the Holy Spirit.
Into your hands, O Lord, I commend my spirit.
   Alleluia, alleluia.

Keep me as the apple of your eye.
Hide me under the shadow of your wings.

Gospel Canticle

Nunc Dimittis (The Song of Simeon)

Save us, O Lord, while waking,
and guard us while sleeping,
that awake we may watch with Christ
and asleep may rest in peace.

1   Now, Lord, you let your servant go in peace:
    your word has been fulfilled.

2   My own eyes have seen the salvation
    which you have prepared in the sight of every people;

3   A light to reveal you to the nations
    and the glory of your people Israel.

Luke 2.29-32

Glory to the Father and to the Son
and to the Holy Spirit;
as it was in the beginning is now
and shall be for ever. Amen.

Save us, O Lord, while waking,
and guard us while sleeping,
that awake we may watch with Christ
and asleep may rest in peace.

Prayers

Intercessions and thanksgivings may be offered here.

The Collect

Visit this place, O Lord, we pray,
and drive far from it the snares of the enemy;
may your holy angels dwell with us and guard us in peace,
and may your blessing be always upon us;
through Jesus Christ our Lord.
Amen.

The Lord's Prayer (see p. 325) may be said.

The Conclusion

In peace we will lie down and sleep;
for you alone, Lord, make us dwell in safety.

Abide with us, Lord Jesus,
for the night is at hand and the day is now past.

As the night watch looks for the morning,
so do we look for you, O Christ.

[Come with the dawning of the day
and make yourself known in the breaking of the bread.]

The Lord bless us and watch over us;
the Lord make his face shine upon us and be gracious to us;
the Lord look kindly on us and give us peace.
Amen.

REFLECTIONS FOR **SUNDAYS** (YEAR **C**)

Reflections for Sundays offers over 250 reflections on the Principal Readings for every Sunday and major Holy Day in Year C, from the same experienced team of writers that have made *Reflections for Daily Prayer* so successful. For each Sunday and major Holy Day, they provide:

- full lectionary details for the Principal Service
- a reflection on each Old Testament reading (both Continuous and Related)
- a reflection on the Epistle
- a reflection on the Gospel.

This book also contains a substantial introduction to the Gospel of Luke, written by Paula Gooder.

£14.99 • 288 pages
ISBN 978 1 78140 039 5

Also available in Kindle and epub formats

REFLECTIONS ON THE **PSALMS**

£14.99 • 192 pages
ISBN 978 0 7151 4490 9

Reflections on the Psalms provides original and insightful meditations on each of the Bible's 150 Psalms.

Each reflection is accompanied by its corresponding Psalm refrain and prayer from the *Common Worship Psalter*, making this a valuable resource for personal or devotional use.

Specially written introductions by Paula Gooder and Steven Croft explore the Psalms and the Bible and the Psalms in the life of the Church.

These two shortened editions of *Reflections* are ideal for group or church use during Advent and Lent, or for anyone seeking a daily devotional guide to these most holy seasons of the Christian year.

They are also ideal tasters for those wanting to begin a regular pattern of prayer and reading.

REFLECTIONS FOR **ADVENT 2018**

Monday 26 November – Monday 24 December 2018

Authors:
Graham James, Gordon Mursell, Angela Tilby, Margaret Whipp

Please note this book reproduces the material for Advent found in the volume you are now holding.

£2.99 • 48 pages
ISBN 978 1 78140 089 0
Available August 2018

REFLECTIONS FOR **LENT 2019**

Wednesday 6 March – Saturday 20 April 2019

Authors:
Jan McFarlane, Kate Bruce, Paula Gooder, Jeanette Sears, Graham Tomlin

Please note this book reproduces the material for Lent and Holy Week found in the volume you are now holding.

£4.99 • 64 pages
ISBN 978 1 78140 092 0
Available November 2018

REFLECTIONS FOR DAILY PRAYER
App

Make Bible study and reflection a part of your routine wherever you go with the Reflections for Daily Prayer App for Apple and Android devices.

Download the app for free from the App Store (Apple devices) or Google Play (Android devices) and receive a week's worth of reflections free. Then purchase a monthly, three-monthly or annual subscription to receive up-to-date content.

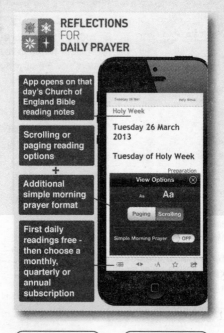

RESOURCES FOR DAILY PRAYER

Common Worship: Daily Prayer

The official daily office of the Church of England, *Common Worship: Daily Prayer* is a rich collection of devotional material that will enable those wanting to enrich their quiet times to develop a regular pattern of prayer. It includes:

- Prayer During the Day
- Forms of Penitence
- Morning and Evening Prayer
- Night Prayer (Compline)
- Collects and Refrains
- Canticles
- Complete Psalter

896 pages • with 6 ribbons • 202 x 125mm

Hardback	978 0 7151 2199 3	**£22.50**
Soft cased	978 0 7151 2178 8	**£27.50**
Bonded leather	978 0 7151 2277 8	**£50.00**

Time to Pray

This compact, soft-case volume offers two simple, shorter offices from *Common Worship: Daily Prayer*. It is an ideal introduction to a more structured personal devotional time, or can be used as a lighter, portable daily office for those on the move.

Time to Pray includes:

- Prayer During the Day
  (for every day of the week)
- Night Prayer
- Selected Psalms

£12.99 • 112 pages • Soft case
ISBN 978 0 7151 2122 1

Order now at www.chpublishing.co.uk
or via **Norwich Books and Music**
Telephone **(01603) 785923**
E-mail **orders@norwichbooksandmusic.co.uk**